UNEASY ACCESS
Privacy for Women in a Free Society

NEW FEMINIST PERSPECTIVES SERIES
Rosemarie Tong, *General Editor*

CLAIMING REALITY
Phenomenology and Women's Experience
Louise Levesque-Lopman

MANHOOD AND POLITICS
A Feminist Reading in Political Theory
Wendy L. Brown

UNEASY ACCESS

Privacy for Women in a Free Society

Anita L. Allen

Rowman & Littlefield
Publishers

For Paul

ROWMAN & LITTLEFIELD

Published in the United States of America in 1988
by Rowman & Littlefield, Publishers
(a division of Littlefield, Adams & Company)
81 Adams Drive, Totowa, New Jersey 07512

Library of Congress Cataloging-in-Publication Data

Allen, Anita L., 1953–
  Uneasy access : privacy for women in a free society /
Anita L. Allen.

(New feminist perspectives)
  Includes index.
  ISBN 0-8476-7327-8.   ISBN 0-8476-7328-6 (pbk.)
  1. Women's rights—United States. 2. Privacy, Right of—
United States. I. Title. II. Series.
HQ1236.5.U6A44   1987   305.4′2′0973—dc19
    87-16465

5 4 3 2 1

Printed in the United States of America

Contents

Acknowledgments

I WOULD LIKE TO ACKNOWLEDGE those to whom I am most indebted, beginning with the Harvard Law School, which supported my work with a Mark DeWolfe Howe Fund fellowship in 1984. I am indebted to Carol C. Gould for inviting me to contribute the precursor of this book, "Women and Their Privacy: What Is at Stake?," to her edited volume *Beyond Domination: New Perspectives on Women and Philosophy* (Rowman & Allanheld, 1984). I owe gratitude to Mary Vetterling-Braggin for encouraging me to write a book on women's privacy, to Martha Minow for written comments on my earliest attempts to work out some of the perspectives developed here, and to Nadine Taub for reading and criticizing the first manuscript draft.

Discussions with students in my "Privacy in American Law" seminar at the University of Pittsburgh School of Law in 1986 and 1987 stimulated and informed my thinking about some of the issues discussed in this book. So too did audience discussion at my presentations on aspects of women's privacy at the 15th National Conference on Women and the Law in Los Angeles, and at the Colloquium on Feminist Moral, Social and Legal Theory at the University of Cincinnati College of Law in 1986.

I wish to recognize law students Sarah Kerr, Fred Longer, Angela Gilmore, Paul Boyton, and Karen Gable, who helped with legal research. Finally, I want to thank LuAnn Driscoll and the Word Processing staff of the University of Pittsburgh School of Law for providing excellent technical assistance.

Preface

THIS BOOK IS DESIGNED to introduce readers to women's quests for personal privacy. One of the book's major goals is to identify a broad range of the privacy and privacy-related problems confronting American women. It strives to clarify what is meant by women's privacy when it is referred to in various specific contexts. It also seeks to illuminate the interests and values at stake—the difference it makes—when a woman possesses or lacks particular forms of privacy. In addition to its significant descriptive content, this book offers views on the moral implications and philosophical underpinnings of some of the laws and social practices that bear most significantly on women's ability to secure and exploit personal privacy. It serves to place into perspective recent philosophical, legal and, to a limited extent, social science research relating to women and their privacy.

Concern for women's privacy has been a leading impetus behind the development of theories about the definition and value of privacy. The felt need of recent generations to demarcate the limits of intervention into the privacy and private lives of women has done more than even the information technology boom to inspire analysis of privacy and the moral right to it. Concern for women's privacy has also had a significant role in the development of American tort, statutory, and constitutional privacy law. Case law decided during the last one hundred or so years reveals that courts have sometimes had to struggle to formulate principled grounds for granting or rejecting privacy-related claims brought by or on behalf of women. As discussed in this book, case law also reveals that "women's privacy" has recently acquired new meanings.

A century ago, the phrase "women's privacy" evoked norms of restricted access to women, reflecting what were widely thought of as distinctly female virtues, female sensibilities, and female social roles. It evoked modesty and chastity, marital and maternal intimacy. It brought to mind the expectation of peaceful seclusion within the domestic sphere. While these traditional connotations have not entirely disappeared, "women's privacy" today is likely to first suggest decisional privacy, especially freedom of choice respecting abortion and contraception.

Indeed, in popular parlance "women's privacy" is sometimes a euphemism for "freedom to choose abortion." How women's privacy came to be identified with abortion rights is no mystery. In *Griswold v. Connecticut*, 381 U.S. 479 (1965), the United States Supreme Court developed a constitutional privacy rationale invalidating state laws barring married women's lawful access to contraception. Then, in *Roe v. Wade*, 410 U.S. 113 (1973), and *Doe v. Bolton*, 410 U.S. 179 (1973), the Court relied on constitutional privacy grounds when it declared that state laws criminalizing abortion prior to fetal viability were unconstitutional. These decisions, along with more recent decisions for which they serve as precedents, have fired scholarship, political activism, and even violence. They have catapulted abortion rights into the minds of the public as *the* women's privacy issue.

While the availability of abortion can make a critical difference to the capacity of a woman to achieve and enjoy personal privacy, women have a great many other privacy interests and concerns deserving careful attention. Therefore, while one chapter of this book is largely devoted to privacy issues raised by abortion practices, each of the other five chapters deals with its own set of concerns.

Chapter 1 is devoted to the conceptual underpinnings of any careful discussion of privacy. I note the lack of universal agreement about how "privacy" is defined, and that different purposes and assumptions about the nature of definitions explain much of the disagreement. Turning to "restricted-access" definitions, to which a plenitude of theorists now subscribe, I defend a "restricted access" definition of privacy as, roughly, the inaccessibility of persons, of their mental states, and of information about them. I explain the relationship of privacy to concepts such as seclusion, solitude, solace, peace of mind, the right to be left alone, secrecy, confidentiality, anonymity, reserve, intimacy, and modesty. Distinguishing the restricted-access sense of privacy from the decisional sense of privacy, I point out the difference made by the choice of philosophical definition of privacy for what can be plausibly conceived of as women's privacy rights and privacy interests.

Chapter 2 examines five accounts of the instrumental and moral value of privacy. I maintain that privacy per se, conceived as a neutral condition of restricted access, cannot be usefully evaluated. Nevertheless, specific instances or patterns of privacy can be evaluated from a moral point of view.

I do not undertake the defense of either a general theory of the justification of moral claims or a particular political morality. The feminist case I make for women's privacy and private choice is based on ideals of personhood, participation as equals, and contribution in accordance with one's capacities. As I understand them, these ideals are consistent with any number of normative moral theories and with major Western secular ethical traditions. I make an argument for basic opportunities for privacy that crosses the lines of demarcation between differing political moralities, such as between liberalism and socialism.

Liberalism has come under increasing attack by academic theorists, who argue that it is an imprecise, contradictory, and unjust political morality. At the same time, the assumptions and language of liberalism, still heavily relied upon by many theorists, dominate public discussion of moral issues. Although the ultimate fate of liberalism is uncertain, egalitarian interpretations of liberalism are highly compelling and useful tools for communicating feminist concerns. Because we live in a society dominated, more or less, by liberal discourse and liberal ideals of law and government, I pay particular attention to the kinds of moral arguments that should be made in a liberal democracy for women's privacy and private choice.

Chapter 3 looks at the forms of privacy associated with home, marriage, and family. I consider obstacles to women's meaningful privacy in the private sphere. In this connection I analyze feminist objections to privacy as "male ideology" and as repressive confinement of women within the home. I also analyze the important post-feminist contention that most women do not want privacy, but something better. It is commonly asserted that, instead of privacy as men conceive it, women want intimate contexts in which to exercise their considerable capacities for caring.

Chapter 4 continues examination of the privacy implications of home life. But here the focus shifts to privacy issues related to contraception, abortion, childbirth, and childcare. I show the practical connection between having decisional privacy—liberty or free choice respecting reproduction and the discharge of familial obligations—and having privacy in the restricted-access sense. I point to a number of underemphasized privacy interests threatened when decisional privacy is preempted by governmental, spousal, parental, and other outside interference. To clarify the sense in which reproductive concerns are privacy concerns, I organize my discussion and arguments around the particular forms of privacy and decisional privacy implicated by reproductive and parental rights policies.

In Chapter 5 the private sphere and its norms of restricted access are left behind as I discuss privacy in the public sphere. I consider, first, privacy in public places and second, privacy in public roles and relationships. I argue that there are legitimate claims to privacy in public places. Although the public is a sphere of de facto easy access, restrictions on accessibility should be recognized. Women do not give up moral entitlement to privacy when they throw off traditional conceptions of female modesty and seclusion to enter public places, or assume extrafamilial relationships and roles. Included in this chapter is discussion of privacy concerns raised by sexual harassment in public places and by the public display of pornographic images of women. Also discussed are the general reasons why women are particularly subject to privacy invasions at work, at school, and in other institutional settings. Chapter 5 concludes with a brief consideration of group privacy as a "reverse privacy" problem for women barred from participation in men-only clubs and organizations.

A final chapter considers the privacy and decisional privacy of, first, rape victims; second, women who are arrested, detained, or incarcerated; and, third, women in prostitution. These diverse topics are tied together by a common theme. Each topic relates to privacy losses that occur because of the vulnerability caused by gender when women, whether blameless crime victims, culpable prisoners, or moral outcasts, find themselves in the hands of our legal system.

The six chapters of this book do not raise every privacy issue relating to women, nor could they reasonably do so. All aspects of human privacy are ipso facto aspects of women's privacy. In addition to the topics discussed in this book, topics related to women's privacy have been referred to in writings on subjects as varied as adoption, surrogate mothering, domestic violence, polygraph testing, fair credit, pregnancy leaves, the rights of welfare recipients, medical examinations, forced sterilization, rape, cable and telephone pornography, non-consensual publication of nude photographs, public breast-feeding, and women in the church. I have selected topics that broadly reflect the kinds of privacy problems women experience in everyday life. To others or another occasion I leave the rest.

UNEASY ACCESS
Privacy for Women in a Free Society

CHAPTER 1

Defining Privacy

P RIVACY PROBLEMS ARE UBIQUITOUS and have a well-recognized presence in virtually every arena of American life. They are present in intimate relations, employment, education, business, medicine, and law. Respect for personal privacy is now a widely accepted moral constraint on the way we treat one another and are governed. And so it should be. For while the value of privacy is easily romanticized, and while a great deal that is worthwhile has been accomplished by individuals with little personal privacy, possessing a high level of privacy can make a critical difference in the quality of a human life. The difference privacy can make in the lives of American women is the subject of this book.

Basic opportunities for privacy and the free exercise of privacy-related liberties are human goods that contribute to the flourishing of individuals.[1] In what sense are opportunities for privacy and the exercise of privacy-related liberties human goods? Instrumentally speaking, it would make sense to describe such opportunities as goods to the extent they are something human beings desire or need as conditions of survival, or as conditions of individual or aggregate happiness or well-being. Privacy and privacy-related liberties are not needed for bare human survival in the sense in which air and water are needed. Yet the prevalence of privacy customs in diverse cultures seems to indicate that the quest for a degree of privacy and privacy-related liberties arises in response to a socially created need. Privacy and privacy-related liberties allow individuals to cope with the requirements of living among others. It seems likely, then, that well-being and happiness depend upon there being a degree of privacy in a human life. It is an open question just how much privacy and what forms of privacy individuals need in given contexts.

Liberal contractarian theorists treat as human goods resources every rational person is presumed to want because they "normally

1

have a use whatever a person's rational life plan."[2] In *Theory of Justice* John Rawls referred to human goods in this sense as "primary goods", distinguishing "natural primary goods" (for example, innate intelligence) from "social primary goods" (such as rights, opportunities, and wealth).[3] Opportunities for privacy and the exercise of privacy-related liberties appear to fit Rawls's concept of social primary goods and also David A. J. Richards' concept of "general good."[4] Richards likened his concept of general goods to John Locke's concept of civil interests, which included interests in "life, liberty, health, and indolency of body; and the possession of outward things, such as money, lands, houses, furniture, and the like."[5] In *Toleration and the Constitution,* Richards made a persuasive contractarian case that privacy and privacy-related liberties number among the general goods meriting constitutional protection. Where privacy goes unprotected by fundamental legal rights, Richards argued, individuals are unjustly deprived of opportunities for the independent exercise of their moral powers. Some contemporary theorists have made an even bolder claim for personal privacy. They have maintained that privacy and the conditions of life that enable human beings to exist as morally autonomous persons are coterminous. On their view, the fundamental requirement of respect for persons presupposes conditions of privacy sufficient for personhood.[6]

Privacy's value is not limited to what it contributes to individuals in isolation from others. Opportunities for individual privacy help make persons fit for lives of social participation and contribution; opportunities for shared privacy facilitate bonds of affection and common interest. Privacy thus has value for friendships, families, organizations, and democratic government.[7]

The quest for privacy can have salutary and benign consequences. But privacy has a darker side. Moral risks accompany the pursuit of privacy and the exploitation of privacy rights interpreted as permission to dominate and ignore. Further risks are risks of indifference, of repression, of physical harm, and of degradation. The possibility that privacy might be used for condemnable ends does not eliminate respect for privacy as a moral constraint.[8] It does, however, create the need to monitor the consequences of human privacy. To what extent should respect for privacy serve as a moral constraint? This question has a recurring role in controversies about the degree of privacy to which individuals are entitled.

This book examines controversies about the degree of privacy *women* ought to be afforded in several important contexts. Women have not always had adequate opportunities for personal privacy, neither in the private sphere of home, marriage, and family, nor in the public sphere. The private sphere has been no guarantor of individual forms of personal privacy. For some women, male hegemony and repressive confinement to the private sphere have stood as obstacles to genuine privacy and the exercise of privacy-related liberties. Other women have freely embraced motherhood and caretaking roles that undercut individual forms of privacy at home. Nor has the public sphere proven to be a guarantor of personal privacy. When women spend time away from home as workers, students, entrepreneurs, and consumers they also experience unwanted and needless diminutions of privacy unique to their gender. With respect to both the public and private realms, women are asking how much privacy they should choose for themselves and how much privacy they are due.

On the threshold of any serious discussion of what respect for women's privacy requires of individuals and government are philosophical questions about the definition of the term "privacy." What does it denote? What senses and connotations does it carry? A great deal has already been accomplished in the courts and on the pages of scholarly legal, philosophical, and social science publications without achieving definitive, precise, and adequate answers to these questions. This chapter will be devoted to questions of definition first, because they are at the philosophical forefront, presupposed by conceptions of women's moral and legal privacy rights and interests, and second, because they have inspired significant scholarly debate.

Two foci warrant highlighting. First and foremost, this chapter elaborates a conception of privacy. It defends my reliance upon a particular philosophical definition of "privacy" and, to an extent, my general reliance upon the particular class of definitions to which it belongs. I refer to the class as "restricted-access" definitions. Restricted-access definitions have been advanced by theorists from diverse disciplines. On the definition I adopt, "privacy" denotes a degree of inaccessibility of persons, of their mental states, and of information about them to the senses and surveillance devices of others. As explained below, privacy is a descriptive, neutral concept denoting conditions that are neither always desirable and praiseworthy, nor always undesirable and unpraiseworthy. Moreover, privacy is a parent concept, the broadest of a family of narrower concepts. The concepts of seclusion, secrecy, confidentiality, and anonymity are included in the privacy family. Because these narrower concepts also denote conditions of personal inaccessibility, I interpret them as forms of privacy. Increasingly, law and morality have been deemed to take as one of their special concerns respect for the forms and degrees of privacy that matter most. Protection of important privacies most clearly requires the inaccessibility of that which shared sensibilities and culture regard as personal and intimate. But, as we shall see, the protection of important forms of privacy has further, and more controversial, requirements.

The definition of privacy adopted here is very similar to definitions advanced by other restricted-access theorists, to whom I am indebted. My aim is to contribute, first, an original account of why "inaccessibility" is a particularly appealing and appropriate term of definitional analysis for "privacy" and, second, some criticisms of published objections to restricted-access theories that show why such objections fail. Restricted-access definitions are stronger and better motivated than their advocates have demonstrated. As elaborated below, restricted-access definitions are suggested by the connotational ties between "privacy" and "inaccessibility" that have arisen by virtue of the practical link between creating and protecting privacy, and creating and protecting conditions of inaccessibility. They are further suggested by the semantic reality that in many characteristic contexts, conditions of privacy are aptly described as conditions of inaccessibility. The converse is also true: conditions of inaccessibility are often aptly described as conditions of privacy. Finally, the near synonymy of "privacy" and "inaccessibility" is highly significant to a defense of the particular restricted-access definition I adopt. For senses of "inaccessibility" there are senses of "privacy" with similar meaning and uses.

As its second focus, this chapter briefly points to ways in which the choice of a theoretical definition can have practical import. How "privacy" is defined will determine the plausibility of claims about what protecting privacy requires, and hence what protecting women's privacy and privacy-related interests requires. A number of philosophers and legal writers have argued that what is popularly designated as "decisional privacy" in the reproductive rights context is no such thing. They assert that liberty, not privacy, is at stake in legal policy debates over reproductive free choice. If one traces the implications of my own and similar restricted-access definitions, one must concede that women's "privacy" is sometimes a misnomer for what would be better designated their "liberty." Yet, to concede this purely definitional point is to leave open all substantive women's rights questions. Moreover, in crucial respects, conditions appropriately designated as conditions of privacy for women are profoundly at stake in debates over abortion choice and other reproductive liberties. For this reason, appeal to the concept of privacy rights in the context of reproductive rights advocacy is not, as has been alleged, deeply misguided.

Some readers may not care to labor over detailed analyses of the definition and value of privacy. These readers are invited to skim the remainder of Chapter 1 and Chapter 2, then proceed to Chapter 3. There substantive topical themes are first developed. Later, should specific questions about definition or value arise, appropriate sections of Chapter 1 or Chapter 2 can be more closely examined.

A UNIVERSAL DEFINITION?

There is no universally accepted philosophical definition of "privacy." Attempts to give an account of the meaning of "privacy" have been almost as varied as they have been numerous.[9] Perhaps this should come as no surprise. Neither are there universally accepted accounts of the meaning of "liberty," "freedom," "justice," or "equality," terms standing for concepts about which a great deal more has been written and which, like "privacy," have disparate moral, legal, political, and descriptive uses. What merits surprise is the extent to which proffered definitions of "privacy" have differed.

Struck by the difficulty of defining what has been characterized as a warm, emotional term, theorists have concluded that the concept of privacy is vague, elusive, infected with pernicious ambiguities, and even indefinable.[10] Many scholars and non-scholars have written about privacy without first attempting to define it.[11] Attempting conceptual clarification of privacy, others have offered definitions, but without explaining their definitional assumptions. A small minority have focused closely on what it takes to define a term adequately.[12]

The explanation for the considerable lack of agreement about how "privacy" is defined is not simple. Variation in definitional accounts is largely attributable to the confluence of three factors: (a) variation in the use and denotational and connotational meanings of "privacy"; (b) variation in the purposes for which definition of "privacy" is undertaken; and (c) variation in approaches taken to the task of definition itself.

Variation in Use and Meaning

"Privacy" is a term with referential meaning; that is, it is typically used to refer to or denote something. But "privacy" has been used to denote many quite different things and has varied connotations. To those who have sought a systematic understanding, the concept of privacy has seemed uniquely elastic. Edward Shils observed twenty years ago:

> Numerous meanings crowd in the mind that tries to analyze privacy: the privacy of private property; privacy as a proprietary interest in name and image; privacy as the keeping of one's affairs to oneself; the privacy of the internal affairs of a voluntary association or of a business; privacy as the physical absence of others who are unqualified by kinship, affection or other attributes to be present; respect for privacy as the

respect for the desire of another person not to disclose or to have
disclosed information about what he is doing or has done; the privacy of
sexual and familial affairs; the desire for privacy as the desire for
privacy as a desire not to be observed by another person or persons; the
privacy of the private citizen as opposed to the public official; and these
are only a few.[13]

Variation in the denotational and connotational meanings attributed
to "privacy" can thus be readily appreciated. "Privacy" is used to
denote phenomena as disparate as a quiet evening at home and the
non-disclosure of corporate records. To a computer engineer working to develop technical safeguards to prevent access to a commercial
databank, "privacy" can carry connotations palpably different from
those carried by the same expression when used by a lesbian mother
fighting a child custody battle.

The particular thing "privacy" is said to denote is subject to variation stemming from disparate meaning and usage. Thus, "privacy"
has been characterized alternatively as a neutral condition or state of
affairs; a desired condition or state of affairs, a psychological state; a
claim; a right; and a moral argument "for a certain measure of moral
space . . . extending well beyond the bodily self."[14] So wide-ranging
are its everyday uses, meanings, and senses that two theorists setting
out to formulate general definitions of "privacy" may fail to have the
same *definiendum* in mind.

Variation in Purpose

Definitions of "privacy" also vary according to the different purposes for undertaking the task of definition. Two major categories of
purpose can be distinguished. Definitional pragmatism, practiced by
journalists, policy-makers and lawyers, is definition in the context of
practical tasks such as reporting, advocacy, or legislation. These
activities breed rough and ready, ad hoc, stipulative definitions that
are not intended to be subjected to meticulous theoretical scrutiny.
The second category of purpose is definitional prescription. Most
definitions offered by philosophers and legal scholars have this purpose. Prescription-oriented theorists recommend definitions that reflect considered judgments about the fundamental meanings and
conceptual boundaries of "privacy." They urge definitional accounts
of "privacy" they deem best in relation to abstract theoretical standards such as clarity, simplicity, internal consistency, and loyalty to
relevant data. In recommending definitions, prescription-oriented
theorists have also taken into account the practical goals of articulat-
ing the basis of rights and making enforceable laws.[15] Richard Parker,
for example, defined "privacy" as "control over when and by whom

the various parts of us can be sensed by others."[16] He defended this definition as meeting the theoretical criteria of simplicity, fitness to data, and applicability by lawyers and courts.

Prescription-oriented theorists sometimes reject popular usage of "privacy" and propose alternative usage limited by narrow or highly technical definitions. These carefully crafted definitions may lack verisimilitude to laymen, but they are responsive to one or more abstract theoretical demands for circumspect usage. Thus, W. A. Parent narrowly defined privacy as "a condition of not having undocumented personal information about oneself known by others."[17] Other prescription-oriented theorists offer less technical and more inclusive definitions of "privacy" deemed broad enough to encompass each and every condition, mental state, act, occurrence, or value that plausibly falls under the ambit of the concept. These inclusive prescriptivists bring under the privacy umbrella concepts or phenomena that other prescription-oriented theorists would leave out. For example, compared to Parent's definition equating privacy with unknown undocumented personal information, Ruth Gavison's definition of privacy as "limited access in the senses of solitude, secrecy and anonymity" was highly inclusive.[18]

Few definitions have been as broadly inclusive as Judge Thomas Cooley's definition of privacy as "being let alone." Quoted by Samuel Warren and Louis Brandeis in 1890 in their noted *Harvard Law Review* article,[19] the definition of "privacy" as "being let alone" has been influential among practical and theoretical writers for nearly a century. This definition has been influential despite its evident overbreadth. If privacy simply meant "being let alone," any form of offensive or harmful conduct directed toward another person could be characterized as a violation of personal privacy. A punch in the nose would be a privacy invasion as much as a peep in the bedroom. Nonetheless, the Warren and Brandeis plea for the legal protection of what they called "inviolate personality," through recognition of a right to be let alone, must be credited with inspiring theoretical interest in understanding the meaning and value of privacy. In the 1960s, 1970s, and 1980s, the proliferation of information technology and concurrent developments in the law of reproductive and sexual liberties have inspired further and more sophisticated theoretical interest in the meaning and value of privacy.

Parenthetically, it should be apparent that to describe a prescriptive definition as inclusive or exclusive, broad or narrow, as I have done here is to offer an interpretation of the definition. For example, my contention that "being let alone" is too broad a definition of privacy involved a two-step interpretative process. First, a particular set of meanings was implicitly attributed to "being let alone" and to "privacy." The judgment was then made that, notwithstanding common members, the sets are not identical. Members of the former set are significantly more numerous than the members of the latter set. In particular, intentional injuries are all examples of not "being let alone" but are not all examples of privacy intrusions. On this basis I concluded that being let alone is a broader concept than privacy, one too inclusive to serve as its definition.

While the characterization of privacy adopted by Warren and Brandeis was too broad, a much-cited definition presented by Alan F. Westin in his path-breaking *Privacy and Freedom* (1967) is too narrow. Westin defined "privacy" as "the claim of individuals, groups, or institutions to determine for themselves when, how, and to what extent information about them is communicated to others."[20] Westin's definition approximates only what is meant by informational privacy. Other definitions of privacy have followed Westin's to the extent of identifying privacy with exclusive possession or control of information, especially what theorists have referred to as "personal," "confidential," "secret," or "undocumented" information. This type of definition might be all that is needed were Richard Posner correct that ours is an age in which, when people "decry the lack of privacy . . . it is not because they want more seclusion" but only because "they want more concealment of information about themselves that others might use to their advantage."[21] But in the minds of many, "privacy" denotes a great deal more than exclusive control over information. Contemporary reactions to employers' drug and alcohol testing, abortion control legislation, and laws criminalizing sodomy between consenting adults indicate that concealment of information is not the only felt privacy problem. As we shall see, seclusion, anonymity, and other noninformational forms of privacy are still aims of the privacy quests of men and women in diverse segments of society.

The two purposes for definition modeled here as pragmatism and prescription do not exhaust the range of purposes for which a writer might be led to define "privacy." A third purpose is often at play, description. A definition can have as one of its purposes the goal of describing what is generally referred to when a term is used by a community of speakers, whether or not such usage is philosophically or jurisprudentially optimal.

Those who attempt to define privacy typically have mixed rather than unific purposes. Idiosyncratic responses to the competing constraints imposed by mixed pragmatic, prescriptive, and descriptive purposes for undertaking definitional tasks further accounts for the considerable variation in definitions of privacy. The purposes behind my definitional efforts in this chapter are best characterized as mixed. They are largely prescriptive. To give foundation to my own and similar conceptualizations of privacy, I defend and recommend a definition that, I maintain, elucidates the referential meaning of "privacy" and does so better than dissimilar definitions advanced by theorists. The restricted-access account I defend is broad, straightforward, and nontechnical. As intended, in addition to prescriptive and descriptive validity, it proves to have pragmatic suitability for the immediate task of explaining philosophical positions that bear on women's privacy in the chapters ahead.

Variation in Approaches

Finally, differences in approaches to the task of definition help explain variation in definitions of "privacy." Lexicology—reporting etymology and proper word usage—is a nonphilosophical approach to definition. So too is stipulation, specifying the meaning an expression will carry in a particular context. Some legal theorists who have written about privacy and its meaning have expressly relied on lexicological evidence and largely stipulative definitions.[22] For some pragmatic purposes, lexicological and stipulative approaches to definition are adequate. For prescriptive purposes, philosophical approaches to definition are required.

In privacy scholarship, a favorite philosophical approach to definition has been the formulation of what could be called "nominal definitions":[23]

> We use nominal definitions to enable someone to understand the defined expression which was incomprehensible to him. A nominal definition fulfills this task if it gives a translation of the defined expression into an expression constructed exclusively of expressions understood by the person in question. If it fails to do this, the definition is flawed.[24]

To elaborate, nominal definitions are those that offer terms with discernible meanings through which the denotational meanings of "privacy" can be better understood and in terms of which questionable uses of "privacy" can be assessed. Phrases like "being let alone," "control over information," and "lack of unwanted access by others" have been offered as the *definiens* of privacy. The success of a nominal definition so conceived depends upon the ability of the *definiens* to be an informative translation device. The *definiens* must clarify what the *definiendum* refers to and do so in terms the intended audience can be expected to understand.

In principle, one's approach to the task of definition could be mixed. Idiosyncratic admixtures of definitional approaches, like admixtures of definitional purposes, is one of the reasons definitions of "privacy" have varied greatly. The approach to definition I take here is intended to be philosophical, rather than merely lexicological or stipulative. I have attempted to define "privacy" by appeal to a nominal definition consisting of a *definiens* with a clear meaning and an ability to illuminate the extension of "privacy" and guide its use.

Some privacy theorists have construed philosophical definition as a search for necessary and sufficient conditions for the proper use of a term. In this mode, Lubor C. Velecky declared himself "prepared to regard as a definition of a term any statement which encapsulates the necessary conditions for its use."[25] Similarly, Tom Gerety rejected definitional analysis that merely "limits the valid applications" of a concept in favor of a form of definition that also "identifies the necessary and sufficient conditions for any application of the concept defined."[26] Arguments raised by Parent against particular definitions of "privacy" plainly entail an assumption on his part that a definition is not adequate unless it states necessary and sufficient conditions for the use of the term.[27]

I have not attempted to define "privacy" by stating necessary and sufficient conditions for its use. I doubt such an effort could ever hope to bear the ultimate fruit. Although Velecky, Gerety and Parent each supposed that an adequate definition would state necessary and sufficient conditions, none of them can be credited with a plausible definition of that type.[28] Language use is complex, and privacy is, again, a notably elastic concept. I suspect that any definition of "privacy" resulting from a serious effort to identify necessary and sufficient conditions for its proper use—or necessary and sufficient conditions for the proper application of the concept it refers to— would be dauntingly prolix. The effort might require the formal apparatus of logic or linguistics. Such a definition would be unable to elucidate the concept of privacy for any but the most astute and patient of theorists. In contrast, an informal nominal definition can do much to communicate a specific, plausible conception of what "privacy" refers to.

Attempting to identify necessary and/or sufficient conditions can have heuristic value in the context of definitional analysis. Such an attempt can lead to the discovery of conditions that are among those necessary or sufficient for the application of a term. I am persuaded, and believe it can be convincingly illustrated, that a degree of inaccessibility is an important necessary condition for the apt application of "privacy." That is, the conditions that "privacy" is properly used to describe are conditions in which, to some extent and in some respect, accessibility is restricted. This is one of the important reasons restricted-access definitions are so plausible and appealing.

RESTRICTED-ACCESS DEFINITIONS

While no definition of "privacy" is universally accepted, definitions in which the concept of access play a central role have become increasingly commonplace. These "restricted-access" definitions characterize personal privacy in terms of restrictions on access to individuals, to their mental states, and to information about them.

Restricted-access definitions have identified privacy with a limitation on others' access to the individual;[29] the condition of being protected from unwanted access by others;[30] lack of access to information related to intimacies;[31] selective control over access to oneself or to one's group;[32] an existential condition of limited access to an individual's life experiences and engagements;[33] the state of limited access by others to certain modes of being in a person's life;[34] a limitation on access of one or more entities to an entity that possesses experiences;[35] and as the exclusive access of a person to a realm of his own.[36] Privacy as a political ideal has been interpreted in restricted-access terms as an individual's freedom to secure conditions free from unwanted access.[37] The concept of private affairs has been explained as being those activities and concerns of an individual that ought to be protected by limited access.[38] Finally, group privacy has been defined in terms of restrictions on others' access to one's group.[39]

Each of the enumerated restricted-access definitions makes use of the expression "access" or the cognate expressions "accessibility" and "inaccessibility." It might be possible to formulate a restricted-access definition that relies on the concept of access but does not utilize the term "access" or etymologically related words. But for the sake of simplicity, I am limiting my attention to the most recognizable restricted-access definitions, namely, those that do contain "access" or one of its cognates. These can be grouped according to whether they identify privacy with (a) access control, (b) limitations on unwanted access, or (c) limited access or inaccessibility. Although well motivated by the practical and conceptual links between privacy and restricted access, the first two types of restricted-access definitions ultimately fail (for reasons I will explain later in this chapter). Definitions falling into the third group, limited-access or inaccessibility definitions, are highly tenable. I will present one such definition and show that it can be defended against the objections raised by a major critic.[40]

A Practical Link

A strong practical link between protecting privacy and creating conditions of inaccessibility is a clue to the popular appeal of restricted-access definitions. Practical links are evident between protecting privacy and restricting access. For example, practical discussions about protecting privacy at home focus on alternative methods for limiting access. Walls, drapes, shrubbery, and fences are used to restrict access. These measures are not always adequate to shield the sights and sounds of home life. Restricting access to the homes of celebrities may require the addition of guards and electronic monitors. In another area, restricting access to patient records maintained by abortion providers is a means of minimizing privacy losses. Similarly, discussions of privacy and the computer invariably reach questions of information access. Restricting the accessibility of computerized data systems maintained by government, employers, and the financial and insurance industries has been put forward as one way of minimizing offensive and economically injurious losses of personal privacy.

While restricting access to data banks, confidential records, and the home may be motivated by a desire to protect personal privacy, it frequently has other goals. Preventing and deterring theft, personal injury, and trespass underlie restricting access to residences. In the business and financial sector, law enforcement purposes are furthered by legislation criminalizing unauthorized computer accessing. Law enforcement purposes are also furthered by programs and electronic devices that restrict access to computers and stored data. In the medical sector, limiting access to patient records protects privacy but may also bear on the success of treatment, as in the case of mental health records. Limiting access to medical records of individuals who have or may be perceived to have a communicable disease serves the purpose of shielding the patient from employment discrimination and unwarranted social opprobrium. Devices similar to those used to limit access to homes are also used to limit access to public buildings such as libraries, museums, county jails, and town halls, and for analogous reasons. Limiting access serves the privacy goal of keeping public records, such as personnel files, criminal histories, and adoption records, confidential. But limiting access to public buildings also helps to prevent economic losses that would otherwise result from theft and vandalism, and to provide security for public employees and individuals in state custody.

Two senses of access restriction are relevant to achieving privacy. Access can be restricted in the physical sense of being limited by physical conditions and physical objects. A remote location, a locked gate, and a clever software design can each restrict access to persons, states of mind, and information. Access can also be restricted in another, normative sense. Moral prescriptions and legal rules, such as the moral rule against eavesdropping and legislation against wiretapping, are both normative restrictions on access.

Physical and normative restrictions are used to regulate as well as prevent access. Suppose, for example, that when visiting hours are over at Vatican City, locked doors and human guards prevent physical access to the Roman Catholic pontiff. A tour group admitted for a special "after hours" papal audience may find physical restrictions to access in the form of red velvet cordons. The cordons are employed not to prevent access, but to regulate it by directing the group and helping to keep its movement orderly. Normative restrictions on access, like physical ones, can be used alternatively for prevention or regulation. A state may seek to prevent government wiretaps by legislating absolute prohibitions. Or it may merely regulate surreptitious interception by passing legislation that permits wiretapping on the condition that a valid search warrant or court order is first obtained.

It is plain that neither physical nor normative restrictions protect privacy perfectly. Distances can be traveled, locks picked, computer codes disencrypted, laws broken, and moral dictates ignored. Nevertheless, restrictions on access can and do protect privacy. The consequent practical link between privacy and restrictions on access explains the popular appeal of restricted-access definitions. The strong practical link does not entail that any or all restricted-access definitions adequately capture what "privacy" means. Still, the practical link has given rise to connotational links, forged by social practices, between "privacy" and "inaccessibility," in virtue of which the two terms and the concepts they stand for have overlapping associations. Both, for example, can signify conditions of safety. Moreover, privacy numbers among the ordinary associations of the term "inaccessibility," and inaccessibility numbers among the ordinary associations of the term "privacy." These connotational ties contribute to making inaccessibility a plausible, as well as an appealing, concept around which to frame a nominal definition of "privacy."

Characteristic Uses

Of greater justificatory import for restricted-access definitions is that "privacy" is commonly used to denote conditions of limited access. In its characteristic uses the expression "privacy" refers to conditions of inaccessibility. For example, we speak of privacy at home. When a person is alone at home, physical structures limit access to behavior. The structures creating conditions of inaccessibility referred to as "privacy" can be as thick as concrete or as thin as an eyelid, as when privacy is afforded within the family by closed eyes or an averted glance. The walls that form residential dwellings are designed to make it difficult to detect what is being done or undone inside. Some building materials do this better than others; common materials are unable completely to exclude intruders utilizing surreptitious surveillance devices such as binoculars, microphones, cameras, or recorders.

Placing distance between ourselves and others, even in the absence of physical impediments, can create conditions of inaccessibility referred to as "privacy." In the name of privacy, co-workers who share office space may place their desks on opposite ends of a room, because they know distance makes behavior less discernible. The inaccessibility created by physical distance can reduce privacy concerns.

Lack of access to a person's emotions, beliefs, habits, and past conduct is also termed "privacy." Because the external self can reveal the internal self, inaccessibility to persons' bodies and products of their bodies may be needed to keep the private self private.[41] Facial expressions, gestures, and body movements can give us away. Happiness and anger, approval and disapproval, sincerity and deception are often discernible by external inspection. Arguments marshaled against polygraph testing include privacy arguments. Polygraphers contend that heart rate, blood pressure, and perspiration are reliable indicators of deception. Their opponents contend that it is an affront to human dignity and the moral right to privacy to compel submission to tests designed to circumvent the public self and make the internal, private self directly accessible. Drug testing based on analysis of urine and blood are opposed on essentially the same privacy grounds. Consensual analyses of products of our bodies—blood, urine, and feces—are routinely performed for our benefit to aid physicians' assessment of our health. When used by government and private employers, such tests are potentially consented to under duress and can be used to reveal past private conduct, habits, and states, to our detriment.

The inaccessibility of information contained in written or electronic form is also described as a condition of privacy. In general, where information about a person is protected by conditions of inaccessibility, the person is said to possess privacy. Secrets contained in a locked diary are inaccessible to persons without the book and the key. Information contained in a computer file may be inaccessible to those who lack technical know-how, equipment, and codes. In general, where information about a person is protected by conditions of inaccessibility, the person is said to possess privacy.

These examples illustrate the soundness of the assertion that in many of its characteristic uses, the expression "privacy" denotes what are aptly described as conditions of inaccessibility. They illustrate "privacy" as denoting limited access or degrees of inaccessibility of persons, their mental states, and information about them to others.

Privacy as Inaccessibility

My own restricted-access definition of "privacy" is this: personal privacy is a condition of inaccessibility of the person, his or her mental states, or information about the person to the senses or surveillance devices of others. To say that a person possesses or enjoys privacy is to say that, in some respect and to some extent, the person (or the person's mental state, or information about the person) is beyond the range of others' five senses and any devices that can enhance, reveal, trace, or record human conduct, thought, belief, or emotion.

My privacy-as-inaccessibility definition entails that a degree of inaccessibility is a necessary condition for "privacy" aptly to apply but is not a sufficient condition for the proper use of "privacy." Is a degree of inaccessibility also a sufficient condition for the proper application of the concept of privacy? It is not clear that it is, nor is it clear what it would take to establish that it is or that it is not. This uncertainty is inadequate grounds for doubting that the restricted-access definition I am adopting has prescriptive, pragmatic, and descriptive validity.

Several examples will illustrate why one cannot maintain in any simplistic way that inaccessibility is a sufficient condition for the proper use of "privacy." A book published in an archaic language or technical vocabulary is aptly described as inaccessible but cannot be aptly described as private. A second example makes the same point. Mary, an individual with pre-school-age children, commits a crime and is incarcerated. Behind locked bars, Mary is largely inaccessible to her children. This inaccessibility does not entail total privacy. Even so Mary substantially lacks privacy due to perpetual surveillance by prison guards and close contact with fellow inmates.

Proponents of the view that a definition of privacy must state the necessary and sufficient conditions of its use might be tempted to view examples like these as proof that restricted-access definitions are untenable. Yet the first example shows nothing more than that "inaccessible" and "private" are neither precisely synonymous nor interchangeable expressions. Of the second example, opponents of restricted-access definitions might say: "Since Mary is inaccessible but lacks privacy, inaccessibility is not a sufficient as well as necessary condition for the use of 'privacy.' " But to take the prisoner example as proof that inaccessibility is not a sufficient condition is to fall prey to the fallacy of equivocation. Such examples show only what no one doubts: inaccessiblity in one respect does not always entail privacy in other respects. Inaccessibility to one social unit (the family) in a given instance is not a sufficient condition for privacy respecting a different unit (the prison community). While we would not ordinarily think of it in these terms, it is accurate to say that, relative to her children,

Mary possesses a high degree of privacy. Her condition of inaccessibility entails privacy (albeit unwanted privacy) respecting them.

A basic, implicit criterion of adequacy for a philosophical definition of the type I am offering is that the *definiens* not be arbitrary. It is not arbitrary to identify privacy with degrees of inaccessibility. Why? First, because there is a practical and connotational link between privacy and inaccessibility; second, because in its characteristic uses, "privacy" in fact denotes what can be aptly described as conditions of limited access or, what I take to be the same thing, degrees of inaccessibility; and third, because, as we shall shortly see, "privacy" and "inaccessibility" have many near-synonymous uses. Beyond being nonarbitrary, a philosophical definition must tell us something about a term that significantly elucidates its referent and its proper application. The definition of "privacy" in terms of inaccessibility tells us that, where "privacy" is properly used, conditions of privacy denote conditions of inaccessibility. This, I believe, illuminates the broad meaning of "privacy."

"Inaccessibility" is the most apt, least arbitrary single expression in our language to use in clarifying privacy's meaning. The privacy-as-inaccessibility definition capitalizes on the rough synonymy of "privacy" and "inaccessibility." If "privacy" and "inaccessibility" were strictly synonymous, "privacy" could not be illuminated by appeal to the concept of inaccessibility. Of course, "privacy" and "inaccessibility" are not strictly synonymous; that is, they do not carry precisely the same meanings and connotations in each and every context. "Privacy" has many "warm" associations, "inaccessibility" many "cold" ones. We cannot exchange every occurrence of "privacy" in an English-language sentence with "inaccessibility" and preserve the truth, value, and meaning of the sentence. Yet, because conditions of inaccessibility are entailed by conditions of privacy and because some (but not all) familiar uses of "privacy" are interchangeable with familiar uses of "inaccessibility," inaccessibility is an apt term of definitional analysis for "privacy."

One way of displaying the rough synonymy of "privacy" and "inaccessibility" is through an examination of the ambiguity of "inaccessibility." The ambiguity of "inaccessibility" might arouse doubt about its value for clarifying privacy, a notoriously elastic concept. In fact, its ambiguity is not a discommendation. The ambiguities of "privacy" and "inaccessibility" closely parallel one another, thereby corroborating the notion that they are roughly synonomous expressions.

A person can be inaccessible in at least three senses: physically, dispositionally, and informationally. A person is physically inaccessible if others are unable to experience her directly through at least one of the five senses. Conversely, a person whose body can be directly seen, touched, tasted, heard, or smelled is physically accessible. Persons who are physically inaccessible by virtue of physical structures or distance possess the form of privacy called "seclusion" and sometimes "solitude." Thus, some familiar senses of privacy do correspond to the first familiar sense of "inaccessibility."

Even a physically accessible person can be inaccessible in the second or dispositional sense. Some of the people we describe as "inaccessible" may be unforthcoming. Individuals are said to be inaccessible in this sense when their beliefs, desires, values, tastes, background, or character cannot be discerned by virtue of their silence, intentional concealment, deception, incomprehensibility, inscrutibility, or reserve. The privacy objection to polygraph and drug testing is that, if the testing procedures work at all, they circumvent the boundaries that allow dispositional inaccessibility. It is significant that reserved, unforthcoming individuals are aptly described as "private" as well as "inaccessible." Clearly, another distinct sense of inaccessibility corresponds to one of the definitions of privacy.

The amnesiac, once a recurring character in daytime television drama, is a good example of a person who, although physically and dispositionally accessible, may be informationally inaccessible. The amnesiac may be disposed to "tell it all" but, because she lacks relevant memory, can share no information. A person is informationally inaccessible to the extent that facts about her beliefs, desires, values, states, background, or character are unknown or unknowable by others. The inaccessibility of information, whether stored in the human brain or in computer files, is widely considered a major requirement of privacy. As noted earlier, for some theorists, the inaccessibility of personal information is virtually what privacy means.

Basic Features

Now I will fill in the basic features of my definition. On the privacy-as-inaccessibility account, privacy losses occur when a person (or the person's mental states or information about the person) is to some degree or in some respect made more accessible to others. The consequences of increased access may be trivial or they may be profound. Access may be either direct or indirect. Direct access is possible through one of the five senses unaided; indirect access is possible through a surveillance device capable of contemporaneous sensory enhancement (for example, binoculars) or recordation (such as a tape recorder). Direct and indirect access of these two sorts has been called "causal" access.[42] Disclosure of information about a person, like disclosure of the physical person, can be an assault on dignity and feelings. As I shall allow, restricted-access theorists generally allow that privacy is lost when others have no "causal" access to the physical person but have what has been termed "interpretative" access to the person through access to information about the person.[43]

Restricted-access accounts generally construe privacy as an ethically neutral descriptive concept. This construal avoids preempting ethical questions about privacy's value. I, too, maintain that privacy is neither a presumptive moral good nor a presumptive moral evil. Thus, one's enjoyment of the privacy of a cabin in the woods may merit moral approval as part of a plan to recover from a nervous breakdown, but disapproval as part of a plan to neglect a dying spouse, abandoned and alone at home.

Restricted-access accounts generally regard privacy as a matter of degree rather than as an all-or-none concept. Again I follow the lead of similar theories. Hence, a person undressing behind a solid brick wall may be said to possess privacy in virtue of his being outside another's range of vision, but a person undressing behind a translucent rice paper screen can also be said to possess privacy. Others' vision is softly obscured by the thin divide. Along another dimension, the quick peek of a peeping Tom diminishes privacy, as does long-term surveillance by a team of government agents.

The Forms of Privacy

It is not uncommon when defining "privacy" to specify its meaning further by identifying the most important forms of privacy. This practice has led privacy theorists to designate seclusion, solitude, anonymity, confidentiality, secrecy, intimacy and/or reserve—collectively referred to here as the "p-concepts"—as forms, that is, states, conditions, aspects, or senses, of privacy. In *Privacy and Freedom,* under the description "states of privacy," Westin identified what he took to be the basic forms of privacy: solitude, anonymity, intimacy, and reserve.[44] Subsequent definitional accounts of privacy exhibit the influence of Westin's helpful analysis.

While theorists agree that the concept of privacy and the p-concepts are related, they disagree dramatically on the question of how they are related. Privacy is best viewed as a kind of parent or umbrella concept to those p-concepts that denote a person's conditions of inaccessibility to the senses and surveillance devices of others. These particular p-concepts have the status of forms of privacy. I embrace as forms of privacy those p-concepts that can themselves be defined in terms of inaccessibility. To the extent that it is reasonable to define "privacy" broadly in terms of inaccessibility, it is reasonable to characterize as forms of privacy concepts of more limited scope that can also be defined in terms of inaccessibility.

Theorists who agree that privacy is a parent or umbrella concept may nevertheless disagree whether a particular p-concept is a form of privacy. For example, they disagree whether intimacy and secrecy are forms of privacy. As explained below, secrecy should be deemed a form of privacy because it denotes certain conditions of inaccessibility, namely, those characterized by the intentional concealment or withholding of information. Intimacy would seem to fall outside the privacy concept as denoting a degree of openness to communication or contact with selected others, rather than a degree of inaccessibility.[45] Yet, when viewed as a condition of selective disclosure, intimacy also denotes inaccessibility. In practice, seclusion and intimacy are closely related. Conventional mores dictate that many types of emotional and physical intimacy not be displayed in public places. Intimacy is thus facilitated by and closely associated with the form of privacy known as seclusion.

Theorists also disagree about whether reserve is a form of privacy. Few privacy theorists have followed Westin in designating reserve as a basic form of privacy. The reason may be this. On one rendering, reserve is a character trait, a proclivity toward non-disclosure of information. One result of the character trait of reserve is dispositional inaccessibility, in the sense explained earlier. As a character trait, reserve does not entail that what a person is or knows will remain private in particular instances. Reserve can falter and be broken down. Construed as a character trait "reserve" denotes psychological proclivities whose expected consequence is a degree of informational privacy. It does not denote a condition of informational privacy. Reserve can be construed instead as specific conduct rather than as a character trait. So construed, reserve consists of particular instances of withholding information by persons who may or may not be generally described as reserved. Viewed as specific conduct, reserve accomplishes a degree of informational privacy.

Modesty is a particular kind of reserve. To be modest is to be reserved about oneself; in particular, to be reserved about one's own praiseworthy attributes and achievements. As a character trait, modesty is the disposition to refrain from ostentation and self-praise. Modest persons are modest with respect to what they themselves regard as praiseworthy and what they believe others will regard as praiseworthy. As specific conduct, modesty consists of acts of refraining from ostentation or self-praise.

Feminine modesty is a somewhat different concept than modesty *simpliciter*. A woman's special virtue, feminine modesty denotes exhibiting a manner of speech, dress, and behavior calculated not to attract attention to one's body, to one's views, or to one's desires. A modest woman avoids self-exposure and ostentation, especially in the presence of men. Feminine modesty is thus a kind of obligatory, social disappearing act that shields a woman in a mantle of privacy.

In nineteenth-century Europe and America, the concept of feminine modesty severely limited even the access of a physician to his female patients' ailing bodies. Lois Banner (*Women in Modern America,* 1984) has noted that:

> The most common argument for professional medical and legal training for women . . . was that women patients and clients had the right to consult professionals of the same sex in order to protect their womanly modesty.

The ideal of feminine modesty also provided an argument against the publication of a woman's name or photograph. Yellow journalism aimed at his socially prominent wife and daughter precipitated Samuel Warren's co-authorship with Louis Brandeis of their celebrated *Harvard Law Review* article, "The Right to Privacy" (1890). In 1902, in the case of *Roberson v. Rochester Folding Box Company,* the New York State Court created a stir by refusing to award $15,000 to a woman claiming invasion of privacy, severe nervous shock, and injury to her good name when her portrait appeared without consent in advertisements for flour marketed by Franklin Mills Company. In a dissenting opinion, Judge Gray argued that it was inconceivable that a young woman should have no basis for relief against those who forced her to submit to "mortifying notoriety." Soon after *Roberson* was decided, Judge Gray's sentiments were vindicated. The New York legislature enacted a statute making nonconsensual use of a person's name or likeness unlawful.

Like media publicity, public speaking offended the nineteenth-century ideal of feminine modesty. Elizabeth Cady Staton (1815–1902) complained in her journals of hypocritical socialities who donned bare-shouldered ballgowns and danced in the arms of strangers but who, on the ground of modesty, balked at the idea of speaking out for women's rights in public forums. When minister Anna Howard Shaw, president of National American Woman Suffrage Association (1904–1911), was asked to deliver her first sermon, she feared telling her family. She knew they would view the invitation to take to the pulpit as a disgrace rather than an accomplishment.

The concept of feminine modesty has a residual presence in American society and often competes with contemporary conceptions of privacy and liberation for women. This is perhaps nowhere better illustrated than in female prostitution decriminalization controversies. There the old ethic of feminine modesty and the new ethic of sexual privacy for consenting adults are at loggerheads. The tension between the old ethic of feminine modesty and the new ethic of female liberation was commercially exploited by the teen rock idol Madonna. She combined an authentic Catholic name and cruciform jewelry with bordello garb, and her stardom began with a popular musical message that it is better to feel like a virgin than to be one.

Two alternatives have been stated to my view that privacy is a parent concept. First, it has been argued that, although they are members of a common family of concepts, privacy and each p-concept are conceptually distinct from one another, and none is a parent or form of another. Second, it has been argued that privacy is a form of secrecy, which is deemed the broader, parent concept. The views of W. A. Parent represent the first alternative. According to Parent, privacy is a narrow concept wholly distinct, not only from secrecy, but also from seclusion, anonymity, and other conditions commonly described as forms of privacy. Under Parent's narrow definition, privacy is "the condition of not having undocumented personal information about oneself known by others."[46] This definition restricts the application of "privacy" to a limited class of information non-disclosures. While the need for conceptual clarity is sometimes a reason to favor narrower over broader definitions, Parent's definition is so narrow that it violates a first principle of conceptual analysis to which he himself ascribes: philosophic definitions must strengthen and clarify, not eviscerate, concepts they seek to define.

Parent's definition and the collateral notion that privacy is not a parent concept must be rejected. Parent's definition represents a number of problems beyond its narrowness. It emphasizes the possession of knowledge, a concept subject to its own perennial definitional difficulties. According to one popular understanding of what it means to possess knowledge, it would not be clarifying to define privacy in terms of others' lacking undocumented personal knowledge about a person. Knowledge that a statement is true requires belief that it is true and requires that one be justified in that belief. Suppose it is widely publicized in literary magazines that W, an eminent writer, keeps a secret diary of interwoven saucy facts and fantasy about his romantic life. S, a stranger to W, hears of W's diary, covertly seizes an opportunity to read it, and broadcasts what he reads to others. Both by reading and by discussing the diary, S has certainly diminished and wrongly violated W's privacy. But does S have knowledge of undocumented personal information? The answer is surely that he does not, since he has no reason to believe that any particular assertion in the diary is true. S can speculate whether this or that statement is informational, but S does not know what is fact and what is fiction.

Only if S had an independent source of knowledge to corroborate his speculations about what he read in the diary could he be said to have knowledge.

Another difficulty with Parent's definition is that it implies that there can be no invasion of privacy unless knowledge of undocumented information is obtained. By "undocumented" information he means, roughly, unpublished or unpublicized information and information that is not contained in the public portions of governmental records. Hence, the writer's diary referred to in the above hypothetical is a potential source of "undocumented" information. It is curious that Parent would want governmental decisions about whether to designate record information open to the public or closed to help determine, from a philosophical perspective, what could constitute a loss of privacy. A problem for his definition is that he conditions the application of "privacy" on bureaucratic classifications that may or may not be consistent and principled. Even if his aim is a definition of privacy for tort law or constitutional law, it would not follow that the status the government gives a document ought to be largely determinative of whether its publication is a wrongful invasion of privacy.

It is also a problem for his definition that it entails that publication of facts from the distant past does not diminish privacy. Parent maintains that there is no privacy diminution where information about a person is retrieved from public documents and republished.[47] This is a point of disagreement. Even if republication from the public record can be defended on the grounds of current newsworthiness or past publication, the possibility that privacy is diminished is not ruled out, for a new generation of readers will thereby have greater interpretative access to the person about whom previously publicized facts are made newly available. The memories of those who knew the facts but had forgotten are refreshed, and their interpretative access to the person is restored. Moreover, republished information about a person from today's *New York Times* is much more accessible—unless one has a computer retrieval system at one's fingertips—than information in a ten-year-old newspaper on microfiche in a public archive. The increased accessibility of the information means privacy is diminished. (If fresh attention is drawn to a living person, there may be further grounds for characterizing republication as a privacy loss.) Whether the diminution is justifiable from the moral point of view would depend upon other factors. If the old information pertains to some current newsworthy event, giving rise to a "public right to know," its republication could be warranted. If the old information is of a type the republication of which would plainly be hurtful, embarrassing, or a breach of confidence, and if there is nothing more than curiosity-seeking to motivate republication, moral disapproval would be in order.

On the basis of his flawed, narrow definition, Parent denied that any p-concept is a form of privacy. It is remarkable that he nevertheless asserted that the p-concepts are part of what he termed a "privacy family, a family whose unifying idea is something like unrelatedness or inaccessibility."[48] This telling remark indicates that while Parent purported to reject restricted-access accounts of privacy, he recognized that the concept of inaccessibility may unify the group of related concepts he saw fit to label the "privacy family."

Seclusion and Solitude

One key form of privacy is seclusion. Privacy in the sense of seclusion is the inaccessibility that obtains by virtue of modes of physical separation that impair observation and other forms of sensing. The condition of seclusion can exist either by virtue of physical distance or by virtue of intervening physical structures such as fences, walls, or curtains. A person's actions may be as effectively hidden by a canvas partition as by a tenth of a mile of unobstructed roadway. Seclusion may bring with it desired solitude (aloneness), but it can also bring loneliness and isolation. In many instances seclusion will be closely related to solace (peace of mind) and intimacy (selective disclosure) as a means to an end. While seclusion is no guarantor of either solace or expressions of emotional and physical intimacy, it can facilitate achieving them.

Westin included solitude but not seclusion on his list of the basic forms ("states") of privacy. This was an unacceptable omission, since seclusion is an important and distinct form of privacy. Seclusion is a broad enough concept to include solitude, but the converse is not true. As its etymological roots suggest, the concept of solitude imparts the idea of being alone. When one is alone one is secluded, if only in virtue of physical distance between oneself and others. When one is secluded, however, one can be alone or with others with whom one shares one's seclusion. Shared seclusion is a lesser degree of privacy than solitude. Including solitude but not seclusion on a short list of the forms of privacy can be deemed to include solitudinous seclusion, but problematically omits shared seclusion as a basic form of privacy.

Anonymity and Limited Attention

A second key form of privacy has been characterized by philosopher Sissela Bok as protection from unwanted attention, and by legal theorist Ruth Gavison as anonymity.[49] These amount to inaccessibility in the sense of limited attention paid to the person. In public places and in the homes of large families, the inaccessibility resulting from and constituted by limited attention takes on special importance. (I will examine the inaccessibility of limited attention paid as a form of privacy in some detail in later chapters in connection with intrafamial privacy and women's privacy in public places.)

Non-disclosure, Confidentiality, and Secrecy

Information non-disclosure, the inaccessibility of information, is the third major form of privacy. As species of information non-disclosure, confidentiality and secrecy are forms of privacy. Confidentiality is achieved where designated information is not disseminated beyond a community of authorized knowers. Secrecy is information non-disclosure that results from the intentional concealment or withholding of information.

"Private" and "personal" are sometimes used as synonyms or as adjectives to describe a type of information. If one recognizes that individuals' dignitarian interests in the non-disclosure of information about themselves goes beyond information relating only to the culturally defined "personal" realm, one can define informational privacy, as do several restricted-access theorists, without appeal to the concept of the personal. This is the path I follow. It is an approach that circumvents discussions of what is and is not truly personal and goes directly to broader questions about whether particular information disclosures (and non-disclosures) are ethically warranted.

The relationship between secrecy and privacy appears unsettled in the privacy literature. On my view, secrecy is a form of privacy that entails the intentional concealment of facts. Much the same view was relied upon by social scientists Carol Warren and Barbara Laslett. Warren and Laslett studied families and homosexual communities they interpreted as arenas of privacy and secrecy, respectively.[50] They defined privacy *and* secrecy in terms of limited accessibility, yet, they explained secrecy as implying intentional concealment of negative facts. They maintained that "secrecy implies the concealment of something negatively valued by the excluded audience and in some instances by the perpetrator [secret holder] as well."[51] Secrecy, they wrote, is "a strategy for hiding acts or attributes others hold in moral disrepute, . . . a means to escape being stigmatized for them."[52] This view of "secrecy" captures one of its uses. But secrecy does not always involve the concealment of negative facts. Secrets are also used to conceal positive facts, such as the plan to throw a surprise party or award a prize.

Bok defined secrecy as the result of "intentional concealment" and privacy as "unwanted access." Since privacy need not involve intentional concealment, she argued, privacy and secrecy are distinct concepts. Privacy, Bok explained, involves boundaries to physical access to our bodies, information about personal matters, and attention drawn to personal matters or one's person. Privacy and secrecy are so often equated because "privacy is such a central part of what secrecy protects."[53] Bok thus viewed secrecy as a device for protecting privacy. A similar view of why privacy and secrecy are often equated was put forward by Carl Friedrich.[54] But, ironically, Friedrich maintained that "privacy is a special form of secrecy," a view Bok implicitly rejected in favor of the view that privacy and secrecy are distinct concepts, and that I have rejected in favor of the view that secrecy is a special form of privacy.

Both Bok and Friedrich err in their analysis of the relationship between secrecy and privacy. Bok correctly perceives that privacy and secrecy are distinct concepts. However, I believe they are overlapping rather than wholly distinct. For although secrecy but not privacy essentially entails intentional concealment, secrecy can be understood as a form of privacy in that it too involves boundaries to personal access. In particular, it involves access to information about persons and their engagements. Privacy is not a form of secrecy, as Friedrich maintained, because privacy is the broader concept and need not involve intentional concealment or withholding of facts.

OBJECTIONS TO RESTRICTED-ACCESS DEFINITIONS

I have identified the appeal of restricted-access theories and described a particular restricted-access theory that identifies privacy with degrees of inaccessibility. Furthermore, I have explained seclusion, limited attention paid or anonymity, and information non-disclosure as major forms of privacy. Finally, I have placed solitude, solace, intimacy, reserve, modesty, secrecy, and confidentiality on a conceptual map. I now turn to objections that have been made to restricted-access accounts of the meaning of privacy. Recall that there are three distinct types of restricted-access accounts: limited access or inaccessibility accounts, access control accounts, and limitations on unwanted access accounts. I will show that access control and limitations on unwanted access theories must be rejected.

Access Control

Access control type restricted-access definitions of "privacy" are susceptible to the same problems as all definitions that identify privacy with forms of control. Privacy-as-control definitions are those that identify personal privacy as the measure of control individuals have over (a) information about themselves, (b) intimacies of personal identity, or (c) sensory access to themselves or information about themselves.[55] Definitional theories of these types have been criticized and rejected by Gavison and Parent.[56]

The problem shared by access control and other privacy-as-control definitions is this. To say that an individual controls access to herself or the flow of information about herself is not to say how she chooses to exercise that control. An individual with control over access may choose to spend her time in a public square, increasing her physical accessibility to others. In general, a person with control over access may, as Gavison has pointed out, "choose to have privacy or give it up."[57] Since a person can exercise control over access in the direction of making herself more accessible rather than less accessible, privacy itself cannot be identified with control over access.

While it is necessary to reject the definition of privacy as control over access, it bears emphasis that the ability to control access for the sake of achieving desirable states of privacy can be exceedingly important. Achieving desired privacy is facilitated by legal and cultural norms that afford control over access to oneself and sources of information about oneself. Requiring consent as a condition of information disclosure is one way individuals are afforded control over information access. Naturally then, what we mean by a right of privacy "includes the notions of control and voluntariness in denoting individuals' claims of entitlement to the recognition of their interests in privacy."[58]

Parent rightly rejected access-control definitions of privacy, but for the wrong reason. He relied on the puzzling ground that entitlement to control over access is contrary to the liberal way of life. He argued that definitions that identify privacy with control over access to oneself confer an "extraordinary kind of sovereignty" that "permits each person to define unilaterally, his relationships with others."[59] He wrote:

> I cannot understand how A could exercise his privacy, on this view, without *eo ipso* depriving others, those persons whose access to A was either allowed or denied, of their privacy! Surely such a view of human behavior is incompatible with the much more liberal ideal of relationships founded on mutual accord and respect.[60]

The problem Parent sees is a problem only if access-control definitions are interpreted to imply that any exercise of control over access is ipso facto morally justified. Yet, the implication that individuals are morally entitled to precisely the access control they want cannot be fairly attributed to access-control theorists. A better interpretation of their view is this: although conditions of privacy are aptly described as conditions of control over personal accessibility, it is an open question how much access control (privacy) the individual ought to be accorded by law, morality or other social practice. The ideal of equal respect for individuals that underlies liberal political morality requires that each person have a degree of inaccessibility and sovereignty that includes control over aspects of his or her life deeply related to personhood. Since each individual is entitled only to a degree of sovereignty consistent with others having the same, the liberal principle of equal respect is preserved. The losses of privacy we care about, and especially those offensive enough to be cognizable in a civil court, are typically those that result from assaults on the sphere of justified self-sovereignty. Hence, while access-control definitions fail, they do not fail because of fundamental incompatibility with liberalism.

Unwanted Access

Sissela Bok defined "privacy" as the "condition of being protected from unwanted access by others." Evaluating Bok's definition raises the question whether "privacy" is better defined in terms of conditions of inaccessibility *simpliciter* or conditions of being protected from unwanted access. One of the things that makes the legal right to privacy significant is that it represents an enforceable right against unwanted intrusions or disclosures of one's affairs. It represents a degree of freedom to limit and define the nature of one's involvements with others in accordance with one's own wishes. It does not follow from this that the concept of privacy should be defined in terms of unwanted access.

When a person retreats into seclusion out of a desire to be "far from the madding crowd," her privacy is accurately described as a condition of unwanted access. A person who is secluded in an attic study is protected by its walls, shutters, stairs, and remoteness. While there, if she begins to crave contact with others, she no longer wants the inaccessibility she possesses. Yet, she is still in a condition of privacy; the same conditions of seclusion and protection are in place. The same walls, shutters, stairs, and remoteness shield her from others. Thus, the unwanted-access definition must be rejected as imposing an unwarranted constraint on uses of "privacy." Privacy aptly describes even some conditions of unwanted inaccessibility.

Unsuccessful Counterexamples

While they both contain important insights, the definitions of privacy in terms of control over access and unwanted access ultimately fail. In this section I will show that the definition of privacy in terms of inaccessibility or limited access can withstand important objections.

Again, Parent is the major published critic. Relying on a counterex-

ample, Parent in effect concluded that any restricted-access definition—including my privacy-as-inaccessibility account and Gavison's
similar privacy-as-limited-access account—will fail because restricted
access is not a sufficient condition for the existence of privacy:

> Suppose A taps B's phone and overhears several of B's conversations.
> From these A discovers some very personal things about B. Official
> restraints have been placed on A's snooping, though. For instance, he
> must obtain permission from a judge before listening in. Here is a case
> where the definiens . . . is satisfied. But we certainly do not want to say
> nor should we say that under these circumstances B retains his privacy.[61]

Parent's putative counterexample erroneously assumes (a) an unduly simplistic interpretation of the *definiens* of restricted access
theories and (b) a conception of philosophical definition whereby
restricted-access definitions are without merit unless they state the
necessary and sufficient conditions for the use of "privacy." Because
of the first assumption, Parent fails even to prove that restricted-
access definitions do not state sufficient conditions. Because of the
second assumption, Parent fails to assess the merits of restricted-
access definitions conceived as informal nominal definitions rather
than as statements of conditions necessary and sufficient for the
proper use of the term "privacy" and the concept for which it stands.
To explain why the putative counterexample is inconclusive, I draw
on the distinctions I made earlier between normative and physical
restrictions on access, and between preventing and regulating access.

Parent's example posits a normative (in this case, legal) requirement
implemented to regulate (rather than prevent) access to another's
private telephone conversations. A legal regulatory norm can cease to
be merely normative when conduct in conformity with the norm
results in a physical condition of restricted access. The admission that
Parent's putative counterexample forces is that legal rules limiting
access in the normative sense are consistent with lost privacy. This
admission does not logically entail that restricted-access definitions
are untenable. Moreover, only with obvious equivocation can the
admission be deemed to entail that limited access or inaccessibility is
not a sufficient condition for privacy. It entails, at most, that a
normative limitation on access to a person is not a sufficient condition
for complete privacy, something no restricted-access theorist would
have reason to deny.

Suppose Parent's putative counterexample had involved a physical
limitation on access, rather than a normative one, as follows: A is a law
enforcement official and B and C suspected co-conspirators in crime.
A intends to tap B's office phone, a fact C gets wind of. C places an
antiwiretapping device on B's office phone. At the last minute A taps

B's home phone instead and thereby obtains personal information. Privacy was lost, even though access to *B* was limited. For this to constitute a counterexample to restricted-access definitions we have to suppose that asserting "privacy was lost even though access was limited" is to assert a contradiction. There is no contradiction, however. What the example presents is a case in which *A*'s access to *B* was limited in one respect (via the antiwiretap device on his office phone) even though it was not limited in another respect (via his home phone).

Another objection Parent raised to restricted-access theories was this one. Privacy cannot be defined in terms of inaccessibility, because *A* could have unlimited access to *B* or information about *B* but choose never to take advantage of it.[62] The idea here is that, in theory, a person can be wholly physically and informationally accessible, and yet possess complete privacy. This objection fails. Conditions of complete though unexploited accessibility are not adequately described as conditions of privacy. Two examples illustrate the inadequacy. *A* performs calisthenics each morning at 4 A.M. in front of her apartment building. All her neighbors have complete access to her, but they do not exploit it and probably never will. No one wants to get up that early or come home that late; they have better things to occupy their time than watching *A*. In a sense, *A* is completely observationally accessible—others can look at her if they really want to. It even makes sense to say *A* exercises in public. In another sense, however, *A* is completely inaccessible—others never view her exercising. This is why it also makes sense to say *A* enjoys privacy when she exercises.

Similarly, suppose Big Brother has mounted roving-eye cameras everywhere, but has not turned them on. Under these circumstances, in one sense Smith is completely inaccessible when he is alone in his bedroom, for no one knows what he does there. In this respect it makes sense to say Smith possesses privacy when he is alone in his room. But this Orwellian world is susceptible of a contrary description. In another sense Smith is completely accessible to Big Brother, since the roving eye monitor can be switched on at Big Brother's option. Correspondingly, it is appropriate to say that Smith lacks privacy, or at least that he lacks the high degree of privacy that he would have if the roving-eye monitors had not been installed.

Examples such as these positing "unexploited access" and "threatened privacy loss" reveal that a person can be in one respect accessible and in another respect inaccessible at the same time. They also reveal that a person aptly described as lacking privacy in one respect can, on the same facts, be aptly described as possessing substantial privacy. Thus, far from proving that privacy cannot be defined in terms of restricted access, these examples illustrate a point made earlier. The expressions "privacy" and "inaccessibility" have parallel applications, some near-synonymous uses in virtue of which restricted access definitions are elucidating and tenable.

DEFINING WOMEN'S PRIVACY

There is one last task for this chapter. I now consider what difference it makes for understanding and addressing women's privacy problems that privacy is defined in restricted-access terms.

In a recent interview on National Public Radio, an etiquette expert was asked what question she was most frequently asked about conventional American manners. She responded that it was a question about privacy, namely, what one should do when others invade one's privacy by allowing their cigarette smoke to drift, especially during a meal in a public place.

Cigarette smoke is frequently offensive, but does it invade privacy? On the restricted-access definition I have defended, it is clear that inhaling drifting smoke would not qualify as a loss of privacy. If your smoke blows my way, I am not more accessible to your senses or surveillance devices. Therefore, my privacy is not invaded. Your smoke is something I may reasonably regard as a nuisance. It may interfere with my enjoyment and peace of mind, but it does not diminish my privacy. A restricted-access theorist who defined privacy in terms of the inaccessibility of persons to others, rather than as inaccessibility of persons to others' senses and surveillance devices, as I have, would be free to construe "others" to include the annoying by-products of others' behavior, such as cigarette smoke, noise, or junkmail. Indeed, it is fairly common to postulate a "private space," whose penetration by odors, sounds, and objects of human origin is deemed an invasion of personal privacy. This is precisely what the etiquette expert seems to have done.

Where the purpose of defining "privacy" is to prescribe more circumspect usage, careful attention to the kinds of experiences a definition entails to be diminutions of privacy is of paramount importance. Responding to broad, inconsistent, and confusing uses of "privacy" in the law and in everyday discourse, theorists have devoted a substantial amount of scholarship to prescribing ideal usages for "privacy." For some, formulating what should and should not count as losses of privacy has been a prelude to formulating what interests privacy rights ought to protect. While few have focused on whether foul smells and loud noises diminish privacy, considerable attention has been paid to whether governmental regulation of abortion, contraception, sexual lifestyle, and families can be coherently said to diminish privacy.

What Privacy Includes

Ruth Gavison, a prescription-oriented restricted-access theorist who aimed at a definition of "privacy" adequate for the law, construed privacy as limited access in the senses of solitude, secrecy, and anonymity. On her view, "privacy" is a measure of the extent to which an individual is known, the extent to which an individual is the subject of attention, and the extent to which others are in physical proximity to an individual. Her definition of "privacy" was intended to include:

> such "typical" invasions of privacy as the collection, storage, and computerization of information; the dissemination of information about individuals; peeping, following, watching, and photographing individuals; intruding or entering "private" places; eavesdropping, wiretapping, reading of letters, drawing attention to individuals, required testing of individuals; and forced disclosure of information. [It expressly excluded] exposure to unpleasant noises, smells, and sights; prohibitions of such conduct as abortions, use of contraceptives and unnatural sexual intercourse; insulting, harassing, or persecuting behavior; presenting individuals in a "false light;" unsolicited mail and unwanted phone calls; regulation of the way family obligations should be discharged; and commercial exploitation.[63]

How did she arrive at these lists of inclusions and exclusions? Notably, she excluded "prohibitions of such conduct as abortions, contraceptives [and] regulation of the way family obligations should be discharged."

It is apparent that Gavison's inclusions and exclusions were not wholly arbitrary. For the most part her exclusions fell into discernible categories. She excluded those forms of behavior that she believed to be encompassed by other distinct legal concepts such as nuisance, trespass, and deprivation of liberty. Why is required testing a loss of privacy? Would it not depend upon the nature of the tests? Why is calling attention to someone a loss of privacy but harassment not? How then do we classify harassment-by-drawing-attention-to? What about harassment-by-interference-with-seclusion? In Chapter 5, I identify forms of harassment that include drawing and paying attention to women in ways that interfere with anonymity and seclusion. I maintain that these forms of harassment are invasions of privacy.

Following the lead of the U.S. Supreme Court, many regard abortion and contraception rights as the preeminent women's privacy issues. David A.J. Richards has been steadfast and unapologetic in his application of the concept of privacy to the analysis of abortion, contraception, and homosexuality cases.[64] Yet, as exemplified by Gavison's discussion of privacy, a major theoretical question occupying privacy theorists in the fields of philosophy and law is whether the rights and interests labeled "privacy rights" and "privacy interests" by the Supreme Court and approving liberal theorists might be better described as "liberties" and "liberty interests." As we shall consider in detail in Chapter 4, some theorists have emphatically contended that it is inaccurate and confusing to view questions of the proper limits of state intervention in freedom of choice respecting sex, childbearing, and the discharge of familial obligations as questions about privacy. They maintain that such "decisional privacy" is not privacy at all. Along these lines Gavison argued that unless a bold line is drawn between privacy and liberty, the concept of privacy loses its theoretical distinctness.

Concerned less about conceptual clarity for its own sake than about sound adjudication, some legal theorists portray the Supreme Court's privacy analysis in leading reproductive rights cases as constitutional legerdemain. John Hart Ely, for example, has criticized the Supreme Court's privacy analysis as overreaching substantive, due process adjudication.[65] Philosophers join in, too, arguing that laws preempting the choice of citizens are coercive.[66] Because such laws are coercive, some say they involve a denial of liberty and are appropriately evaluated against the Fourteenth Amendment procedural standard that citizens shall not be deprived of liberty without due process of law, rather than against a putative, substantive standard of fundamental rights of privacy.

Another Usage

Like Gavison, I have adopted and prescribed a definition of "privacy" on which what has been termed "decisional privacy" can be defined neither as privacy itself nor as a form of privacy in the restricted access sense.[67] While decisional privacy does not fall within the parameters of the restricted-access conception of privacy, another conception of privacy helps to explain why certain liberty interests affecting sex, reproduction, and families are so commonly labeled "privacy" interests.

The use of "privacy" in connection with governmental interference with sexual, reproductive, and familial free choice seems to derive from the concept of "the private" utilized in the public/private distinction,[68] rather than from the concept of privacy as restricted access. Under the public/private distinction, the public is the sphere of activity that is or ought to be a matter of governmental (that is, public) concern. The private is the sphere of activity that is or ought to be left to non-governmental (that is, "private") interests. In reliance on the public/private distinction, "privacy" has been used to refer to spheres of activity that are, or ought to be, free of governmental involvement. Decisionmaking concerning noncommercial heterosexual adult sexuality, procreation, and families is generally supposed to fall largely within the private sphere. The usage whereby "privacy" means "freedom from governmental involvement" is not always carefully distinguished from the restricted-access usage that has been the focus of this chapter. Yet it should be, for the latter usage is a more distinct one. On the former usage the expression "privacy" refers to aspects of liberty rather than to conditions of restricted access. It refers to freedom from coercive outside interference.

As I will explain in Chapters 3 and 4, decisional privacy is an important requirement of women's freedom, their social equality, and their privacy as well. Decisional privacy is an aspect of liberty, but it contributes significantly to women's ability to achieve paradigmatic forms of privacy. Privacy is centrally at stake in reproductive rights controversies.

The senses in which abortion and contraceptive rights issues are privacy issues has not always been fully appreciated. Most discussion of privacy in connection with the abortion issue focuses on decisional privacy, the freedom of choice whether to terminate or not to terminate pregnancy. Equally important are the implications of decisional privacy for privacy in these paradigmatic senses: solitude and limited attention paying at home; secrecy and confidentiality in personal and medical relationships; and anonymity in governmentally mandated abortion record-keeping and reporting. These bear on self-determination, bodily integrity, satisfaction, and fulfillment in private life, and on authority in relationships with others. As a practical matter, as long as appropriate attention is given to the privacy implications of reproductive liberties, the resolution of the theoretical debate over whether decisional privacy is liberty or is privacy matters little.

Or does it? The definition assigned to "privacy" constrains what one can term a condition of privacy, an invasion of privacy, and a loss of privacy. The moral rhetoric of fundamental rights of constitutional proportions and the rhetoric of privacy have helped to keep reproductive rights concerns near the top of the public policy agenda. To define reproductive issues beyond the realm of privacy discourse carries with it the threat that these concerns will seem less urgent. It is conceivable that the desire to take women's issues out of the public eye has even on occasion been a motive for insisting that "privacy" be narrowly defined to exclude reproductive concerns.

In the final analysis, the close ties between reproductive liberties and personal privacy take much of the point away from insisting that political advocacy of permissive abortion policies be purged of privacy talk. Privacy diminution is part of what is wrong with governmentally imposed obstacles to decisionmaking respecting birth control, abortion, and the discharge of childcare duties. Women understand that their liberty, their equality, their moral authority, but also their privacy is at stake.

CONCLUSION: FROM DEFINITION TO VALUE

The concept of privacy is central to this book. Toward clarification of the concept, Chapter 1 has offered a survey of some of the issues that attend philosophical definition. Despite a striking lack of consensus in the scholarly literature about how privacy ought to be understood, numerous theorists have settled upon what I have termed "restricted-access" definitions. This chapter has defended a particular restricted-access definition: privacy denotes a degree of inaccessibility of persons, their mental states, and information about them to the senses and surveillance devices of others. This definition is pragmatically well suited to maintaining clarity and consistency in the discussions ahead. But it has even more significant virtues. It has validity as a descriptive account of what "privacy" is generally used to denote. Most important, it can be defended as a prescriptive recommendation for circumspect usage.

I have distinguished the restricted-access usage of "privacy" from a second popular usage. This one is derivative of the public/private distinction. Under this usage, "privacy" refers to freedom from coercive governmental or, by extension, other outside interference with decisionmaking. The decisional privacy usage can lead to a blurring of the conceptual lines that should be drawn between "privacy" and "liberty." It is a usage that some philosophers have rejected and some legal scholars associate with heavily criticized Supreme Court opinions I consider in conjunction with reproductive liberties in Chapter 4. Focusing on the distinction between privacy in the restricted-access sense and privacy in the decisional sense, theorists have overlooked the important ties between the two. I will attempt to elucidate these ties in the pages ahead.

Thus far I have only hinted at the moral value and social significance that opportunities for personal privacy have for women. The next chapter takes up questions of value, addressing leading accounts of the value and risks of personal privacy in general. It is a necessary prelude to subsequent topical discussions of the importance of women's privacy and privacy-promoting liberties.

CHAPTER 2

The Value of Privacy

T HE EXPRESSION "PRIVACY" applies to a broad range of conditions that go by such names as "solitude," "secrecy," and "anonymity." They have at least one thing in common: all are conditions character- ized by a degree of personal inaccessibility.

How important is privacy? Social scientists have concluded that practices to protect privacy are present in virtually all human cultures and function as devices to limit observation and disclosure inimical to individual and societal well-being.[1] Philosophers and legal theorists maintain that respecting privacy is paramount for human dignity, personhood, and workable community life.[2] They have argued that a right to privacy must be viewed as a fundamental moral right. Law has been counted as one of the means through which a society can promote the privacy deemed beneficial from philosophical and social science perspectives.[3] In the last three decades personal privacy has emerged in the United States as a preeminent legal policy concern. A substantial body of state and federal case law and statutes now protects individual privacy. Between 1970 and 1980, Congress enacted no less than seven major pieces of legislation aimed at the information and surveillance practices of the private sector and the federal government.[4] Significant new federal legislation aimed at protecting privacy was enacted in the 1980s.

The high accolades for privacy and privacy rights have been neither unqualified nor unanimous. Legal privacy rights have been criticized as trivial and construed as less important than efficiency, accountability, and keeping the public educated and informed. In another vein, privacy has been causally linked to loneliness, aliena- tion, social irresponsibility, and the repression of women and chil- dren. Detractors opposed to individualism have viewed individual privacy rights as inextricably grounded in an untenable political

35

morality. Even some proponents of liberalism see the idea of privacy and privacy rights as fundamentally out of place in a discussion of the ethics of family life and procreation. In addressing these negative assessments of privacy, this chapter conveys my belief that, without adequate privacy, individuals have a severely diminished capacity to live as individuated persons and equal participants in the good family and the just society.

Opportunities for individual forms of privacy have practical and moral value for women. Some feminists appear to reject this view. Catherine MacKinnon, for example, has portrayed privacy as an ideal in the service of ideologies that have helped to subjugate and confine women to the domestic sphere.[5] Despite the inimical uses to which the concept of privacy may be put, I believe opportunities for privacy and the exercise of liberties that promote privacy have special importance for women. Privacy can strengthen traits associated with moral personhood, individuality, and self-determination. It can render a woman more fit for contributions both in her own family and in outside endeavors.

In *The Second Sex,* Simone de Beauvoir sought to explain why Western women have not contributed more to art, literature, and philosophy. She argued that women need liberty and opportunities for privacy if they are to exercise their creative and intellectual capacities to the fullest. They must be free of social practices that perpetually interfere with "sovereign solitude":

> The restrictions that education and custom impose on woman limit her grasp on the universe; when the struggle to find one's place in the world is too arduous, there can be no question of getting away from it. Now, one must first emerge from it into a sovereign solitude if one wants to regain a grasp upon it. . . . What I desire is liberty to go walking alone, to come and go. . . . You believe you can profit by what you see when you are accompanied by someone, when you must wait for your companion, your family! . . . Thought is shackled. . . . That is enough to make your wings droop.[6]

The quality of group culture and individual lives is improved if women have the meaningful opportunities for privacy that foster larger and more varied contributions.

This chapter has two purposes. First, it will offer a critical taxonomy of the general accounts of the moral and instrumental value of privacy that have been set out in the scholarly literature. It stands to reason that the most useful assessments of the value of privacy would be particularized assessments. That is, they would be assessments framed as inquiries about the value of specific instances or patterns of particular forms of privacy. Although particularized assessments would seem to be most worthwhile, numerous philosophers and legal theorists have turned their attention instead to very general moral or instrumental assessments of privacy—and left it there.

The second purpose of this chapter is to suggest why wholesale rejection of privacy motivated by feminism and antiliberalism is unwarranted. Women have had too much of the wrong kinds of privacy. But they very much need certain beneficial privacies. This chapter is most directly concerned with the value of privacy in the restricted-access sense. It also recognizes the value of decisional privacy. "Decisional privacy" stands for aspects of liberty, especially procreative and sexual liberty. One of the claims I shall make is that decisional privacy can promote privacy in the restricted-access sense. For this reason, the moral argument for privacy is also, to a great extent, an argument for some important types of decisional privacy. Moreover, as we shall see, the moral arguments made for decisional privacy, like the moral arguments for paradigmatic forms of privacy, relate closely to values of personhood and self-determination.

Accounts of privacy's value discussed in the scholarship of philosophers and legal theorists can be grouped as follows: (a) intrinsic value accounts, (b) reductionist accounts, (c) functionalist accounts, (d) personhood-creation and personhood-enchancement accounts, and (e) relationship-creation and relationship-enchancement accounts. Accounts of type (a) and (b) are not sufficiently explanatory and are thus untenable. Type (c), functionalist accounts, usefully stress that the many forms of privacy serve diverse, instrumentally valued ends. But the accounts of type (d) and (e) best get to the root of privacy's moral value.

INTRINSIC VALUE ACCOUNTS

To describe privacy as having intrinsic value implies that it is unnecessary to state any justificatory basis for privacy sanctions: human privacy ought to be promoted by individuals and government because it is irreducibly worthy of respect.[7] As evidenced by their accounts of the meaning and value of privacy, theorists generally overlook the possibility of an "intrinsic value" account of the value of privacy.[8] Little harm is done by overlooking the possibility of an intrinsic value account. It is implausible to suppose that all conditions of privacy, regardless of time, place, and circumstance, are either useful or merit moral approval. It is equally implausible to suppose the opposite: that conditions of privacy invariably lack utility and moral worth. It is surely sometimes a good thing—the healthy, sensible, fair, virtuous, or morally best thing—to seclude oneself, to have secrets, to remain anonymous. By the same token, conditions of privacy are surely sometimes pathological, foolish, unjust, despicable, or morally wrong.

The account one gives of the definition of "privacy" bears importantly on the account one can give of privacy's value. A definition might prescribe or stipulate that "privacy" be applied only to morally praiseworthy conditions of limited access. For example, were privacy defined in terms of the degree of inaccessibility from others a person ought to have—ought relative to a system of moral norms—then the question whether privacy is a morally valuable thing would have been definitionally preempted. This definition of "privacy" would entail that privacy means a morally good thing.

Something of an intrinsic value account of the value of privacy tied to a value-laden definition of "privacy" can be seen in Carl D. Schneider's definition of "private affairs" as those which ought to be protected by limited access.[9] Schneider's definition preempts the question of whether access to private affairs ought to be limited. Sissela Bok, whose definition was evaluated in Chapter 1, defined "privacy" as the condition of being protected from unwanted access by others.[10] Bok's definition preempts the question of privacy's subjective desirability but not the question of its moral value. Nonetheless, because liberal political morality gives presumptive validity to each person's self-regarding desires, a liberal embracing Bok's definition would come closer to preempting questions about the moral value of privacy than would a liberal embracing either my purely neutral privacy-as-inaccessibility account or similar limited access accounts offered by David O'Brien and Ruth Gavison.[11]

Where "privacy" is defined neutrally to denote conditions of inaccessibility, the moral value of a specific condition of privacy will depend upon its morally relevant implications or consequences. What one takes to be the morally relevant implications or consequences of privacy will depend, of course upon one's underlying moral theory.

For many, morality is essentially a matter of religion. Religious precepts dictate what consequences or implications of conduct are morally relevant. Religious teachings dictate whether particular conditions of privacy and those who seek them out are good or evil. It should be noted that the concept of an omniscient, omnipresent God poses an interesting privacy problem: one is never truly alone.[12]

Secular philosophical moralists are commonly grouped in accordance to whether they judge conduct or a rule of conduct principally on the basis of (a) its ability to promote designated consequences or ends or (b) its consistency with fundamental moral duties. Moralists who judge conduct or rules principally on the basis of whether they promote designated consequences or ends are described as "teleologists." Moralists who judge principally on the basis of consistency with categorical or prima facie moral duties are termed "deontologists." A good deal of scholarly controversy has concerned the soundness of competing deontological and teleological approaches. Attempts have been made to reconcile the two in theories that draw on the best insights of both.[13]

Following Immanuel Kant, Kantian deontologists view a principle of respect for persons as the fundamental moral duty constraining human actors.[14] Moral respect requires that persons never be treated solely as means to an end. Kant maintained that we are duty-bound never to treat ourselves or other individuals as mere things. Correlatively, individuals have a right to be treated with dignity as ends in themselves. It not always clear precisely what conduct is permitted by the abstract Kantian guideline.[15] Conduct that is physically injurious, cruel, demeaning, or degrading would presumably count as immoral.

From the Kantian perspective, treatment with moral respect is called for by traits of personhood. For Kant himself, rationality, free will, and autonomy were the key traits.[16] They entail that one is entitled to moral respect as an individual and may be held to a high standard of conduct. For contemporary Kantian ethicists, self-consciousness, moral agency, and the capacity to form life plans have been deemed the traits in virtue of which individuals are entitled to moral respect.[17] Kantian deontologists judge privacy on the basis of whether it represents satisfaction of duties, principles, or rules called for by due regard for the traits of personhood in virtue of which individuals have a special dignity and ought to be accorded respect. Contemporary social contract theorist David A. J. Richards has tied the value of decisional privacy to what could be interpreted as a Kantian principle of equal respect for the independent exercise of moral powers. In *Toleration and the Constitution* he argued that this principle requires governmental non-interference with decisionmaking respecting reproduction and sex. In *A Matter of Principle*, legal philosopher Ronald Dworkin has similarly argued that without decisional privacy, individuals as possessors of a moral right to equal respect and concern have a diminished ability to put into play their own ideas about the best circumstances for human flourishing.

Utilitarianism is the most discussed teleological approach to the moral evaluation of human conduct. Philosophers have identified numerous varieties of utilitarianism, some more plausible than others.[18] According to classical utilitarian teleologists Jeremy Bentham and John Stuart Mill,[19] maximizing human pleasure or enlightened happiness for the greatest number is the end of moral conduct. The moral value of particular instances of privacy would be assessed by reference to their consequences for bringing about a greater balance of aggregate pleasure over pain, or happiness over misery.[20]

Utilitarianism has been frequently criticized as a nominally moral theory that sometimes requires immoral conduct. For example, it has been argued that utilitarianism demands killing innocent persons if their deaths would result in the greatest aggregate happiness. At least some forms of utilitarianism do seem to call for sacrificing the good of the one for the convenience of the many. To put it differently, utilitarian teleologies seem to be inconsistent *in principle* with a conception of individuals as having rights that trump arguments of social utility.

Nonetheless, John Stuart Mill's *On Liberty* is an influential source for the principle often relied upon by liberal utilitarians and non-utilitarians alike to justify decisional privacy rights protecting procreative and sexual choice from interference by government. On behalf of the decisional privacy principle, Mill argued that the individual is normally the best judge of his own good; that freedom of choice promotes the exercise of informed judgment by individuals; and that allocating decisional rights to individuals wherever possible avoids the evil of a needlessly powerful government. Consequently, the individual should not be accountable to society for his actions insofar as they are self-regarding, that is, insofar as they are harmless to others and concern the interests of no person but himself.

Like utilitarianism, the ethical philosophy of the Greek philosopher Aristotle can also be described as teleological.[21] For Aristotle, conduct is to be judged from one context to the next in accordance to whether it exemplifies the exercise of role-related virtues required by the goals of individual character and harmonious communities.[22] A modern Aristotelian could be expected to judge instances or patterns of privacy in relation to the requirements of a good character and a good society.

Privacy can be used for good or ill, to help or to harm. For example, if Jane is secluded alone in her home, we need to know something about her and the reasons she is in seclusion before we make a moral judgment about her privacy. This is true no matter what our moral theory or religion. Is she getting deserved relaxation? Is she indulging in destructive self-pity? Is she writing letters to good friends? Is she praying? Is she selfishly neglecting commitments to others who depend upon her?

Yet, when we hear that so and so's privacy was invaded we readily assume that something morally reprehensible has occurred. We sometimes speak of privacy as if it were unquestionably of positive moral value. We speak as if losses of privacy are always bad, gains always good. How can our doing so be reconciled with my observation that what are aptly denoted conditions of privacy are not always good from the moral point of view?

When we hear others complaining about privacy invasions we assume they are referring to a wrongful, nonconsensual diminution of the forms and degrees of inaccessibility one can reasonably expect to enjoy. We commonly use "invasion of privacy" as a shortcut for a highly value-laden concept: intentional deprivation of a reasonably expected, desired type and amount of privacy to which a person is morally entitled. Reflection reveals that privacy is not itself a value and not itself intrinsically valuable. Nevertheless, in many contexts we can speak of it as if it were, in reliance upon shared conceptions of desirable, legitimate, reasonable forms and levels of privacy.

REDUCTIONIST ACCOUNTS

A reductionist account of why privacy is of moral importance is one that attempts to show that privacy interests are identical to other familiar interests.[23] The term "reductionist" signifies that the value of privacy is deemed reducible, that is, equivalent to the value of other treasured conditions of life. Philosopher Judith Thomson was among the first to set out a reductionist account of privacy rights and interests.[24] Her account implied that the moral importance of privacy could be explained by reference to other familiar interests she construed as more fundamental.

The right to privacy, she argued, is actually a cluster of rights all of which are derivative of property rights, rights to the integrity and physical safety of the person, and established rights of confidentiality. It follows that privacy interests are an amalgam of interests in property, the person, and confidentiality; and that the value of the many forms of privacy is to be found in the value of undisturbed possession and control of property, personal safety and peace of mind, and informational non-disclosure.

Thomson's reductionism has been rightly criticized on the ground that, as an attempt to clarify privacy's value, it obscures the distinctive meaning of "privacy."[25] It also ignores the extent to which social rules, norms, conventions, and practices define the parameters of what is considered private. Note that this is a criticism in principle to reductionism. It insists that it is not possible for a reductionist to rehabilitate her account, as long as the essentially reductionist tact of dispensing with the concept of privacy in favor of other, putatively adequate concepts is preserved.

FUNCTIONALIST ACCOUNTS

Functionalist accounts of the value of privacy are an improvement over reductionist accounts that treat privacy as a superfluous concept. Functionalists maintain that privacy is a distinct, complex concept.

They maintain that there are many different forms of privacy whose value relates to aspects of social and economic flourishing, personhood in the moral sense, and to ideals and requisites of a liberal democratic society.

Alan F. Westin's *Privacy and Freedom* (1967) was the inaugural treatise of the present generation of privacy scholarship. Westin argued in the functionalist style that privacy is achieved through solitude, intimacy, anonymity, and reserve. Privacy is to be valued because it functions to promote personal autonomy, to afford emotional release and release from public roles, to promote self-evaluation, and to allow for limited and protected communication.[26] Westin tied the function of personal privacy to the ideals and requirements of the liberal state. The structure of his argument shows that for Westin, the value of privacy chiefly derives from its instrumental import relative to the ends of a liberal democracy. The liberal society does not require absolute privacy, Westin argued, but only sufficient privacy consistent with a good life for the individual. That life will include substantial areas of interest apart from political participation. It would include time to devote to sports, arts, literature, and similar nonpolitical pursuits. Westin suggested that liberal democracy requires the degree of privacy implied by a strong commitment to the family as a basic and autonomous unit with claims to physical and legal privacy against the state.[27]

Ruth Gavison's functionalist analysis of the value of privacy similarly stressed the multipurposive character of privacy.

> The best way to understand the value of privacy is to examine its functions. . . . These justifications for privacy are instrumental, in the sense that they point out how privacy relates to other goals. The strength of instrumental justifications depends on the extent to which other goals promoted by privacy are considered important.[28]

On Gavison's account, privacy furthers a number of valued interests of individuals respecting their own persons and their lives as social and sexual beings. Individual autonomy, mental health, creativity, and the capacity to form and maintain meaningful relationships with others are some of the specific interests to which privacy contributes. According to Gavison, privacy, understood as secrecy, solitude, and anonymity, promotes relaxation and intimacy by removing persons from view; it relieves pressure to conform, promotes freedom of thought and (hence) of action, and promotes inventiveness and creativity. Privacy also limits unfavorable social responses to a person's actions, history, or plans, such as ridicule, moral censure, adverse decisions, and the formation of negative opinion. Finally, privacy is an integral part of the franchise (in secret ballots) and of democratic institutions (political organizations).

Functionalist accounts of the value of privacy usefully point out the many respects in which privacy can be utilized to further the interests and goals of individuals and groups. But, as Gavison herself could see, functionalism does not answer the question of what moral significance the interests and goals furthered by privacy have. As a result functionalism underemphasizes the close and special connections moralists have stressed between and among privacy, personhood, and fitness for social participation and contribution.

PRIVACY FOR PERSONHOOD, PARTICIPATION, AND CONTRIBUTION

Personhood-creation and personhood-enhancement accounts of the value of privacy ("personhood" accounts, for short) are consistent with functionalist accounts, except that they seek to identify the most fundamental and morally significant ends promoted by individual forms of privacy. On personhood theories, privacy is described as a condition or set of social practices constituting, creating, or sustaining boundaries that should be drawn between ourselves and others in virtue of our status or potential as persons. In short, personhood theories maintain that the value of privacy is that it creates, sustains, or enhances personhood. Not all personhood accounts go the step further to explain the moral value privacy has relative to fitness for social participation and contribution. To do so would be to provide the most complete, fundamental, and explanatory account of the moral value of opportunities for individual privacy.

Personhood Enhancement

Moral philosophers have distinguished being a human being from being a person in the moral sense.[29] To be a human being is to be a member of the human species. To be a person in the moral sense is to possess traits in virtue of which one is entitled to a high standard of treatment and to be held to a high standard of conduct. Self-consciousness, free-will, rationality, moral agency, and the ability to form life plans are traits that have been regarded by Anglo-American ethicists in the Kantian tradition as essential traits of personhood.[30] As explained by S. I. Benn in connection with his personhood-enhancement account of the value of privacy, to recognize that a human being is a person in the moral sense is to recognize that he is a "subject with a consciousness of himself as an agent, one who is capable of having his projects and assessing his achievements in relation to them."[31]

Benn argued that a moral right to privacy worthy of legal protection flows from the "principle of privacy," that any individual who desires not to be an object of scrutiny has a reasonable prima facie claim to immunity. The justificatory ground of the privacy principle is that the self-regarding choices and desires of human persons, which often include the desire to be free of scrutiny, deserve moral respect. According to Benn, "the very intimate connection between the concepts of oneself and one's body," combined with the cultural norms of our "possessive individualist" society, firmly ground the privacy principle as a moral reason for respecting privacy.[32]

The possessive individualist cultural norms to which Benn appeals to help explain the importance of privacy are not self-justifying norms. An "individualistic society" has been defined as:

> one where individualism prevails and where control over behavior and thought is vested in the individual relatively more than in custom, tradition and consensus (as is the case in primitive and traditional societies), and relatively more than in authority (as in command economies and authoritarian societies). ["Individualism" has been defined as] the perception of the individual distinguished from his social group, the definition of the individual in terms of qualities that are distinctively his own as contrasted to group qualities, and the evaluation of the individual separate from the evaluation of the group.[33]

As traits of an individual and the ethos of a society, individualism can be taken too far. Yet, a high degree of individualism is warranted by the fundamental conception of human persons as morally unique, each presumed worthy of treatment with moral respect for his or her own sake, each presumed morally responsible. To let a person's own desires and preferences seldom dictate how she should be treated, and instead to allow the will of the state or the majority always to govern, is to treat her as a mere instrument of others' ends. A society whose legal and social systems presuppose the high degree of individualism called for by respect for moral personhood may not justly deny opportunities for privacy to its members. The moral case for privacy is buttressed by individualism as a conventional ethos. But it is premised on treatment as an individual as a moral requirement and a requirement of moral justice in a liberal society.

The value of privacy is, in part, that it can enable moral persons to be self-determining individuals. No human being is perfectly self-determining. Genetic and environmental factors beyond our control go a long way to fixing who and what we are; the past and the material circumstances of the present limit us. A self-determining individual is one whose own preferences significantly contribute to his fate. Privacy enhances individual lives by affording undisturbed opportunities to engage in activities that make self-determination a meaningful concept.

Self-reflection and reflection, self-expression and self-enjoyment, self-development and rejuvenation are generic forms of activity fostered by privacy. Self-reflection and reflection include psychological self-analysis, soul-searching, taking-stock, deliberation over important choices, reconsideration, scientific or philosophical speculation, religious worship, and free-floating musing or rumination. Self-expression and enjoyment include some of the activities just listed, but also emotional reaction, auto-sexuality, and artistic creation. Self-development and improvement may involve the expressive activities mentioned, but include, as well, planning, study, and practice. Rejuvenation includes previously named mental, expressive, and developmental activities, but also rest, relaxation, and meditation.

Personhood Creation

Does privacy merely enhance individuality or does it actually create individuals? Jeffrey Reiman has advanced a notable personhood creation theory. He characterized privacy as a complex social practice that enables individuals to identify themselves as persons.[34] Without these privacy practices, Reiman argued, human young would not learn that their bodies are their own; they would not learn that they have "moral title" to their existence. Reiman argued for the existence of a right to privacy understood as a right to the existence of a social practice that makes it possible for individuals to think of their existences as their own. Reiman's right to privacy is intended to be more basic than rights of property or over the human body, since there would be no person, in the moral sense, to whom any rights could be meaningfully ascribed were it not for the boundary-drawing, person-creating, social rituals we call privacy.

Reiman's account leaves unclear just what the social rituals of privacy are and how they bring about individuals who believe they have and ought to be respected as having "moral title" to their existence. Many practices that are not typically regarded as having anything to do with privacy appear to confer "moral title". For example, practices that restrain physical assault and battery create and promote personhood. Moreover, Reiman's notion that persons have a right to a way of life that confers "moral title" to their existence is ambiguous. It could mean that individuals should be encouraged to view themselves as having proprietary interests in their bodies, talents, and work products.[35] More plausibly, individuals understanding their existence as their own might be thought to consist in their having a certain conception of themselves as continuous, distinct, self-determining persons.

Whether privacy is a strict prerequisite of personhood, as Reiman believed, or whether it is not, opportunities for individual privacy are a prerequisite of the self-determination and the individuation that is called for by compelling conceptions of human dignity:

> The man who is compelled to live every minute of his life among others and whose every need, thought, desire, fancy or gratification is subject to public scrutiny, has been deprived of his individuality and human dignity. Such an individual merges with the mass. His opinions, being public, tend never to be different; his aspirations, being known, tend always to be conventionally accepted ones; his feelings, being openingly exhibited, tend to lose their quality of unique personal warmth and to become the feelings of every man. Such a being, although sentient, is fungible; he is not an individual.[36]

We promote and protect privacy to show moral respect for individuals and to confer moral dignity.

Social institutions and practices that promote individual privacy can be justified ultimately on the grounds that privacy is crucial to sustaining and enhancing personhood in the moral sense. Respecting privacy in everyday life means affording individuals what is often described, in terms of territorial metaphors, as a domain, sphere, or zone of privacy. The concepts of "the intimate," "the personal" and, less common today, "the decent" or "the sacred" are appealed to to further characterize the most important corners of privacy's territory. Singling out "the intimate," Gerety has written that "invasions of privacy take place whenever we are deprived of control over . . . intimacies of our bodies and minds so as to offend what are ultimately shared standards of autonomy."[37] Through this observation it is possible to see that invasions of privacy in the restricted-access sense and interference with decisional privacy affecting procreation and sexuality ultimately raise the same moral concerns. Both offend values of personhood. Deprivations of either privacy or decisional privacy can be occasions of offense and injustice. Deprivations of either can arouse feelings of anguish, shame, fear, and anxiety. To lightly impose these experiences on a person is a grave moral wrong.

Women and Personhood

Assuming privacy has the value personhood-creation and enhancement theorists contend it has, it is of critical importance that women have privacy too. Charles Fried has remarked that "the deepest moral principle is that each man in some sense belongs to himself." Feminists have argued that Western society has only recently begun to recognize the principle that each woman also "belongs to herself," that each woman has the same "moral title" to her own existence that each man has to his. "Belonging to oneself," best construed as a metaphor for possessing a degree of autonomous self-determination, is helped along by the exercise of liberties. But it is also helped along by opportunities for privacy.

Not only does belonging to oneself call for privacy, but so too does belonging to others in the sense of participating in the world and using one's talents for positive contributions. As Simone de Beauvoir understood, privacy and liberty spawn independence of thought and perception needed to grasp the universe and one's place in it. From this can come self-satisfaction and distinguished contributions to science, the humanities, government, art, commerce, medicine, and social services.

Interpersonal Relationships and Social Participation

Analogous to personhood-creation and personhood-enhancement accounts of the value of privacy are relationship-creation and relationship-enhancement accounts. A relationship-creation account maintains that certain relationships are not possible without privacy, and that privacy is therefore of crucial social importance. In this vein, Fried once contended that privacy is a necessary context for relations of love, friendship, and trust.[38] Robert Gernstein has argued that privacy is essential for the existence of intimate relationships.[39] James Rachels has argued that while privacy performs a number of important functions, including the prevention of embarrassment and the disclosure of incriminating or damaging information, its most important function is that it enables us to secure the variety of relationships with others we want to have.[40] Privacy, Rachels contended, allows us to control information about ourselves and thereby shape relationships, allowing some to become intimate, keeping others at a distance. A frequent and well-taken criticism of relationship-creation theories such as these is that, while privacy can foster and promote intimate, loving, trusting interpersonal relationships, it is not a strict prerequisite for such relations. Thus, relationship-enhancement accounts (that privacy is of value because it enhances interpersonal relationships) are more plausible than relationship-creation accounts.

Is the view that privacy is a means to personhood or enhanced personhood true, while the view that privacy is a means to certain relationships or enhanced relationship false? All of these views seem to embody a part of the truth of the matter. Privacy can promote *both* individuals' personhood interests *and* their interests in relationships with others. All four accounts treat privacy as a means to another end, namely, either (a) personhood per se or enhanced personhood, or (b) relationships per se or enhanced relationships.

One could argue that personhood is a more fundamental moral end than the intimate relationships, associations, and communities individuals form. For example, libertarians seem to take this view, adding that consenting adults may bind themselves to others through contracts and commitments into relationships whose moral significance is that they are embodiments of the wills of autonomous persons formed in expectation of mutually self-interested gain.[41] Yet, even were it to be granted that moral persons are ends in themselves and that similar claim could not be made for any group or relationship, it would not follow that the most adequate account of the moral value of individual privacy is one that relies solely on the idea of the moral value of persons apart from others.

To give a complete account of privacy's moral value, it is necessary to consider the social character of human existence. The concept of privacy is not abused if applied to describe the condition of the hypothetical last person on the planet. But privacy would be a pointless concept in a universe of one. Absent others, privacy has a definition—inaccessibility to others—but no real significance. We "know ourselves as separate only insofar as we live in connection with others and . . . we experience relationships only insofar as we differentiate others from self."[42] Privacy signifies contexts of self-determination. It signifies conditions in which the "I" presupposed by "we" can be morally individuated, that is, in which individuals can develop character, personality and skills. These traits can enrich subjective experience and qualitatively enhance participation in intimate relationships and group life. The moral value of privacy is tied to the fact that opportunities for privacy make individuals more fit for social participation and contribution. Privacy restrains but also benefits group life.

The Darker Side of Privacy

The need for privacy arises because human survival, and perhaps humanity itself, requires life in a society.[43] Opportunities for privacy satisfy a need for relieving the strains of our inherently social condition. Studies of a broad range of human cultures indicate that in all human groups there are patterns of social interaction whereby individuals sometimes seek companionship and sometimes seek privacy through distancing, avoidance, restraint, and reserve.[44]

Patterns of privacy vary across cultures. Some cultures, such as contemporary America, put a great emphasis on privacy. In fact, some Americans probably have more privacy than they need. In other cultures there is a greater emphasis on social rather than individual values.[45] What is treated as private is subject to cultural variation. Many cultures treat the female genitalia and some aspect of religious ritual as private.[46] But whether and to what extent genitalia, limbs, faces, homes, religious rites, sex acts, childbirth, death, menstruation, etc., are treated as suited for privacy greatly varies. Privacy patterns vary in accordance with the economic bases of societies, and they vary over time. It is commonly said, for example, that with Western industrial capitalism came new opportunities for privacy and new expectations of privacy.[47] Within a given society privacy patterns vary as a function of age, role, sex, and individual tastes and preferences. For instance, in a number of cultures, women's traditional caretaking roles and nurturing values appear to have resulted in a lesser degree of privacy at home for them than for their male counterparts.[48]

The romanticization of privacy has led to its being both overvalued as sacred and condemned as a particularly dark social menace. It is sometimes objected that privacy is a retreat from valuable social intercourse and social responsibility.[49] But this objection is overly general. While episodes of privacy sometimes constitute antisocial retreat, apathy, or abrogation of duties, this is not always the case. To maintain otherwise neglects "the full range of reasons why conscious persons seek privacy."[50] It also neglects the full range of reasons why a just society would bestow opportunities for privacy on its members. I have already noted Mill's argument that a just society ought to bestow privacy promoting liberties on individuals to limit government power. Another overly general objection to privacy is that it is a source of loneliness, fear, and alienation.[51] Again, privacy can represent these states, but does not always and need not. Privacy can be the welcome, restful retreat of a happy, socially active individual.

As these examples show, objections to excessive privacy and mis-used privacy have on occasion been styled as objections to privacy itself. Affording individuals opportunities for freedom carries the risk that freedom will be used for harmful, offensive, or self-destructive conduct. So, too, affording individuals opportunity for privacy carries the risk that privacy will be used as occasions for malign ends. It makes no more sense to reject privacy because of the risks it carries than to reject freedom wholesale in virtue of its familiar risks.

Liberalism and Privacy

By "liberalism" I shall mean here and throughout this book the dominant (if amorphous) political morality of the United States, currently reflected in its Constitution and in the views of the bulk of its people.[52] Liberalism is a political morality that regards each person as a subject of rights.[53] Liberalism starts with the assumption that individuals are endowed with basic rights protecting dignity, free-dom, well-being, and property. Government and private persons alike are obligated in virtue of these rights to accord prima facie validity to the choices individuals make respecting their own lives and interests.

The liberal conception of justice requires that, despite the risks, individuals be accorded wide-ranging personal freedoms, economic rights, and privacies. Social and political liberty can make harmful, offensive, and self-centered conduct possible; economic rights can be used to dominate and oppress; privacy can shield such conduct from observation and interference. Liberalism does not entail that all of the injurious consequences of freedom, property, and privacy are morally self-justifying. Egalitarian interpretations of liberalism hold only that there is a moral presumption in favor of the degree of freedom and privacy entailed by ideals of fundamental equality. On Ronald Dworkin's well-developed egalitarian interpretation of liberalism, protection of freedom and privacy is called for by the fundamental Kantian ideal of equal respect and concern, and by a derivative ideal, government neutrality.[54] Leaving others alone is a way of allowing individuals to exercise their own preferences and to live according to their own conceptions of a good life.[55]

A defender of the liberal democratic conception of justice could not reject the idea of rights protecting privacy. J. Ronald Pennock was correct when he wrote that the "sense of privacy and a demand for areas of life that are sacro-sanct . . . is an important component in the individualistic complex."[56] Nevertheless, there is broad room for disagreement within the liberal framework about, first, just how much privacy respect for individual rights requires and, second, whether privacy claims are invariably outweighed by claims of social utility. Moreover, it is consistent with liberalism to criticize Americans for exaggerating the value of individual privacy.

Not all proponents of liberalism place a *high* value on personal privacy. Indeed, differences regarding the importance placed on particular forms of privacy and privacy-promoting liberties are among indicia relied upon to sort liberal politicians, activists, jurists, and theorists into camps. Labels such as "liberal," "welfare state liberal," "conservative," "libertarian," "moral majoritarian," and "liberal feminist," are employed to identify individuals with clusters of policy perspectives on privacy and other matters. Richard Posner, a conservative who couples liberalism with a keen enthusiasm for a free market economy and powerful, decentralized government, maintains that personal informational privacy is less valuable to society than civil libertarians and liberals believe.[57] It is a hallmark of the conservative to place a premium on autonomy and privacy for the traditional family, but not on individual sexual privacy. For example, some conservatives view homosexuality as obscene, degrading conduct, properly subject to state investigation and criminalization. Supporting sexual privacy rights for lesbians and gays is associated with liberals and civil libertarians; supporting sexual privacy for women, with liberal feminism; and supporting government funding to create the economic basis for privacy for the poor is a mark of what is disparagingly labeled "welfare-state liberalism" or even "socialism."

It can never be taken for granted that an adherent of liberalism will place a high value on particular forms of personal privacy and privacy-promoting liberties. Placing a high value on particular forms of privacy is consistent with some interpretations of the broad principles of liberalism, inconsistent with others. This implies that valuing privacy and privacy-promoting liberties highly is not a peculiarly liberal phenomenon—not peculiarly liberal in practice nor peculiarly liberal in principle.

Plainly, privacy is not merely a liberal value. The need for opportunities for personal privacy cannot be dismissed by opponents of liberalism on that ground. Nor is privacy a capitalist value, if by that one means that capitalism is the only economic order under which individual privacy would have a purpose and a place. Of course, economists and entrepreneurs will be heard to extol privacy as something of special value to players in commercial enterprises whose ability to manage and profit is diminished by compliance with disclosure and reporting requirements, by industrial espionage, and by loss of trade secrets. But the critique of privacy is a separate project from the critique of private property, the market economy, and the concept of individual rights.[58]

Liberals praise individual privacy and decisional privacy as prerequisites of individualism. Nevertheless, any communitarian or collectivist political morality on which communities are viewed as ends must also place a high value on individual forms of personal privacy. Opportunities for individual forms of personal privacy make persons more fit for social participation and contribution to the pool of resources and assets available to all. Some personal privacy is inevitably sacrificed to the demands of social control, efficient bureaucracy, and centralized planning in collectivist economies. However, privacy for the poor, unemployed and homeless who cannot afford to purchase it is inevitably sacrificed in capitalist economies. Moreover, in our society individual privacy is sacrificed for the sake of accountability, the free press, and the public's "right to know." The American economy encourages individuals to voluntarily give up informational privacy for the privilege of consumer credit, insurance and employment. The value of privacy relative to the ends of particular economies and political regimes is anything but straightforward.

Feminists of all stripes have grounds for ambivalence about certain types of privacy. Privacy can denote isolation, and women have been isolated in the private sphere. Liberal feminists find it easier than feminists on the left to forgive privacy its past transgressions. Liberal feminists are aware of the ways in which forced isolation has thwarted women's self-development and cut them off from others with whom they might organize for making the personal become the political. But liberal feminists embrace privacy and decisional privacy today as a means to achieving the individual self-determination called for by human dignity, autonomy, and well-being.

Judged by the character of their activism, liberal feminists view greater privacy in women's personal lives—won through decisional privacy rights and more egalitarian styles of sex, marriage, and home life—as one of the tools women can employ as individuals to further personal and collective interests. By contrast, feminists on the left for whom women's liberation is a collective, class-centered, struggle may find privacy suspect. They may reject privacy on the ground that it is a mechanism for preserving private property, status, and privilege inimical to economic justice. Feminists may reject privacy on other grounds, including the putative ground that women value attachment and caretaking over individual modes of being. Yet, for the reasons I will explore in the next chapter, suspicion must give way to a recognition of the value that opportunities for individual forms of personal privacy have for social contribution and participation as equals.

CONCLUSION

What is the value of privacy? This question has a thoroughly conditional answer: it depends. It depends upon what form and what instance or recurrent pattern of privacy we are talking about; it depends upon whether we are talking about instrumental value or moral value. It is possible, however, to make a few generalizations about the value of privacy. One such generalization is suggested by the work of Westin and Gavison. The many forms of privacy— seclusion, solitude, secrecy, confidentiality, and reserve—have numerous practical uses. Some uses are moral and legal, some are immoral and illegal.

I offer a second generalization about the value of privacy. Opportunities for individual forms of privacy and the exercise of privacy-promoting liberties enhance persons and personal relationships in ways that cannot be ignored by those who feel ethically constrained to treat persons as more than things. Since the quality of a community is a function of the quality of its members, we need not view respect for individual rights or the satisfaction of individual needs as constituting the whole argument for individual forms of privacy. Not only the individuals extolled by liberals, but also the communities extolled by communitarians and socialists will benefit by opportunities for personal privacy.

Women's abilities to participate and contribute in the world as equals and on a par with their capacities are limited where laws and customs deprive them of opportunities for individual forms of personal privacy. Feminists rightly oppose particular inequitable instances and patterns of privacy. But a strong feminist case for adequate opportunities for privacy rules out wholesale rejection of privacy. What is a morally adequate amount of privacy for women? Degrees of privacy are not readily quantifiable. It is clear that spending time at home in domestic and caretaking roles does not assure women the privacy demanded by moral respect. The coming chapters will examine the ways in which opportunities for privacy and the exercise of privacy-promoting liberties promote female well-being, self-determination, participation, and contribution.

CHAPTER 3

Privacy at Home

THE TWOFOLD PROBLEM

F OR PEOPLE WHO WANT PRIVACY, there may be no place like home. Whether an ordinary row-house or an extraordinary houseboat, the residential dwelling is where American custom and law generally allow one the greatest freedom to look, speak, and behave as one pleases. Business and amusement outside the home call for a mode of conduct and appearance calculated to avoid unwanted attention and interference. In the workplace, punctuality, productivity, skill, and decorum are closely monitored by employers and co-workers. It is easy to covet the privacy of the superrich, the superannuated, and those, typically women, who stay home to keep house or rear children. Yet, for women with families to care for, staying at home is not always a privacy blessing. Marriage, motherhood, housekeeping, dependence, and her own moral ideals of caretaking and belonging have made many a woman's home life a privacy bane rather than boon.

The recurrent problem of privacy for women at home is twofold. First, women face the problem of overcoming inequitable social and economic patterns that substitute confinement to the private sphere for meaningful privacy. Second, women face the problem of enjoying and exploiting individual privacy without sacrificing worthy ideals of affiliation and benevolent caretaking to self-centeredness.

CONFINEMENT

Feminists have pointed out that subordinate and caretaking roles at home have deprived women of the experience of meaningful privacy.[1] Although their lives have been centered in the nominal privacy of the family home, women have rarely had the opportunity to experience and take full advantage of privacy. Feminist critiques of

54

women's privacy stress the undeniable: that the privacy of women secluded at home without powers of effective decisionmaking concerning sex, pregnancy, vocation, and lifestyle has been something of "an injury got up as a gift."[2] Since the early nineteenth century, many American women, especially married middle-class women, have been relegated to the private household in economically dependent and legally subordinate positions.[3] Traditionally, men have served both as heads of the household and as architects of social policy, doubly powerful arbiters of how women's time and personal resources at home could be expended.

In 1986, 55 percent of American women—46.6 million women—were in the labor force, not at home. But many of these wage-earners, even professionals and businesswomen, went home to onerous caretaking and housekeeping roles inconsistent with meaningful opportunities for individual forms of privacy. There is still a privacy problem for women related to their roles within the private sphere,[4] even though half the female population now works outside the home. It is no wonder, then, that some feminists look upon the concept of privacy with skepticism and view the public/private distinction itself as entailing sexual injustice.[5]

In recent decades, rights against governmental interference with effective decisionmaking in the areas of contraception and abortion, often described as "decisional privacy" rights, have increased women's ability to achieve and make use of beneficial degrees of privacy at home. Nonetheless, noted feminist legal scholar Catherine MacKinnon has rejected what she disparagingly labels the "ideology of privacy," arguing that the personal privacy right espoused by liberal theorists and the U.S. Supreme Court in *Roe v. Wade* is only "a right of men 'to be let alone' to oppress women one at a time."[6] The gist of MacKinnon's critique of privacy is that even though women officially have privacy and "free choice," men actually dominate their private lives, control sexual intercourse, and decide women's sexual and reproductive fates. Between 1970 and 1986 the number of women living alone increased 73 percent. This group included the increasing percentages of divorced and unmarried women. If MacKinnon is correct, to the extent that these women interacted with men, they enjoyed less control over their private lives and, in one sense, less privacy than their unmarried status first suggests.

Critiques of privacy such as MacKinnon's go wrong at the point where the historic unequal treatment of women and the misuse of the private household to further women's domination is taken as grounds for rejecting either the condition of privacy itself or the long-overdue legal rights to effective decisionmaking that promote and protect that condition. Privacy, here broadly defined as the inaccessibility of persons, their mental states, or information about them to the senses and surveillance devices of others (see Chapter 1), does not pose an inherent threat to women. Nor do sex, love, marriage, and children any longer presume the total abrogation of the forms of privacy a women might otherwise enjoy. On the contrary, women today are finally in a position to expect, experience, and exploit real privacy within the home and within heterosexual relationships. The women's movement, education, access to affordable birth control, liberalized divorce laws, and the larger role for women in politics, government, and the economy have expanded women's options and contributed to the erosion of oppressively nonegalitarian styles of home life. These advances have enhanced the capacity of American men and women, but especially and for the first time women, to secure conditions of adequate and meaningful privacy at home paramount to moral personhood and responsible participation in families and larger segments of society. Instead of rejecting privacy as "male ideology" and subjugation, women can and ought to embrace opportunities for privacy and the exercise of reproductive liberty in their private lives.

SELF-CENTEREDNESS

All this implies, of course, that a degree of individual privacy is a morally good thing. Yet, privacy has moral opponents who view it as largely hostile to important moral, social, and political goals.[7] Like private property and individualism, privacy and the high value placed upon it have been denounced from the left as products of capitalism and its political ideology. Even some proponents of liberalism cast the condition of privacy and the value placed upon it as extreme tendencies within modern societies, major causes of social alienation and loneliness, and all-too-convenient "moral" excuses for moral and social irresponsibility. Most significant for our purposes is opposition to privacy grounded in the notion that privacy is inconsistent with the value most women are believed to rightly place upon family, caring, intimacy, and community. It is now being suggested that women value concerned personal affiliation and intimacy over individual forms of privacy.[8]

Two strands of opposition to privacy directly related to women warrant careful examination. One was just stated: opposition grounded in the notion that, as a self-centered value, privacy is inconsistent with women's affiliative and caretaking ideals. The other, previously identified line of opposition calls for the rejection of privacy as a historic condition of subjugation through confinement to the home and a lack of autonomy in the private sphere. Both strands of opposition point toward a feminist devaluation and deemphasis of privacy. Yet, as responses to women's twofold privacy problem, deval-uation and deemphasis are mistakes. While there is a frank tension between privacy and concern for others, and while in the past women have been unfairly and wastefully confined to the domestic sphere under conditions of inequality, privacy and privacy at home are distinctly beneficial to women. This chapter reveals that opportunities for meaningful privacy and privacy-related liberty are beneficial to women for reasons that include the familiar moral reasons feminists used to insist that equality is beneficial to women. Hence, far from advocating rejection of privacy as a condition and a concept, it is important that feminists suggest answers to the gender-related pri-vacy questions women repeatedly encounter in their private and their public lives: How much privacy should we choose for ourselves? How much are we due?

This chapter begins an examination of privacy in the private sphere that will continue with a different focus in Chapter 4. Developing both strands of feminist opposition to privacy, this chapter argues from a feminist perspective that the solution to the twofold privacy problem women face begins with promoting greater emphasis on opportunities for individual forms of privacy, rather than in rejecting privacy. I start from the premise that, despite the decline of the nuclear family household and privacy losses stemming from the use of information and surveillance technology, the home remains, cul-turally and legally, the center of privacy in American life. Real privacy at home is possible for women to the extent that sexual privacy rights, innovative approaches to marriage, childcare, housekeeping, and their alternatives are tools women can use to secure the privacy home life can bring. Focusing on women's historic lack of privacy and the value of privacy for women is a way of exposing the myth that God, nature, morality, and the family require that women lead cloistered lives in the private sphere of the home, but without meaningful and adequate individual forms of personal privacy.

CENTERS OF PRIVACY

For many Americans the home is a center for the experience and enjoyment of privacy. This is no mere platitude. Our homes are the places we most expect to be let alone in solitude or to deal selectively with others. While the expression "home" can be used to denote a physical structure that serves as a residential dwelling-place, it has come to connote what home life can procure: being let alone, relaxa-tion, candid expression, affection, sexual enjoyments, and familial ties.

Privacy at home can have deep significance for an individual's sense of well-being, dignity, and identity. Heinrich Böll's novel *The Lost Honor of Katharina Blum* powerfully depicts the consequences of lost privacy of the home for an independent young woman. Divorced and living alone, Katharina enjoyed a peaceful, well-ordered home life. It ended when Katharina's apartment was searched without her consent by police, who accused her of abetting a criminal suspect with whom she had spent a night. Following the police intrusion, a distraught Katharina wondered:

> Why does one suddenly find one's own study so repulsive, everything upside down and dirty although there is not a speck of dust to be seen and everything is in its proper place? What makes the red leather armchairs, in which one has clinched many a good business deal and had many a confidential chat, in which one can be really relaxed and listen to music, suddenly seem so repulsive, even the bookshelves disgusting and the signed Chagall on the wall downright suspect, as if it were a fake done by the artist himself?[9]

Katharina lost her ability to identify with her home and possessions. Public inspection of her financial and sexual affairs eventually caused her to feel she had no private life of her own, no self apart from the public's perception of her as cold, radical, and unchaste.

Böll's Katharina lived alone, her entire apartment was her special private place. In many cases, only a part of a home, such as a bedroom or study, is one's center of privacy. Toni Morrison's Sula, the young heroine of her novel by the same name, found privacy behind a roll of linoleum in the attic of "a household of throbbing disorder, constantly awry with things, people, voices and the slamming of doors."[10] Sula's widowed mother had no room of her own in "that crowded house" and hence had "no place for spontaneous lovemaking." Hannah sought privacy "down in the cellar in the summer where it was cool back behind the coal bin and the newspapers or in the winter [in] the pantry."[11]

It is a fact of life in our society that privacy at home is subject to consensual and nonconsensual quotidian losses through the actions of, to name a few, relatives, police, government, insurance investigators, peeping-toms, media, salespersons, reformers, pollsters, plumbers, and neighbors. The demoralizing intrafamilial constraints on privacy experienced by Sula and Hannah are profound, though commonplace. The dramatic losses of privacy and integrity suffered by Katharina Blum are atypical.

Legal Protections

The customary expectation of privacy at home is reinforced by state and federal law. Unlike the United Nations Universal Declaration of Human Rights and the European Convention on Human Rights, the U.S. Constitution does not expressly provide for a right to privacy of the home.[12] Indeed, no express right to privacy of any sort is contained in the Constitution. Yet, the privacy of the home is protected by a number of constitutional provisions. The Third Amendment, which prohibits the quartering of soldiers in private homes in peacetime, reflects the idea of the home as a place in which citizens are entitled to enjoy undisturbed seclusion.[13] Embodying James Otis's colonial-era sentiment that "A man's house is his castle,"[14] the Fourth Amendment guarantees individuals the right to be secure in their houses against unreasonable search and seizures.[15] It has been held also to protect individuals' "reasonable expectations of privacy," which naturally extend to privacy in the paradigmatic sphere of privacy, the home.[16] Relying on the Fourth and Fifth Amendments,[17] the Supreme Court held late in the last century that the Constitution limits "invasions on the part of the government and its employees of the sanctity of a man's home and the privacies of life."[18] Since then the Court has held that Fourteenth Amendment liberty includes the right of the individual "to marry, establish a home, and bring up children,"[19] and that obscenity prohibitions do not reach "the privacy of one's home."[20] In the reproductive rights and sexual privacy cases of the past quarter-century, the Court has established that a constitutional right of privacy subsisting in the First, Third, Fourth, Fifth, Ninth and Fourteenth Amendments protects consensual heterosexual intimacy in the home.[21]

Aspects of individual privacy are protected by a growing number of federal statutes, including the Privacy Act of 1974, the Right to Financial Privacy Act, and the Family Educational Rights and Privacy Act of 1974. Aspects of privacy at home are protected by federal statutes limiting wiretapping and surveillance, most notably, by provisions of the Omnibus Crime Control and Safe Streets Act.[22]

State statutes join federal statutes to protect privacy at home;[23] so too does state common law. For example, under principles recognized in every state, the privacy of homes, of the persons who live in them, and of their effects is protected by the law of trespass. The law of trespass presupposes that individuals with possessory interests in real and personal property are entitled to exclude others. Moreover, many states now recognize a right of privacy to be free from intentional interference with seclusion, including, but not limited to, seclusion in the home.[24] With state law protections such as these in place, and with federal statutory and constitutional protections in place, when at home we can anticipate being let alone in our solitude or selective dealings with others.[25]

Domestic Privacies

While home life does not deliver all the privacy a person may want, many homes reliably afford three forms of personal privacy. (The precise sense in which there are forms of privacy was elaborated in Chapter 1.) In characterizing homes as centers for privacy I have had these three forms of privacy in mind. The first two domestic privacies are inaccessibility of the person in the senses of seclusion and anonymity. Anonymity is intended in the broad sense of limited attention paid rather than in the narrower sense of undisclosed identity. The third is inaccessibility of personal information, especially the non-disclosure, through secrecy and confidentiality, of personal facts, opinions, or creative expressions contained in documentary form. Homes serve as the respositories of cherished diaries, correspondence, photographs, audio and video recordings, and other momentos and creative efforts intended for selective disclosure. These documents are deemed personal. Understood in relation to current societal norms, personal documents include those that relate closely to family problems, physical and mental health, sexual experiences, religious beliefs, finances, and performance in school.

Seclusion and anonymity, on the one hand, and inaccessibility of personal information, opinions, and expressions on the other, have a special relationship. Seclusion and anonymity of the physical person provide the opportunity for self-expression that makes its way into correspondence, diaries, and artistic efforts. It also provides the occasion for unembarrassed inspection of momentos and rumination about their significance.

In virtually every society some cultural activity (for example, a religious rite) or some biological function (such as defecation) is deemed unfit for general detection.[26] In our society homes go some distance toward shielding individuals and fostering social exchanges. The architectural design of typical American homes enhances domestic privacies through the use of walls and similar barriers, limiting the accessibility of home dwellers, their possessions, and their guests. Typical homes are designed not only to shut inhabitants off from the eyes, ears, noses, and sensing devices of the outside world, but also to limit access by co-inhabitants to one another. For example, separate bedrooms function as spheres of domestic privacy, separating spouses, parents, children, siblings, and in-laws. Anthropologist Barrington Moore has observed that modern American society is "almost certainly unique in the extent to which it has created space for the privacy of physiological functions through bedrooms, bathrooms, and their associated equipment."[27] In other cultures several families or extended families share the same unpartitioned residence. Privacy needs are addressed by honoring complex patterns of avoidance designed to limit observation and physical contact.[28] Our homes limit the audiences to performances and consequences of urination, defecation, menstruation, and sexual intimacy. Home is also where bathing, dressing, and grooming may be accomplished without general detection and hence with a minimum of embarrassment, shame, or offense. American homes limit the audience for displays of emotion—joy, pride, frustration, fear, rage.

Privacy, Affluence, and Roles

Commenting on cross-cultural empirical studies of privacy, Moore observed that "the taste for privacy as well as the ability to satisfy this taste are very unequally distributed among human societies and within them."[29] It is plain that in the United States domestic privacy is a virtual commodity purchased by the middle class and the well-to-do. Privacy is bought and sold in the form of single-family houses on privately owned land, townhouses, apartments, and recreational second homes in remote locations.

The poor, whose "taste" for privacy may be equally keen, are compelled by economic necessity to accept smaller, thinner-walled, and more crowded accommodations. For New York City tenement dwellers earlier in this century, "privacy was a luxury too ridiculous to be considered."[30] This is true today in some urban communities where low-income individuals live in structures that do not shield co-inhabitants from one another and scarcely shield them from their neighbors. The economically disadvantaged who rely on public assistance or live in public housing face additional obstacles to privacy.[31] Privacy at home is diminished by the mandatory inspections of welfare caseworkers and housing authorities. Periodic and sometimes unannounced visits by agents of the state aim to detect and deter violation of the conditions of entitlement, of aesthetic standards, and of health and safety codes. Their effect is to compel the dependent poor to share privacy with strangers. Economic status can also affect the enforceability of privacy-related rights against trespass and to seclusion at home. The poor may find out of reach the legal aid and neighborhood police assistance needed to enforce the rights that protect and enhance domestic privacy.

Similarly unable to satisfy their taste for privacy are those in all social and economic strata whose homes are, for better or worse, public hospitals, nursing homes, and prisons. These institutions have purposes as different as punishment and health management. Yet in each case the institutional way of life is an artificially communal way of life. Limited resources and cost containment measures usually mean not only sharing, but crowding. The institutional way of life is a

life of unwanted intrusions by others, which affected individuals may
be powerless to control. In hospitals and nursing homes, unwanted
intrusions often have to be tolerated in virtue of their bona fide
health-care objectives. In prisons, institutional security may require
inmate body searches, cell-searches, and surveillance.

Least likely to be able to satisfy their taste for privacy are the
homeless. Urban street-people and bag-ladies sleep, eat, groom, com-
miserate, etc., out-of-doors or in places of public accommodation such
as subways, train terminals, and building stairwells. A large percent-
age of the homeless are unemployed, poverty-stricken, ill, and cut off
from their families. They have no place to go, or no place worth going
to. Temporary shelters, public facilities, woods, fields, caves, or night-
fall are poor substitutes for the more certain privacy of homes. It is
conceivable, but barely, that among the homeless are a few robust
men and women whose taste for domestic privacy is dwarfed by the
taste for the freedom and anonymity of vagrancy.

When a person lives alone, a keen taste for the domestic privacies
can be satisfied. Many adults, however, live with spouses, head more-
or-less "nuclear" two-parent families, head single-parent families, or
share their homes with friends or roommates. The extent to which
privacy can be obtained and exploited in a household will be a
function of the size, type, and location of the dwelling; the number of
inhabitants; and their roles, ages, and needs. Other factors have a role
too, such as attitudes about privacy, mutual respect and cooperation.

Very small children are presumed to lack the self-consciousness
that would mandate respect for their privacy. Indeed, parents may
impose unwanted seclusion upon youngsters expressly to teach them
that privacy ought to be respected. Once the desire for privacy
develops in small children, their parents may justifiably deny them
their desired levels of privacy on paternalistic grounds to assure
discipline and safety. Teenagers living at home are typically allowed
greater privacy than small children. But they may find that their
phone calls and visitors are monitored, their bedrooms shared with
younger siblings, and their diaries read. In a related vein, they may
find that their sexual and reproductive preferences, their "decisional
privacy," is effectively preempted.

Home management and supervision entail privacy losses. Consequently, parents may enjoy fewer private hours at home than their
children. Tending to the needs of children requires spending substantial amounts of time in their presence and directly interacting with
them. So too does the care of infirm adults. All other things being
equal, caretakers enjoy less seclusion than non-caretakers or occa-
sional caretakers. This observation relates importantly to any consideration of women's privacy at home. Women, whose lives at home as

mothers, wives, and daughters often involve caretaking roles, have real problems finding opportunities for privacy.

PRIVACY IN THE WOMAN'S PLACE

Not only is the home recognized as the seat of the private sphere, but Americans commonly view privacy itself "as a set of rules against intrusion and surveillance focused on the household occupied by the nuclear family."[32] However, privacy must not be construed as synonymous with the norms of seclusion governing the separation of the nuclear family household from the larger social world. This point is the starting place for understanding women's problem of privacy at home.

The problem of privacy at home for women is, in part, the problem of overcoming the tradition of inequality through confinement to the private sphere of home and family. A short time ago, the view prevailed in the United States that the family home was a man's castle but a woman's place. The family home was conceived to be a sphere of privacy in two senses. First, it was a realm of privilege beyond the control of public authorities. Within this realm a man was presumed entitled to make decisions affecting himself and members of his economically dependent household. There a man might retreat from the larger world and find repose. Second, the family home, the woman's place, was conceived to be a realm of physical and social seclusion, as well. There a woman was confined to keep house, prepare meals, and rear children. These conceptions of privacy were undoubtedly what Kate Millett had in mind when she remarked that "privacy is about keeping taboos in place."[33] For feminists, the privacy that keeps taboos in place consists of social and legal norms through which a male-dominated society maintains women in a condition of inequality at home. In the name of sexual *equality*, proponents of thoroughgoing sexual justice oppose privacy conceived as a man's castle and a woman's place. In the name of genuine opportunities for personal privacy, they must also oppose this same flawed conception.

History reveals that women's roles in the private sphere have not entailed a plentitude of personal privacy. It is well documented that by the eighteenth century, Western women were economically and ideologically defined as people who cared for and supported others within the private sphere of home and family, rather than themselves being active in the world.[34] Yet in early America the lives of both men and women centered around the home. For example, in early Puritan settlements women's tasks typically included childcare, housekeeping, and food preparation; their husbands' work as farmers, artisans, or shopkeepers kept them close by.[35] Among the Puritan colonists the private sphere was not especially private by contemporary standards. Their religion and the exigencies of aggregate life in an untamed new world rendered closeness and accountability an imperative.[36]

In general, the homesteads of early American colonists offered a degree of seclusion for families and their servants. But the hardworking colonial lifestyle "left little room for privacy or non-conformity even among the free and affluent."[37] Notable among those who were neither free nor affluent were women who earned passage to America as indentured servants or who were brought over as slaves. Sometimes expected to provide sexual services to their masters in addition to domestic and agricultural labor, these women enjoyed "neither privacy nor self-determination."[38] During the Revolutionary War women took over men's work at home, and some even fought alongside men in battle. Nonetheless, both the Constitution of the new American republic and the laws of the individual states accorded women an inferior legal status as private ancillaries of men rather than as public citizens.

As part of the nation's westward expansion, women—wives, missionaries and fortune seekers—endured the hardships of the Oregon Trail alongside men. On their journeys and in their camps they shared mutually dependent lives with fellow travelers, settling for very little personal privacy, even with respect to toilet functions and childbirth. Meanwhile, in the east and south, with the coming of industrialism to the United States and the advent of wage labor, the separation of men's work from the home became more marked.[39] Men increasingly went outside the home to work in industry; women remained behind to labor in the home. Significant numbers of less affluent women also became wage earners. Poor and working-class women worked in the textile industry, the shoe and boot industry, and other industries deemed suitable for women. New England "mill girls" left the relative seclusion of their families to work in the textile industry. Mill girls commonly lived in boarding houses operated by employers, where strict codes of conduct were imposed to keep feminine virtue intact.[40] Poor and working-class women in New York peddled wares from push-carts and worked in garment and needle industry sweatshops. Or they found work as domestic servants as the affluent population multiplied with the growth of the industrial economy. Live-in domestics could work hundred-hour weeks and lacked both "independence and privacy."[41] During the Civil War, women on both sides "managed businesses, farms, and plantations while men went to fight," much as they had done during the Revolutionary War.[42] Southern women revived home industries to compensate for the imported goods cut off by northern sea blockades. Women made clothing and ammunition, taught, nursed, worked in government printing offices, and trailed troops to cook, do laundry, and be prostitutes.[43] A few engaged in the extraordinary professions of teamster and steamboat captain.

Throughout the nineteenth century many women did stay at home. Although women's share of the labor force increased from 7.4 percent to 17 percent between 1830 and 1890, a middle-class model of the family dictated increasingly that the proper place for women was at home.[44] Under the familiar model it was the duty of a man to marry and to earn an income for the support of himself, his wife, and their children. It was the duty of a woman to marry and maintain a clean, cheerful, practical home for her husband and the children she was expected to bear and rear. Politics and commerce were public concerns and the concern of men, whereas housekeeping, food preparation, childbearing and rearing, and intimate relationships were private concerns and the concerns of women. According to historian Barbara Weltzer, nineteenth-century middle-class married American women were virtually hostages to their homes, held captive by pervasive middle- and upper-class ideals of "true womanhood" powerfully reflected in the popular women's literature of the day. "'Who Can Find a Valiant Woman?' was asked frequently from the pulpit and the editorial pages. There was only one place to look for her—at home."[45]

In view of the message it conveyed about the proper place of women in society, Thomas Gisborne's *Enquiry Into the Duties of the Female Sex* could have been published in America in 1897 as easily as in England in 1797. Gisborne warned of the evils to which women who leave home, wandering from place to place and house to house, are peculiarly subject. Women who go out interrupt "domestic habits and occupations" and acquire "an unsettled, tattling, and a meddling spirit." The home is where a woman "may be more known and more respected than she can be in any other place."[46] The nineteenth-century woman was encouraged to believe that in the home she had virtue and the power to set cultural norms and moral standards. In addition, "a stable order of society depended upon her maintaining her traditional place."[47] In a lecture entitled "Of Queen's Gardens," the poet John Ruskin essayed that "the woman's true place" is the home, "the place of Peace; the shelter . . . from all injury . . . all terror, doubt, and division. [In the sanctuary of her home] the woman must be enduringly incorruptibly good; instinctively, infallibly wise . . . wise, not for self-development, but for self-renunciation: wise . . . with . . . modesty of service."[48] Ruskin's opinions must have had an audience, for in George Gissing's novel *The Odd Women* (1893), Edmund Widdowson instructs his young wife to read John Ruskin: "every word he says about women is good and precious."

Charlotte Perkins Gilman is noteworthy for her ability to have seen clearly, even in the 1890s, the flaws in Ruskin's and others' understandings of the role of women. She denied that the ideal of the wife-servant is an ennobling influence in the home. She pointed to the many evident respects in which the middle-class home is not a "place of Peace" for women confined to repetitive labor within it. One of Gilman's special concerns was the ways in which confinement to their homes thwarted women's social potential. She observed that while men "meet one another freely in their work," women work alone at home—too much in privacy.[49] A similar criticism of the confinement of women was made more than sixty years later by Betty Friedman in the *Feminine Mystique.*[50] Contemporary feminists add that "consciousness-raising" and the formation of political bonds that could ground collective efforts for seeking recourse for common grievances is hindered both by the segregation of women into atomistic private households and by the definition of the matters most central to their quest for autonomy and personhood as "private."[51]

In the middle- and upper-income segments of the population, a clear pattern emerged in the nineteenth century that continued through the late 1960s. Women worked, if they had to, but only until they married (although during World War II many women worked outside the home temporarily in the defense-related industries). Working at all, even in secretarial posts in lush offices, was seen by "middle-class moralizers [as] fundamentally incompatible with femininity."[52] Poor families subscribed to the ideal that women ought to remain in the home, in theory if not in practice. Women who had to earn wages often worked at home. They sewed, made artificial flowers, took in laundry, and cared for boarders.

In view of the seclusion made possible by life at home, women in traditional home-making roles might be thought to have enjoyed a privacy boon. This conclusion would seem to follow from Alan F. Westin's analysis of the overall implications of modern industrial society for personal privacy: "The developments associated with the rise of modern industrial societies—such as the nuclear family living in individual households, urbanization and the anonymity of urban life, mobility in work and residence, weakening of religious authority over individuals—all provide greater situations of physical and psychological privacy."[53] Westin's analysis entails that American women in the post-industrial age should have experienced increases in the "physical and psychological opportunities" for privacy thanks to, inter alia, the nuclear family household.

Yet, the amount of "physical and psychological" privacy a person possesses is not solely a function of increases in the number of hours spent in the nuclear family home, or of increases in mobility, urban anonymity, and religious authority. The specific character of life within the nuclear family home is more determinative of the available degree of meaningful privacy. Speaking of home-centered working-class urban women earlier in this century, Kennedy remarked that privacy played no significant role. For "living in crowded tenements, enduring pregnancies they could not prevent, struggling to find means to supplement factory wages . . . working-class women placed their first priority on survival."[54] Nor have middle- and upper-income home-centered wives necessarily enjoyed situations of notable privacy. In the simple words spoken by the heroine of a nineteenth-century novelette to her husband, "You are at your store from dinner to supper, and the hour or two of relaxation you take at home is undoubtedly pleasant. . . . There I am cooped up nearly two whole days every week with the children."[55] Westin's theoretical account of the relationship between post-industrial opportunities for privacy may approximate a description of the consequences of industrial society for men. But as far as women are concerned, it is a misleading oversimplification.

Traditional home life in the United States appears to have fit the pattern observed in diverse cultures around the world. Women, in particular married women with children, "pay the social cost for whatever privacy men obtain in and through the nuclear family."[56] An important social cost women have paid as guardians of the private sphere is inadequate personal privacy and the personal benefits that privacy entails. The lot of many women has been, to borrow Ruskin's words, self-renunciation rather than self-development.

Marriage

Christina Markyate, a thirteenth-century *religieuse* who went on to lead a life of public service through the windows of her cloister, reportedly spent four years in a tiny cell too small to allow for heavy clothing or a blanket.[57] This extreme subterfuge, we are told, was prompted by a desire to escape marriage. For some Christian women of medieval Europe, the monastic life offered a more private, independent, and intellectually stimulating life than marriage.[58]

Marriage has been described as a woman's greatest obstacle to privacy. In an 1819 tract entitled *Family Lectures,* a Mrs. Sproat set out the duties of the married woman in the form of advice to her daughter:

> Your husband demands your first and constant attention. His worldly interest, his peace of mind, and his reputation, you should regard as sacred deposits committed to your trust, for which you will be highly responsible; you are to consider yourself not only as a companion whose smiles must sweeten prosperity, but as a partaker of his cares, as his solace in affliction, his friend in adversity . . . and his patient and faithful

attendant in the hours of sickness and pain. Yet these comprise not the whole of your domestic duties. You should also be an example to your family of all the virtues—amongst which, patience, meekness and moderation, are not the least prominent. . . . But your duties as a wife are not all confined to your family circle; . . . you must do honor to your husband's choice . . . by treating his connections and friends with the most attentive respect.[59]

In Mrs. Sproat's day women were encouraged to take their creative and intellectual development seriously, but subject to strict limitations imposed on the female sex, it was thought, by God and nature. The goal of women's socialization and education was to enable them to preserve their natural piety, moral superiority, chastity, and modesty; to attract a husband; and to adjust to the duties of marriage and child-rearing. But fidelity to Mrs. Sproat's conception of subservient care-taking duties respecting one's husband denied women both the opportunity for solitude and solace in their secluded lives, and the ability to enjoy and exploit the modicum of privacy afforded by their lives as wives.

The notion that married women should unquestioningly place their husbands before themselves has limited currency in the United States today. Marriage remains an important and sought-after relationship, for reasons not difficult to see. Judeo-Christian religious traditions, still a significant force in this country, encourage marriage. Wedding customs lend fantasy and romantic appeal to marriage. In some quarters, family and social pressure to marry is considerable. Given the popular wisdom that children need fathers at home as well as mothers, and given the residual social stigma attached to the unwed mother and "fatherless" child, many women who wish to raise children are unwilling to experiment with single-parenting.

American women today seeking love, sex, motherhood, and the economic security traditionally associated with marriage find that marriage is not the only feasible means to these ends. This may explain why the number of first marriages dwindled between 1950 and 1970, and why the divorce rate doubled between 1960 and 1974 and increased by 80 percent between 1970 and 1986. The number of women heading households has increased 84 percent since 1970.[60]

In assessing what marriage per se means for an American woman's privacy, it is important to keep in mind that "marriage" does not stand for a single, uniform lifestyle. It can denote very different arrangements. The law creates certain limitations. It largely prohibits state-sanctioned lesbian and incestuous marriages, for example. The law also imposes uniformities with respect to taxation, mutual financial support, and responsibility for children. Custom and religion create certain extralegal uniformities. Otherwise, marriage has no fixed format. Women of diverse lifestyle preferences and expectations can flourish within formal marriages and other coupling arrangements of unique design. Whether marriage will be an obstacle to a woman's privacy at home depends upon her actual living conditions after marriage. Virtually any marriage that involves living together entails sacrifices to individual privacy. Young married adults who have always lived with inquisitive parents and in crowded, thin-walled college dormitories may find that living together in a place of their own affords greater opportunities for privacy than they have ever experienced before. How much time she spends with her spouse and with others, the degree of communication and accountability in the marriage, and whether there are children or other relations to be cared for will affect a married woman's privacy.

Love

To the extent that marriage is a love affair, it represents an obstacle to privacy, but one women in love will welcome.[61] In the case of lovers, individual privacy must compete with shared privacy. Lovers relish being secluded and alone together; they share confidences and secrets; they share keepsakes and momentos of their relationship. Lovers enjoy shared privacy at home because it is a realm in which they are known, appreciated, and pampered: "In sharing their privacy, lovers give a significance to whim, desires, and moods that receive no recognition in larger social world. . . . The aim of love is achieved when lover's retreat by themselves to a personal world apart from the world of everyday social and moral life."[62]

Shared privacy at home is a danger to women in love when it replaces individual privacy. Periods of separation from loved ones can promote traits of self-reliance and individuality that actually enrich relationships. The philosopher Montaigne eloquently bade his (male!) readers not to depend too much on their wives and on other external pleasures for their happiness, but to find happiness in time spent alone in solitude in a back shop all one's own:

> We should have wife . . . but we must not bind ourselves to them so strongly that our happiness depends on them. We must reserve a back shop all our own, entirely free, in which to establish our real liberty and our principal retreat and solitude. Here our ordinary conversation must be between us and ourselves, and so private that no outside association or communication can find a place; here we must talk and laugh as if without wife . . . we have a soul that can be turned upon itself; it can keep itself company; it has the means to attack and the means to defend, the means to give: let us not fear that in this solitude we shall stagnate in tedious idleness: In solitude be to thyself a throng.[63]

Montaigne's point is that to build individuality and inner resources, it is important to be able to retreat periodically from others.

Maintaining a literal back shop of one's own is an expenditure most men—and especially most women—can ill afford. Writing of the importance of a place of one's own, feminist Charlotte Perkins Gilman contended that while the "progressive individuation of human beings requires a personal home, one room at least for each person . . . for the vast majority of the population no such provision is possible."[64] Where money is not an obstacle to needed privacy, she continued, socio-sexual norms may be: "The man has his individual life, his personal expression and its rights, his office, studio, shop: the women and children live in the home—because they must."[65]

Speaking of economic dependence, Barrington Moore observed that "Even a strong yearning for privacy can evaporate in the face of an acute awareness of one's dependency on other human beings."[66] The same point could be made respecting the excessive emotional dependence sometimes associated with women in love. Emotional dependence can cause a woman to be unwilling to be separated from her lover or spouse; separations may provoke a high level of anxiety or loneliness that undermines her ability to benefit from time spent alone. Self-reliance can be an unattractive prospect for young women who, under the influence of infantilizing conventions for female behavior, are not prepared to strike out on their own, to utilize private time, or to value emotional independence. In such cases the desire for privacy may be overcome by a felt need and desire for dependency.

THE VALUE OF PRIVACY FOR WOMEN

The preceding descriptive discussion exposed the dimensions of half of the twofold privacy problem faced by American women, the problem of overcoming the tradition of confinement to the private sphere of home, marriage, and caretaking roles as a substitute for and barrier to genuine personal privacy. Liberal feminism represents one response to the problem. By liberal feminism I mean a kind of liberalism that, first, recognizes that gender is not a morally legitimate ground for denying women the legal, economic, and social rights ascribed to men; and that, second, presses for legal and social reform calculated to enhance the status of women as self-determining individuals and valued participants in the socioeconomic realm.

Liberalism and liberal feminism place a high value on personal privacy and embrace the private sphere as occasions for privacy. Liberal feminism rejects forms of home life, sex role stereotypes, and sexual ties that foreclose privacy options for women. Although mindful of the ways in which traditional marriage, family life, and sex roles have resulted in inadequate privacy for women, liberal feminism in principle does not oppose marrying, mothering, and heterosexual relationships. Instead liberal feminism demands that these not be deemed women's only options; and that, in any event, sex, marriage and child-rearing be, to take a phrase from Jean Bethke Elshtain, "reconstructed" consistent with sexual justice, through legal, economic and attitudinal changes. The liberal feminist looks with favor upon decisional privacy in the context of contraception and abortion, because she views it as a tool of female autonomy and privacy.

Catherine MacKinnon opposes the liberal feminist response to women's privacy problem. She rejects the "ideology" of the private because she assumes that it can be understood only in historical terms as referring to conditions of male hegemony and female inequality, conditions reinforced by the liberal democratic conceptions of political morality.

> It contradicts the liberal definition of the private to complain in public of inequality within it . . . The democratic ideal of the private holds that, so long as the public does not interfere, autonomous individuals interact freely and equally. Conceptually, the private is hermetic. It *means* that which is inaccessible to, unaccountable to, unconstructed by anything beyond itself . . . It is personal, intimate, autonomous, particular, the original source and final outpost of the self, gender neutral. It is, in short, defined by everything that feminism reveals women have never been allowed to be or have, and everything that women have been equated with.[67]

To reject the private sphere for the reasons MacKinnon gives is to toss out the baby (privacy itself) with the bathwater (confinement and inequality). MacKinnon rightly condemned women's unequal control of sex and powerlessness to make decisions about matters most closely associated with their own bodies and self-development. She rightly judged that existing conditions of sexual inequality in the private sphere can undercut decisional privacy rights established by law on behalf of women. But these are not reasons to reject privacy, the private sphere, or the decisional privacy right of *Roe v. Wade*.

Decisional privacy rights have done more than supplement male authority over women. Many women still "second-chair" men in sexual relationships, but *Roe* and access to birth control have helped to create new powers, new norms, and new expectations of self-determination among women. Decisional privacy must be recognized as one of the important remedies for the problem of sexual inequality and women's lack of meaningful privacy. Economic equality, by which I mean equal employment opportunity, equal pay, and greater recognition of the economic and social worth of the kinds of work women do, is another essential remedy. Political and governmental power are essential remedies as well. It is as mistaken to dismiss decisional privacy because it is impaired by residual male domination, as it would be to dismiss equal pay and comparable worth because their efficacy is impaired by residual male domination of private relations.

Male hegemony is not a reason to reject decisional privacy, and it is not a reason to reject the idea of privacy and the private sphere. Absent radical social reorganization, to reject the private sphere is virtually to reject the notion of reliable opportunities for seclusion, anonymity, and solitude. As I will argue in Chapter 4, one of the great benefits of decisional privacy respecting birth control and abortion is that it enables women to enjoy important forms of privacy at home. Decisional privacy is a tool women can use to create and control the privacy available to themselves and those with whom they choose to share their private lives. So too are options about marriage, employment, and careers.

To the extent that it ceases to be an obligatory domain of self-renunciation and the lack of privacy for women, the objection to the private sphere based on its being a form of subjugation through confinement is severely blunted. In women's lives today the home potentially serves the function it once was thought to serve for men— the role of a haven, a realm in which the pressures of the larger world are relaxed. Not a haven for the exercise of domination over others, but a haven for solitude or selected intercourse with others. Home will not be a haven, especially not for the 17.5 million working women with children and the 13.8 million with husbands, without changes in attitudes about the importance of privacy for women and public policies that reinforce those attitudes.

SOMETHING BETTER THAN PRIVACY

It is sometimes said that women do not want privacy, but something better than privacy: opportunities for affiliation and caring. Seen as a woman's free choice in an age of options, the rejection of individual forms of privacy can be viewed as an acceptable post-feminist development. Seen as an inauthentic preference shaped by a tradition that relegated women to subservient caretaking roles in the private sphere, the rejection of privacy must be viewed as unacceptable and an occasion for consciousness-raising. In either case, a frank tension of special relevance to feminism exists between the ideal of opportunities for personal privacy and the ideal of active participation in, and contribution to, families and communities.

This tension is the reason for the second half of the twofold problem of privacy at home for women. Two women writing about the psychology and moral values of women have popularized aspects of the problem. Their evidence suggests that women in fact—whether they ought to or not—value concerned affiliation above individual forms of privacy. Psychologist Jean Baker Miller has contended that women do not want autonomy as it is defined for men, but "are quite validly seeking a fuller not a lesser ability to encompass relationships with others, simultaneous with the fullest development of oneself."[68] Women aspire to make themselves more and more accessible to others with whom intimacy is desirable, while achieving goals of self-satisfaction and fulfillment. According to Miller, women have seldom achieved both aspects of this goal. Their roles as subservient caretakers have robbed them of sufficient opportunity for self-development while also narrowing the range of their relationships:

> To concentrate on and take seriously one's own development is hard enough for all human beings. But, as has been recently demonstrated in many areas, it has been even harder for women. Women are not encouraged to develop as far as they possibly can and to experience the stimulation and the anguish, anxiety, and pain the process entails. Instead, they are encouraged to avoid self-analysis and to concentrate on forming a relationship to one person.[69]

Women's caretaking roles may serve to explain why they have seldom been able to experience and enjoy privacy or to develop and enjoy autonomy. Women's caretaking roles may help explain why some women do appear not to value privacy as men define it.

Carol Gilligan's well-known studies suggest that attachment, rather than autonomy, and caring, rather than abstract principles of justice, dominate the moral sensibilities of women.[70] According to Gilligan, men and boys tend to engage in a mode of moral reasoning and moral discourse that emphasizes rights and justice, construed as equal treatment, reciprocity, or fairness. Women and girls tend to engage in moral discourse that emphasizes relationships, responsibilities, and caring. For men, morality is primarily an injunction to respect the rights to life and self-fulfillment. For women it is an injunction to care. For men and boys, morality consists of making and applying abstract rules. For women and girls, morality consists of discerning needs and fulfilling them as contexts demand.

As background for these descriptive claims about moral reasoning, Gilligan advanced three important developmental and psychological theses about women that bear on privacy. First, separation and individuation from mothers is critically tied to the development of masculine gender identity, but not feminine gender identity. Second, women's identities are defined in the context of relations; moreover, women judge themselves by a standard of responsibility and care. Third, developmental maturity in the case of women does not dis-

place the value of on-going attachment and the continuing importance of care in relationships. These three theses seem to entail that
obtaining individual forms of privacy are not moral priorities for
typical women.

Gilligan's studies suggest that for women, being alone can signify
danger rather than peace and solace. (One is reminded of Mrs.
Cadwallader's admonition to a younger woman in George Eliot's
Middlemarch: "You will certainly go mad in that house alone, my dear.
You will see visions.")[71] In one study, women projected violence most
frequently in the only picture portraying a person alone, while the
men most frequently saw violence in the only picture in which people
touched.[72] Gilligan concluded that men and women apparently experience attachment and separation in different ways, and that each sex
perceives a danger the other does not see—men in connection,
women in separation.

According to Gilligan, the desire to maintain affiliation also makes it
plain why American women's new-found freedom to choose involves
new dilemmas:

> When birth control and abortion provide women with effective means
> for controlling their fertility, the dilemma of choice enters a central
> arena of women's lives. Then the relationships that have traditionally
> defined women's identities and framed their moral judgments no longer
> flow inevitably from their reproductive capacity but become matters of
> decision over which they have control . . . However, while society may
> affirm publicly the woman's right to choose for herself, the exercise of
> such choice brings her privately into conflict with conventions of femi-
> ninity particularly the moral equation of goodness with self-sacrifice.
> Although independent assertion in judgment and action is considered
> to be the hallmark of adulthood, it is rather in their care and concern for
> others that women have judged themselves and been judged.[73]

If caring for others in lieu of exploring opportunities for personal
privacy is what women want and believe they ought to want, the
question remains whether that is what they in fact *should* want. The
implication of Gilligan's work for privacy seems to be this. If we want
to put an end to the psychological predisposition of women to care
themselves into oblivion, and if we want to put an end to the belief
that they have a duty to do so, then women's interests in privacy—
restricted assess and decisional privacy—must be strenuously protected by our culture and our laws. This conclusion is in line with
Gilligan's own observation that changes in women's rights change
women's moral judgments. They season feminine caring with respect
for individual autonomy. Or, as she put it, women's rights season
"mercy with justice." Women must be enabled to consider it morally
permissible to care for themselves as well as for others.

As a group, women have done too much caretaking at the expense of their development as individuals. Intrafamilial caretaking duties have required that women forego solitude. The mother of a small child cannot blissfully shut herself off and allow herself to be ignorant of the child's needs. From the point of view of privacy, no matter how much women may enjoy them, motherhood and traditional marriage have a cost. As wives and daughters to men in business and the professions, women have assumed the onerous caretaking duties of social hostessing in addition to intrafamilial duties. Privacy can be a welcome, deserved sanctuary from affected social exchange in which one must observe conventions of politeness and attentiveness. Catherine Talbot, a nineteenth-century writer, recorded her displeasure with the life of social duties as "the life of constant, unremitting mortification and self-denial." She complained that in the company of others, bad and painful dispositions break out at every unguarded moment, selfishness shows its ugly head, little contradictions excite vehemence of temper, useless talk prates away the hours, and good humor must be restrained. Fear of "criminal negligence" and "destructive extravagance mar the social experience," whereas in solitude, "one has nothing to do but to cherish good and pleasing dispositions."[74]

A degree of personal privacy is an important underpinning of a workable, humane family and community. It is also an important underpinning of female personhood. Self-development does not require that women pursue a selfish degree of privacy that precludes concern for others. Women need not abrogate responsibility to enjoy privacy. While Americans may overemphasize privacy to the detriment of shared intimacy and responsive beneficence, the existence of privacy customs, even in human societies that are models of cooperative interdependence, seems to indicate that there is no essential contradiction between privacy and affiliative ideals. The past two decades of increased independence for women have signaled that what is worthwhile in our society can survive without women being forced inhabitants of the private sphere who devote themselves exclusively to caring for others.

PRIVATE TIME

For some women, a private place and private time at home are desirable because they make additional productive work possible. A small group of career women were recently assembled by a residential real estate developer in New Jersey to provide ideas about how new houses could be designed to better accommodate the needs of women in the labor force, many of whom are married (45%) and have children (38%). As reported in the *New York Times,* August 31, 1986, the desire for privacy at home emerged as one of the major themes of the meeting. Two decades ago women who wanted a private room of their own asked for a sewing room. The women at the New Jersey conference said they wanted a study or an office, a place within their homes away from the family bustle to work at their jobs, businesses, or professions.

While private time at home is viewed by some women as an opportunity for additional work, it is viewed by many others as leisure time. Gardening, needlework, and reading number among women's uses of their solitary leisure. The lofty ideals that ground the argument for privacy are no less legitimate in view of the sobering reality that some women, like some men, will choose to devote a portion of their leisure to activities that promote neither careers, health, intellect, good taste, nor human bonds.

Respecting others' privacy does not require that we should each approve how others spend their time. It requires only that we be tolerant.[75] The moral case for privacy does not presuppose relativism about moral good. Without a doubt, certain private conduct, such as sexual child abuse, is immoral and, because of the patent harm involved, should be halted. The moral case for privacy does not presuppose relativism about tastes or about what constitutes human flourishing. *Qua* leisure, some activities (reading a well-written book, taking a walk) show better taste and reflect a better conception of a good life than others (watching reruns of "Gilligan's Island" on television, using cocaine). We rightly encourage our families and friends to aim at a good life by preferring better activities most of the time.

The moral argument for privacy is grounded, inter alia, on the belief that individuals should be permitted to live out their disparate, nonconforming preferences. Control of how others' private time is spent is inimical to pluralism and individuality. Democratic liberalism thus dictates that it be largely left to individual choice whether the opportunities for privacy furnished by custom and law are used for good or bad, high-brow entertainments or low. As John Stuart Mill urged, only where the safety or well-being of others is directly at risk should private life be opened to public scrutiny.

These points are raised here in connection with women's privacy at home with good reason. According to a familiar stereotype, women waste leisure time. They engage in idle chatter, gossip, romantic fantasy, and vanity. This stereotype is not of recent origin. Two hundred years ago, Thomas Gisborne advised that women read books during time not spent on domestic duties or charity. His *An Enquiry into the Duties of the Female Sex* was specific about the kind of books women ought to read. Because tales of love and passion "agitate the human heart," Gisborne exhorted women to steer clear of romances. He instructed them to select instead books from some of the "various branches of elegant and profitable knowledge. . . . Let whatever she peruses in her most private hours be such as she need not to be ashamed of reading aloud to those whose good opinion she is most anxious to deserve. Let her remember that there is an all-seeing eye, which is ever fixed upon her, even in her closest retirement."[76]

Buttressed by a thinly veiled allusion to the omnipresent God of Christianity, Gisborne's advice in essence denies women real private time. He set the standard of public conduct as the test of the legitimacy of conduct performed under conditions of privacy. His advice amounted to a prescription that women dispense with even limited, solitary periods of self-indulgence. He would have had women forego private time of their own to become ladies of perfect virtue.

It is interesting that whether women ought to occupy their leisure time with romance novels continues to be a topic of social concern. Because a lively controversy surrounds what women ought to read, there is also a debate over what women ought to write for women to read. Women who write for the popular Harlequin, Avon, Fawcett, and Ballantine romance novel lines have been targets of criticism.

Romance Writers of America report that the romance book industry earns $250 million annually and can boast a 35 percent share of the paperback market. *Romantic Times* estimated in 1986 that 22 million women read romance novels, some purchasing ten or twelve books at a time. The average romance reader is a college-educated woman between 18 and 45 years old, has a full-time job and a family income above $30,000. She reads one romance every two days, and spends $60 to $150 monthly on the books.[77]

Once romance novels were thought to be a threat to female virtue. They were opposed because they were thought to stimulate sexual fantasy and prompt premarital and extramarital sexual experimentation. Today romance novels are opposed for different reasons. They are accused of perpetuating pernicious stereotypes of men and women in heterosexual relationships. They are said to foster unrealistic expectations of sex and love, expectations that may subvert fulfillment in the real world. Romances are also opposed on the theory that they serve as substitutes for better literature and hence retard women's education. It is argued that more women would read serious books were lightweight romances not so readily available. Against these "censorship" arguments that romances should not be written, sold, or consumed, it is sometimes argued in rebuttal that only anecdotal evidence suggests that women who read romances expect the impossible in real-life relationships. Moreover, readers of romances include self-sufficient, educated women of outstanding intellectual and professional achievement.

The popularity of romance novels gives rise to legitimate concern about their impact on women's sexual and emotional expectations and place in the world. But, any heavily consumed genera of entertainment must give rise to the same concerns. Despite their popularity, the impact of romance novels, compared to that of other influences, is arguably small and all but impossible to gauge precisely. Experts cannot even agree on whether blatantly misogynist obscenity and pornography have serious adverse consequences on their consumers. Romantic images of women compete with realistic images of women projected into the public arena through television, films, books, and magazines. Paternalism about women's reading preferences is probably unnecessary and an affront to women's own exercise of judgment about how they spend a portion of their leisure time.

The notion that women waste their private time is disproven by the outstanding cultural records that have been a product of women's privacy. The diaries and letters of women are valued windows through which the mores of bygone eras can be understood.[78] The notion is also contradicted by outstanding literary achievements. Poet Emily Dickinson, perhaps the most famous female artistic recluse, described the secluded room in her father's house in Amherst, where she wrote, as her "freedom."[79] While some have characterized Dickinson as a bizarre eccentric who shut herself off from public life, others argue that her isolation was imposed from without by conventions of female gentility and a lack of access to the male-dominated literary world. Adrienne Rich has advanced a third view. She has speculated that "Dickinson chose her seclusion, knowing she was exceptional and knowing what she needed." Yet Rich also believes Dickinson was not as secluded as some have imagined, for though she lived in retreat, it was "no hermetic retreat, but a seclusion which included a wide range of people, reading and correspondence."[80]

Rich's description of Dickinson aptly describes the deliberate seclusion of many other creative women, including May Sarton. Sarton's *Journal of Solitude* (1973) chronicled her daily activities during a year of her life as she neared old age. A prolific writer of poetry, novels, stories and non-fiction, Sarton chose to live alone in quiet New Hampshire town. She gave lectures, and attended professional meetings, and maintained ties with friends and neighbors. But Sarton spent most of her time alone. She believed she needed solitude for her work and for her "real life": "friends, even passionate love, are not real life unless there is some time alone in which to discover what is happening or has happened."[81]

Many women both work for wages outside the home and have substantial caretaking obligations at home. Consequently, how to create private time rather than how to avoid wasting it is their more compelling practical concern. One way to find private time is not to spend it on excessive caretaking and housekeeping. Lavishing unnecessary attention on children and spouses is suffocating and thankless. Onerous unnecessary housekeeping can reduce the amount and value of private time. It is easy to waste private time on housework, despite the proliferation of time-saving household appliances. International studies show that more "time-saving" appliances have not resulted in women spending less time at housework.[82] In 1910 the average housewife spent 50 hours a week cooking and cleaning. In 1980, though "armed with dozens of motors and electronic chips, [she] still spends 50 to 60 hours a week cooking and cleaning, shopping and chauffeuring."[83] Even women with full-time jobs average 35 hours a week on housework. One reason for this in our affluent society is that oversized dwellings, high-maintenance furnishings, and bric-a-brac multiply the amount of housework that needs to be done. So too do high standards of personal and environmental hygiene.

Maintaining healthy relationships with those with whom one lives is a way of creating more rewarding private time in busy lives. In addition to having serious psychological and physical consequences, frequent domestic conflicts and violence waste time and waste opportunities for privacy at home. Wife-beating must be counted among practices that have served to deny women the solace and peace of mind they would otherwise enjoy in their private lives. Wife-beating deprives a woman of a sense of her own worth and must undoubtedly "help to emphasize her dependence and make it more difficult for her to face life on her own."[84]

Like beatings, sexual violence in the home can injure women's bodies and spirits. Legal questions have been raised about the extent to which the state may justly and usefully interfere with domestic relations for the sake of deterring and punishing spousal violence. It is increasingly recognized that men and women should not be able to escape punishment for gravely harming one another, solely by virtue of marriage or cohabitation. In 1986, a man convicted of assault and involuntary deviate sexual intercourse under Pennsylvania's Spousal Sexual Assault Statute appealed his conviction. He argued on appeal that the constitutional right to privacy inherent in marriage placed his cruelty toward his wife beyond the reach of the law. Fortunately, the court rejected his argument and upheld the constitutionality of the Spousal Sexual Assault Statute as "another step in the erosion of the common law notion of a married woman as chattel."[85] The privacy of the home and marriage are not properly permitted to shield violence that deprives women of the capacity to utilize opportunities for privacy in the domestic sphere.

Just as family violence can bind one detrimentally to the domestic sphere and result in a wasted privacy fraught with anxiety, so too can the malady known as "agoraphobia." Literally "fear of the market-place," agoraphobia causes its victims to dread leaving and, in severe cases, to be incapable of leaving their homes. Rejecting the theory that agoraphobia is a neurosis or illness, Seidenberg and DeCrow have interpreted it as a form of political protest: the "agoraphobe . . . is vigorously protesting social intimidation, sex-role stereotypes, and oppression. [It] is primarily women's way of fighting back. . . . In their so-called neuroticism [they] are acting out a strong personal political statement about their own plight in a restrictive society."[86] If Seidenberg and DeCrow are correct about its causes, we can expect to see a decrease in the incidence of agoraphobia as women continue to find acceptance as workers and equal participants in the public world. Wasted privacy will be supplanted by opportunities for salutary private time that is not confinement, but, as Emily Dickinson conceived it, freedom.

CONCLUSION

In one sense, women in the United States since the industrial revolution have enjoyed a great deal of privacy. The private house or apartment of the middle- and upper-income classes has separated women from the larger world in a condition of inaccessibility protected by law and social practice. However, as Charlotte Perkins Gilman pointed out a century ago, this privacy does not always represent meaningful opportunities for personal privacy in a woman's life, particularly if her home is a family home in which she assumes the roles of cloistered housewife and mother. The home-bound life furthers ideals of feminine modesty and intimacy. It perpetuates the male-headed nuclear family as a basic social unit. But it is inimical to individual forms of personal privacy and the exercise of privacy-promoting liberties.

Jean Bethke Elshtain, Catherine MacKinnon, Susan Okin Miller, and other scholars have pointed to respects in which the concept of the private sphere has been utilized in Western thought to justify undervaluing women's work and their claims to equality and self-determination.[87] The central criticisms I make of the private sphere—

as constituted by home and family life—are that women have been confined to it and that it has not always been a context in which women can experience and make constructive use of opportunities for privacy. Given privacy's special value, there must be contexts in the lives of women in which they can reliably anticipate meaningful opportunities for personal privacy.

In our culture, homes are designated centers of privacy, and women must be free of inequitable traditions that deny them meaningful privacy at home. I take my argument for real privacy in the private sphere to be consistent with and in the same spirit as the thrust of those feminist objections to the private sphere that equate privacy and "the private" with conditions of female repression. My criticism, however, is only a criticism of a certain poor quality of life within the private sphere and not a rejection of the concept of a separate, private sphere. I leave open the question whether a normative distinction between the public and private spheres can ultimately be drawn, and if so, what principles ought to govern individual, group, and governmental conduct respecting each.

Women have served well their traditional roles as guardians of the private sphere. The social experiences of the sexes in our society are sufficiently different that men and women may have contrasting attitudes about their own privacy. Many women enjoy and relish caretaking roles. Many readily embrace lifestyles that diminish individual privacy. It must not be too hastily concluded on this basis that women are not keen on individual privacy and want to keep it that way. One can only speculate whether women in a condition of full equality would exhibit a stronger or weaker preference for privacy; whether, if free to do otherwise, most would pursue affiliative ideals even to the point of self-oblivion. But it is evident now that many caring women enjoy privacy and would relish more of it for their work and leisure.

How is more privacy in the private sphere possible for women? Insofar as privacy has an economic basis, economic equality is a background condition for greater privacy. But that is not all. In Chapter 4 I argue that contraception and abortion are important privacy control devices to which women ought to have easy access. Decisional privacy to choose whether or not to bear a child affords fertile, younger women a valuable degree of control over the personal privacy they have at home.

CHAPTER 4

Reproductive Liberties

Privacy is commonly pointed to as part of what is at stake in the choice between competing reproductive and parental rights policies. Yet it is not always clear what is meant by "privacy" and hence what forms of privacy are at stake. Is the privacy at stake decisional privacy, individual, autonomous choice free of governmental interference? Is it family privacy, free choice for the family aggregate? Is it seclusion, solitude, or anonymity? Is it secrecy or confidentiality? When it is clear what kinds of privacy are at stake, it may not be clear whether they are important enough to justify, for example, abortion on demand of a viable fetus or a woman's choice to let a handicapped neonate die.

This chapter will identify the most important forms of privacy at stake in the quest for basic reproductive liberties and explain why respect for these forms of privacy should be deemed a major impetus toward policies that maximize women's choices. The task will be undertaken primarily in the context of an examination of arguments for privacy that have a place in the moral evaluation of governmentally imposed constraints on contraception, abortion, childbirth, and neonatal care. Still other moral questions about choosing and foregoing privacy arise for women in connection with pregnancy and parenting quite apart from questions of political morality about the justified limits of governmental intervention. I examine a number of these, as well.

Much of this chapter concerns contraception and abortion. Proponents of permissive contraception and abortion laws have rightly emphasized the concept of privacy in pressing their cause, arguing that the availability of abortion affords women choice and hence control over their bodies and lives. What has privacy to do with choice? Legislative constraints eliminating abortion as a realistic

82

choice are deemed to be assaults on an aspect of privacy. On this view, through passage of laws that prohibit or discourage abortion, government is deemed to enter a zone of free decisionmaking respecting private life, which ought to be the exclusive domain of private parties and beyond the reach of public authorities. This chapter will focus on free choice, construed by many as a decisional form of privacy, as well as on what I will refer to as paradigmatic forms of privacy: seclusion, solitude, anonymity, secrecy, and confidentiality. As we shall see, decisional privacy is an aspect of liberty with deep and definite implications for paradigmatic forms privacy.

MOTHERHOOD AND INTRAFAMILIAL PRIVACY

Seclusion, Solitude, and Anonymity

Complete privacy is as undesirable as its opposite. Nevertheless, a degree of privacy is of value to individuals and the communities to which they potentially contribute. As elaborated in Chapter 1, personal privacy can be characterized as a degree of inaccessibility of persons, their mental states, or information about them to the senses and surveillance devices of others. Seclusion, the inaccessibility of the physical person, is a basic, indeed, paradigmatic form of personal privacy in this sense. Solitude, or being alone, is a particular kind of seclusion, namely, solitary as opposed to shared seclusion. People who live alone normally achieve solitude simply by entering their homes. The story is quite different for co-habitants of a shared residence. Without space or rooms of their own in which to further seclude themselves, they may seldom possess either solitude or the form of privacy known as anonymity.

In a familiar sense of the term, "anonymity" denotes not having one's name or identity known to others. In the broader sense favored by privacy theorists and intended here, "anonymity" denotes not having attention paid one.[1] In this broader sense, anonymity can be a reasonable expectation of privacy even in the context of nuclear family life where, it goes without saying, one's name, identity, and background are known. When attention is being paid a person, it is accompanied by implied pressure to limit conduct to publicly acceptable standards. One seeks to fit in and to avoid opprobrium, shame, embarrassment, and negative sanctions.[2] While conformity to public norms is relaxed considerably within the typical family, there are often further, family norms that govern conduct. Family members reasonably seek periodic relief from such norms. Intrafamilial privacy provides opportunities to be free of the social requirements imposed by both the public and the family.

In the last chapter, I considered respects in which the family home has come to symbolize what it does not in fact always represent—both the shared seclusion of good times spent with others and the solitudinous, anonymous seclusion of good times spent alone. Sharing a home can make seclusion within it anything but satisfying. The burdens and responsibilities that arise out of commitments, dependencies, crowding, incompatible lifestyles, clashing personalities, and emotional conflicts can make a shared residence oppressive. Crowding, for example, diminishes opportunities for solitude and anonymity and can diminish the pleasure of intimate contact. In some cases the most meaningful opportunities for solitude and anonymity in a person's life may be time spent at work in a private office or in a public park, where the obligation to interact with others is circumscribed. Life outside the home may be the truer haven.

Is Motherhood Consistent with Privacy?

The foregoing points are obvious, but have the greatest importance for a woman's decision whether to have a child. Motherhood and family life typically entail that women sacrifice a good deal of their privacy. In many circumstances the birth of a child will entail that too much privacy be sacrificed. Feminist Charlotte Perkins Gilman only slightly overstated the conflict between family life and privacy when, she wrote, in 1898:

> Such privacy as we have at home is family privacy, an aggregate privacy; and this does not insure—indeed, it prevents—individual privacy. . . . The home is the one place on earth where no one of the component individuals can have any privacy. . . . At present any tendency to withdraw and live one's own life on any plane of separate interest or industry is naturally resented, or at least regretted, by the other members of the family. This affects women more than men, because men live very little in the family and very much in the world.[3]

Contrary to Gilman, there *can* be privacy in a family home. Indeed, where family size is limited, space is sufficient, and there are mutual respect, discipline, and cooperation, a household can offer quite a lot of intrafamilial privacy. Family life, however, plainly presents the potential for conflict between adequate privacy, especially solitude and anonymity, and adequate participation in and responsibility toward the family. As shown in Chapter 3, Gilman was correct in her recognition that women's roles as guardians of the private sphere have been a special obstacle to their attainment of adequate privacy.

If I am right that intrafamilial privacy is possible, then it follows that advocacy of meaningful opportunities for privacy and the conditions of life that make them practicable is not a rejection of motherhood and the family. Should motherhood and the family be rejected for other reasons? The family is not beyond reproach as a social institution. The family has been celebrated in Western society in sentimental, moral, and pragmatic terms as both a valuable educational vehicle for the transmission of culture and as an efficient economic unit, satisfying the need for food, clothing, shelter, and productive work. The philosopher who may have been the first to examine carefully the question of the justice of the family was ambivalent about the institution. While he rejected the family as a form of life for the ruling elite of his ideal republic, Plato not only embraced it for the artisans or "working classes," but also prescribed that elites live together in communes and be encouraged to think of themselves as family kin, for the sake of social harmony.[4] Sharing Plato's ambivalence, some modern political theorists have viewed the moral justice of the family for individuals and the aggregate of society as an open question. In *Theory of Justice,* John Rawls suggested that the result of grouping persons into families with unequal social, educational, and economic resources is the imperfect carrying out of what he called the "principle of fair opportunity."[5] This principle requires that social institutions be constituted so as to ensure that each person has a fair chance to enjoy society's benefits. Children from happier and wealthier families tend to have better opportunities than equally deserving children from troubled and poorer families. Rawls maintained that because of the inequalities it perpetuates, the family is consistent with justice only to the extent that it contributes goods that redound even to the benefit of those most disadvantaged by family life.[6]

Ambivalence about the family has also stemmed from recognition of its implications for moral justice toward women. In recent decades feminist theorists have advocated the rejection or reform of the family. With analyses reminiscent of Frederick Engels's *The Origin of the Family, Private Property and the State,*[7] radical feminists have concluded that the male-dominated modern monogamous family has been inimical to social justice for its subjugation of women (and children) and should be rejected. Others have rejected the male-dominated family, but urged that the family is a redeemable institution. In this vein, Jean Bethke Elshtain has argued for family reconstruction. Elshtain perceives the family as a moral imperative for the humane nurturance of children. But she rightly calls for the articulation of a "particular idea of family life that does not repeat the terms of female oppression and exploitation."[8]

While the problem of privacy at home for mothers can be especially severe in the male-dominated family, it exists as well in female-headed families and in egalitarian families where women share decisionmaking authority with partners. Women welcome some of the obstacles to privacy posed by motherhood. Maternal and familial love, like romantic love, make solitude and anonymity less attractive. Mothers often want nothing more than to be in the company of their families and to have their attention. Familial love is an obstacle to privacy. Nevertheless, many women doubtless undertake family life precisely to have and give love. They are anxious to assume the characteristic commitment of responsiveness to the emotional, social, and economic needs of children and partners. These women "no longer want to exist as persons for themselves as they do in the area of abstract right characterized by property, contract, and punishment for injustice, or as mere isolated subjects with their own private resolutions, intentions, conscience . . . but as real social members, living with each other."[9] Still, some obstacles to solitude and anonymity are not welcomed and could not be welcomed, even by women who have voluntarily undertaken family life.

A child can be such an obstacle. While older children are capable of intentionally invading the privacy of those with whom they live, it is not chiefly for this reason that children in general constitute an obstacle to privacy for their mothers. The main reason they are a privacy obstacle is that children must be closely cared for and must have ready access to those who care for them.

Planning for Privacy

Simply put, contraception and abortion can be utilized to assure that children are not born who would constitute an obstacle to the attainment of privacy. Safe contraception is an inexpensive tool for assuring privacy. Abortion, the emotional costs of which are often substantially greater than the emotional costs of contraception, is also a birth prevention tool. It reduces the number of persons with whom a sexually active younger woman is likely to have to share a home and for whom she would be responsible. Absent contraception and abortion, there would be more unwanted pregnancies, more births, and more children to be cared for by women. It is impossible to know precisely how many births are prevented through the use of contraceptives, but we do have a good idea of how many births are prevented as a result of medical abortions.

According to *Abortion Surveillance*, a U.S. Centers for Disease Control study, approximately 1.3 million abortions were performed in 1981. A more recent study by the Alan Guttmacher Institute indicated that total annual abortions were 1.574 million in 1982, 1.515 million in 1983, and 1.508 million in 1984, the latest year for which statistics are available. In 1984 there were 26.8 abortions per 1000 American women. Viewed as a social phenomenon, abortion rights may have the effect of indirectly preventing more births than the number of annual abortions procedures suggests. Kristin Luker, *Abortion and the Politics of Motherhood* (1984), cited empirical evidence that outlawing abortion could turn public opinion against the pill, the IUD and treatment after rape. Public disapproval of birth control could reduce reliance on contraception and raise the birthrate.

Mothers, rather than fathers or couples, still typically assume primary responsibility for the direct care of children. Mothers closely share their lives with each of their children for eighteen years or more. Spouses, fathers, and extended families can relieve women of responsibilities that compete with privacy. Increasingly, due to mobility, divorce, and women working outside the home, such assistance is not readily available. Few birth-mothers, even teen-aged and unmarried birth-mothers, exercise the adoption option afforded by law. Instead, typical mothers choose to retain responsibility for their offspring.

Creating adequate privacy for herself (and any other members of her household) may require financial resources that women with children do not have. Affluent women can purchase professional childcare, babysitters, additional living space, and vacations, all of which allow family members to escape from one another from time to time. However, not all women of means view giving over childcare responsibilities to others as a viable option. Consideration of the child's best interest and of doing what is morally best may preclude apparent options. For example, many thoughtful women reasonably conclude—with expert concurrence—that the well-being and safety of their children should not be entrusted to pre-school day-care centers.[10] As another example, conscientious women may feel morally compelled by traditional secular and religious values to reject day-care and similar options, even at great cost to their freedom and privacy. Moral and religious considerations, as well as financial limitations and considerations for the safety and well-being of the child, help to determine the extent to which having a child obstructs a woman's attainment of privacy.

Sharing a life with a child has a psychological dimension that may undermine a woman's effort to create privacy and freedom by delegating childcare responsibilities. Few women today have fallen prey to the late nineteenth-century middle-class myth that failure to lavish every moment upon one's children could jeopardize the whole of civilization. Nonetheless, a mother's active concern and sense of responsibility do not end when her infant is placed under the charge of a sitter or her child heads off to school or to play. Carol Gilligan and others have pointed out that women with children strongly identify with them and their needs. A mother may cease to define herself as an individual and view herself as the composite of her child and herself. Mothers have been known to feel without purpose and identity when children to whom they have devoted themselves leave home for good.

Sexually active younger women who do not want children, who want no more children, or who want to postpone children must rely on contraception and abortion to preserve and achieve desired levels of solitude and anonymity in their lives. The moral significance of these and other paradigmatic forms of privacy was set forth in Chapter 2. Most deeply, privacy must be valued for promoting individuating traits and well-being called for by personhood, social participation, and contribution. And while individuality is not as important among family members, who inevitably share a common history and many of the same values and aspirations, it goes without saying that respect for personhood, participation, and contribution have value inside the family as well as out.

While solitude and anonymity can represent vacant, non-goaldirected time of one's own, these forms of privacy are often prerequisites for fulfilling educational, artistic, and professional aspirations. Privacy in private life provides the best opportunity in our society for relaxation, rejuvenation, reflection, and nurturing traits that can potentially distinguish one in the larger, public world. Contributions within the private sphere are not to be demeaned, but contributions to the public must not be foreclosed. It is plain why privacy, as opportunity for self-development, is essential for women if they are to continue progress toward social equality.

Contraception

The use of contraception is lawful in the United States. Respect for privacy and privacy-related liberties demands that it remain so. Where the law prohibits contraception, sexually active fertile women are exposed to the possibility of recurrent pregnancies. Each pregnancy represents potential privacy losses for women and others in their households. Laws prohibiting contraception also expose women to privacy intrusions by persons outside the family. Enforcement of laws banning contraception invite law enforcement officials into the seclusion of the bedroom. Beyond that, laws banning contraception would invite the courts to inspect the intimacies and privacies of home life to ascertain whether contraceptive practices measure up to the legal standard.

Supreme Court Justice Douglas raised these privacy concerns in *Griswold v. Connecticut* when he posed the now-famous question "Would we allow the police to search the sacred precincts of marital bedrooms for telltale signs of the use of contraceptives?"[11] Douglas answered the question as he knew his readers would: "The very idea is repulsive to . . . notions of privacy."

With the *Griswold* case, the Supreme Court struck down unconstitutional Connecticut anti-contraception statutes. The statutes provided, first, that persons using any "drug, medicine or instrument for the purpose of preventing contraception" be fined, imprisoned, or both; and second, that any person "who assists, abets, or counsels, causes, hires or commands another to commit an offense," including use of contraception, be prosecuted as if he were the principle offender. The executive and medical directors of the Planned Parenthood League of Connecticut, Estelle T. Griswold and Dr. Charles Lee Buxton, had been arrested and convicted after giving contraception information, instruction, and medical advice to a married couple. Ms. Griswold was determined to test the legality of the state laws criminalizing contraception, and virtually sought out arrest after she opened a birth control clinic in New Haven.[12] In the ensuing Supreme Court proceedings the two directors were found to have standing to raise in their own defense the constitutional rights of the married people with whom they had a professional relationship. On the basis of rights of privacy and repose emanating from the penumbra of the Bill of Rights, the Court held that states may not prohibit use of contraceptives by married couples.

In a later case, *Eisenstadt v. Baird,* the Court went further, holding a Massachusetts statute prohibiting distribution of contraceptives to unmarried persons unconstitutional.[13] Defendant Baird had been convicted of violating provisions of the Massachusetts General Laws after he exhibited contraceptive articles in the course of a lecture at Boston University and gave an unmarried woman a package of Emko vaginal foam. As a result of *Griswold* and *Baird,* the decisional privacy of adult women to safeguard their privacy at home through contraceptive use is now legally protected. The Court has not always taken care to distinguish decisional privacy from paradigmatic forms of privacy, such as solitude and anonymity. It is now evident that they can and should be distinguished, and that decisional privacy is a key to women's attainment of paradigmatic forms of privacy.

Aborting for Privacy

It is conceivable that attempts to enforce laws regulating abortion could lead to intrusions upon the seclusion of women in their homes and in the offices of health-care providers. Seclusion interests number among those privacy interests women have that oppose abortion prohibitions and some abortion control laws. Even so, women's interests in decisional privacy rather than privacy in the sense of seclusion were the focus of pathbreaking abortion rights cases.

In *Roe v. Wade* and *Doe v. Bolton,* the Supreme Court invalidated statutes criminalizing procurement or administration of abortion.[14] *Roe* plaintiff "Jane Roe" was actually Norma McCorvey, a poor, uneducated Dallas woman who had become pregnant as the result of a gang rape. Unable to obtain a legal abortion in Texas, she felt compelled to have the child and put it up for adoption. Her suit alleged that the Texas abortion statutes were unconstitutionally vague and abridged her right of personal privacy protected by the First, Fourth, Fifth, Ninth, and Fourteenth Amendments. Additional *Roe* plaintiffs were a childless couple, "John and Mary Doe," and a licensed physician, Dr. Hallford. The Texas abortion statutes before the Court in Roe provided for prison sentences of up to ten years. Statutes in various states criminalizing attempted abortion were also at issue in *Roe.* For example, under Massachusetts law, attempted abortion was a crime that carried fines up to $1,000.

Writing for the majority in *Roe,* Justice Blackmun explained that while states may assert a legitimate interest in safeguarding health, maintaining medical standards, and protecting pre-natal life, women have a fundamental constitutional right of privacy to decide for themselves in the early stages of pregnancy whether or not to give birth to a child. Their right of privacy—choice free of governmental interference—is implicit in the concept of liberty.[15] As a result of the *Roe* decision and later cases clarifying its meaning, pre-viability abortions are available to adult women "on demand" and to some minors without parental consent. *Roe,* its progeny, and the moral and jurisprudential problems they raise have been extensively analyzed and debated.[16]

Decisional privacy was the focus of *Roe,* but the concepts of seclusion and solitude arose subtly in the Court's opinion in the context of explicating the nature of the pregnant woman's claims against her unborn and the right of the state to interfere on behalf of viable fetal life. Justice Blackmun suggested that the pregnant woman shares whatever condition of physical privacy she enjoys with a developing entity, and that therein lies the problem: "The pregnant woman cannot be isolated in her privacy. She carries an embryo and, later, a fetus. . . . [A]t some point in time . . . [t]he woman's privacy is no longer sole and any right of privacy she possesses must be measured accordingly."[17] This confused passage has doubtless helped to convince opponents of *Roe* that the Supreme Court's privacy analysis is incoherent. Justice Blackmun's words suggest that he subscribes to a non sequitur: as an embryo approaches maturity it becomes progressively less true that the pregnant woman possesses actual physical privacy and therefore less true that she possesses a right to decisional privacy.

Why suppose with Blackmun that a woman's decisional privacy rights diminish as her physical privacy correspondingly diminishes? It is not clear what sense it makes to suppose that her physical privacy is significantly diminished by pregnancy. Here the definition of privacy-as-inaccessibility becomes useful. Privacy means a degree of inaccessibility to the senses and surveillance devices others can employ to learn what we are, do, think, and feel. At no stage in their development do the unborn have the combination of sensory experiences and understanding that could make their presence in the womb a significant privacy diminution for others. A pregnant woman's privacy never ceases to be virtually sole, despite her pregnancy. Thus pregnancy itself cannot have the impact on a woman's privacy that Justice Blackmun suggested it must. Moreover, even if pregnancy did lessen physical privacy, it would not follow as a matter of logic alone that decisional privacy rights have to be compromised.

The point Justice Blackmun sought to make on behalf of the Court was simply that the right of decisional privacy respecting childbirth cannot be deemed absolute. At the point at which the fetus becomes a "viable" entity, it is reasonable for the state to assert an interest in its well-being and put an end to a woman's right lawfully to choose abortion. The decisional privacy rights to decide whether to enjoy heterosexual adult sex or read pornography in the home are less subject to lawful state interference. They are, in Blackmun's words, "inherently different," because they do not normally have the life-and-death implications of abortion. The problem with Blackmun's *Roe* analysis is that viability strikes many conservatives and liberals as an arbitrary, vague dividing line.

In addition to seclusion and solitude other paradigmatic privacy concepts, namely information non-disclosure and anonymity, have joined decisional privacy in playing a role in abortion rights cases. In *Thornburgh v. American College of Obstetricians and Gynecologists,* the Supreme Court found provisions of Pennsylvania's Abortion Control Act ("the Act") unconstitutional.[18] The Act was enacted to discourage abortion by making it expensive, time-consuming, and psychologically burdensome to offer or obtain abortion services. Concern for secrecy, confidentiality, and anonymity motivated invalidating provisions of the Act that required modes of record-keeping and reporting by abortion facilities, which threatened to subject abortion recipients to public exposure and harassment. The Court recognized that protecting these paradigmatic privacy interests was an important means of protecting free choice. Women who fear they cannot obtain an abortion in a context of secrecy, confidentiality, and anonymity are constrained in their decisionmaking. The Court upheld the principle that women are entitled to make the abortion decision, and to make it without undue risk of public scrutiny and its inhibiting consequences: "Few decisions are more personal and intimate, more properly private, or more basic to individual dignity and autonomy, than a woman's decision . . . whether to end her pregnancy."[19]

Four tiers of privacy and privacy-related concerns are implicated by *Thornburgh* and earlier abortion cases. They are (a) privacy at home, (b) bodily integrity and self-determination, (c) decisional privacy, and (d) informational privacy. The first tier, not expressly addressed by the court cases but emphasized here, is privacy at home. Abortion, like contraception, helps women create seclusion, solitude, and conditions of limited attention-paying at home. The second tier, bodily integrity and self-determination, are privacy-related concerns for managing one's own body, a prerequisite of managing one's self. A third tier of privacy and privacy-related concerns is decisional privacy. An aspect of liberty, it protects bodily integrity and self-determination (tier two) and allows women to assure adequate privacy for themselves and their households (tier one). A fourth tier, informational privacy, protects decisional privacy (tier three) and through it bodily integrity and self-determination (tier two), as well as privacy at home (tier one). Secrecy and confidentiality assure that women can elect abortions without fearing that family members or others in possession of the knowledge will cause them harm.

Arguments for permissive abortion policies generally relate to the second, third, and fourth tiers. Can an argument for permissive, woman-centered abortion policies be based on the importance of the first tier of privacy concerns? Yes, but such an argument will not always be persuasive to women who oppose abortion on certain religious, cultural, or moral grounds.

Religion, Character, and Ethnicity

An argument based directly on the value of seclusion, solitude, and anonymity in home life is likely to be unpersuasive to those who oppose contraception and abortion on religious grounds. A woman may believe seclusion, solitude, and anonymity in the family have legitimate significance (as opportunities for meditation and prayer, for example) but view preserving privacy in these senses as less important than the child-bearing and child-rearing duties ascribed by religion. Christian doctrines provide that releasing new souls into the world to do God's work or be put to God's test is a central aspect of women's duties. Likewise, some Christians regard the moral education of the young in a family context to be an aspect of women's religious duty. Religious beliefs such as these cause women to oppose abortion for herself and for others, and to oppose contraception as well.

In addition, some secular opponents of abortion would not be persuaded by an argument for abortion based on the importance to women of privacy at home. Secular moral opposition to abortion is commonplace on such grounds as (a) bearing and rearing children is required by virtue, women's natural duty, or social obligation; (b) human life, even in embryonic and fetal stages, has inherent value; and (c) the unborn have a right to life. The cogency of these grounds has been exhaustively debated, and those debates will not be duplicated here.

The dialectic of one abortion debate is worth noting. The expression "person" is commonly used to mean *human being*.[20] A number of philosophers have argued that only persons in the moral sense have inherent moral value or rights, and that fetuses are not persons.[21] To be a person in the moral sense is to possess consciousness of oneself as a subject of experiences and a minimal rational capacity to view oneself as having a past and a future, qualities that embryos, fetuses, and even neonates do not have. Critics of such arguments have contended that only arbitrary reasons can be given for withholding the protected moral status which pertains to persons from the unborn since they have unquestioned potential to develop traits of moral personhood. One reply to this potential-persons-count-too rejoinder is to concede personhood to the unborn, but to deny that abortion is therefore without justification. Even if the unborn have the highest moral status, the reply goes, women have the same high status. Their moral status countermands that they be required either to sacrifice their bodies, happiness, and potential, or to yield to others decisional authority concerning matters so deeply tied to their individual identities.

While both pro-life and pro-choice activists rely heavily on the language of children's and women's rights, some ethicists have urged that discussion of rights has no place in family and reproductive ethics.[22] The notion of those ethicists—that there are special, onerous, sui generis family obligations—is a potentially self-serving one, too easily used to mandate sacrifices for women. Theories claiming that individualistic rights analysis is appropriate in connection with the public sphere (male world) but has no place at all in the private sphere of family and reproductive concerns (female world) are cause for suspicion. If pregnancy and motherhood impose particular sui generis abstract obligations upon women, it is notoriously unclear what they are. This is not to say that family and reproductive ethics is naught but a battleground of rights in which the arsenal of other ethical concepts guiding human conduct are necessarily unwelcome.

For example, the evaluation of character in the framework of abortion decisionmaking might be appropriate. Having an abortion after deliberately becoming pregnant could indicate a frivolous character. Suppose, for example, a woman sought to obtain an abortion after discovering she would have a girl, because she really wanted a boy. Refusal to bear a child would also show a lack of integrity if one unilaterally decided to remain childless after carefully planning a pregnancy with a devoted spouse. I must add, however, that it is doubtful that the abortion decision is often a product of lapses of character. There is evidence that adult women make the abortion choice carefully. Carol Gilligan's studies of abortion decisionmaking indicate that women agonize over the abortion choice, because they perceive themselves as having serious obligations of caretaking, sacrifice, and benevolence.[23]

Abortion is not always the less sacrificial of the choice between giving birth and abortion. For women who know they are unable adequately to provide for a new child, but who still desire to see their pregnancy through, abortion may be the greater act of self-sacrifice. Character can be presumed to cut inevitably against abortion only where one assumes that electing abortion is inherently of greatest appeal to women without good characters. It is easy to fall prey to this assumption because, traditionally, having a good female character has meant being a woman of saintly sacrifice, rather than a person of temperate and just disposition. In any case, permissive abortion laws may be precisely what is required if reproduction is to be fully within the realm of character. Meaningful exercises of character can occur only where individuals have realistic choices.

Opposition to birth control can arise out of a woman's identification with the traditions of her cultural group. These traditions may expressly oppose abortion, contraception, and laws that permit them. But even if they do not, a woman may nonetheless view herself as having an obligation to sacrifice privacy at home and perpetuate her group by bearing children whom she will rear in its traditions. Thus, some Jewish women view themselves as having special obligations to rear children and to rear them as Jews. To do otherwise would be virtually to continue what Hitler began with the Holocaust. Some black women recognize special obligations to bear children, obligations that arise out of a tradition of large families. Large families serve as a source of pride and as a network of economic and moral support in a hostile world. During the 1960s and 1970s, genocidal concerns not unlike those raised among Jewish women were raised among black women in intellectual circles, who feared emphasis on birth control was less women's liberation than a conspiracy to thin the negro population. More recently, capable black women have come to believe themselves under an obligation to sustain black progress and promote further social and economic improvement by rearing children with racial identity but with the special resources needed for self-help and success in a multiracial society.

The role of felt moral obligations of culture are typically overlooked in scholarly discussions of the morality of birth control. This may be because prevailing political moralities in the United States are, broadly speaking, liberal. Liberalism cannot straightforwardly accommodate the recognition of nonuniversal obligations. Liberals typically recognize universal obligations that are the correlatives of universally ascribed individual rights. The liberal perspective recognizes morally binding laws, but does not recognize publicly cognizable genuine moral obligations binding women as members of particular cultural groups to have children (or to do anything). On the liberal view, the individual is "incapable of membership in any community bound by moral ties antecedent to choice."[24] At most, the liberal would allow that an individual woman could undertake an obligation to have a child through a voluntarily promise or commitment made to a spouse, parent, or community.

If real and not simply felt moral obligations can flow from cultural identity, then the argument that abortion is morally acceptable and ought not be prohibited because the unborn have no independent moral status faces a particularly strong challenge. Yet, the difficulty of knowing what membership in a particular cultural group truly requires is a weak link in arguments from culture against birth prevention. The tendency of such arguments to preserve the status quo, however unjust, is another difficulty that cuts against reliance on culture-based arguments. The acceptance of ancillary child-bearing and child-rearing roles has been a historic feature of what culture after culture has defined as the moral obligation of women. It may be necessary for a woman recognizing strong bonds to a cultural heritage to reject its traditional opposition to birth prevention as a step toward reshaping that heritage in a more equitable direction. Doing so may serve to strengthen the heritage's chances of survival in a world of improved opportunity for women.

Privacy arguments based directly on the value to women of privacy at home can seem to condone selfishness in the same way that economic arguments for abortion can seem to condone materialism. An economic realism argument for permissive abortion and contraception laws is sometimes made by pro-choice activists. They argue that it is morally wrong to allow an unwanted child to be born who will be economically underprivileged and an economic burden to its family. The economic argument is countered by pro-lifers with the claim that human life is more important than economic comfort. It is better to be born poor and unloved, conditions that can be overcome, than to be killed before birth; it is better to suffer the malnourishment and miseducation that poverty entails than to have one's life snuffed out in its inception. This rebuttal pits life against mere money. It suggests that to embrace the economic argument is to condone materialism and demean human life.

Arguments from privacy may not appear persuasive when interpreted to pit the value of privacy at home for women against the value of life itself for the unborn. Mere privacy, after all, cannot be more important than a chance at life itself. Is not the right to privacy surely outweighed by the right to life? Wouldn't Judith Thomson's famous argument have collapsed had the hypothetical kidnap victim decided to detach the ailing violinist (hooked to her in the night without her consent to save his life) merely for the sake of her privacy?[25]

A basic level of privacy is more need than luxury. For this reason the value of privacy is not always outweighed, so to speak, by the value of life. The right to privacy is not always outweighed by the right to life. The strongest possible privacy-at-home argument is one that highlights the importance of privacy by showing its connection to those attributes that give individual lives moral significance. As a practical matter, such an argument is powerless against someone wedded to the premise that mere life is the ultimate, preeminent value, and that public policies ought to be shaped accordingly. Nonetheless, the present generation, more than any other in history, has had its faith in the absolute value of creating and extending life tested. We have seen that death can be better than life spent in a coma or in slow agony aided by technological life supports.[26] That is not something we want for ourselves or for our families and friends. It is not merely life but the quality of the life that merits protection.

Lives ended through abortion, or never begun because of contraception, would not, for the most part, have been valueless lives. This means women's privacy is typically pitted not against altogether dreadful lives, but against crowded, impoverished, stressful, and perhaps unhappy lives. Nonetheless, there is a strong privacy-at-home argument against restrictive abortion and contraception laws. It starts with the premise that lack of abortion choice is detrimental to women's full development, and that the personal development of women is every bit as important as the personal development of the unborn. What gives human life its special value is that it can be an experience in which persons find happiness and satisfaction through self-directed participation and contribution. Lives spent bearing and rearing children and without adequate solitude and seclusion from others are stunted lives. These lives can lack the levels of fulfillment and satisfaction that are the hallmark of happiness; such lives may be lives of sacrificial contribution, but they are lives that fall far short of those that might otherwise have been. Women are justified in refusing to bear children to the extent that the privacy they need to be happy, to participate, and to make their most meaningful and best contributions would be obstructed by motherhood. The argument from privacy at home asserts that it is better to have a population of adult women who are satisfied, fulfilled participants and contributors than simply to have more people. It further asserts that it is worse to perpetuate a social order in which some persons are unhappy, stunted, and inferior because of their sex, than to permit termination of human life prior to birth.

DECISIONAL PRIVACY

Thus far I have emphasized seclusion, especially anonymous and solitudinous seclusion, as the form of privacy threatened by laws placing constraints on the availability of abortion and contraception. But free choice regarding whether or not to bear a child, choice free from governmentally imposed constraints, is the "privacy" more often emphasized in connection with reproductive rights. Strictly speaking, in the sense set forth in Chapter 1, free choice is not a form of privacy. Solitude, anonymity, and information non-disclosure are aptly described as forms of privacy, because they designate respects in which persons, their mental states, and information about them are to some extent inaccessible to others. Free choice is not a form of privacy, even though it relates to one's capacity to control one's privacy, one's private life and one's own body. Free choice designates the absence of governmental (in that sense, "public") interference with decisions made by individuals and families about aspects of life deemed unsuited to such interference. Decisional privacy, that is, nongovernmental decisionmaking, is an important part of what autonomous choice is all about.

The Supreme Court relied mainly on decisional privacy rights in stating the rationales for leading reproductive rights cases in the 1960s, 1970s, and 1980s. Thus, in *Eisenstadt* Justice Brennan wrote, upholding the right of single women to birth control, that "If the right of privacy means anything it is the right of the *individual*, married or single, to be free from unwarranted governmental intrusion into matters so fundamentally affecting a person as the decision whether to bear or beget a child."[27]

Decisional privacy has distinct implications for women's ability to secure important forms of privacy. The free choice implied by decisional privacy can be exploited to promote privacy interests. Whether or not the right to free choice—the right to be free from unwarranted governmental intrusion into the decision whether to bear a child—is aptly construed as a right to privacy, it is a right whose recognition and protection have profound implications for women's ability to achieve privacy. Seclusion, solitude, anonymity, and information non-disclosure are forms of privacy implicated by free choice and the right to free choice. Thus we must strenuously reject the conclusion of George Sher that "despite what the Supreme Court has said about [the right to privacy], its connection with abortion seems too tenuous and indirect to be credible."[28]

Liberty versus Privacy

A number of legal scholars and philosophers have sought to drive a wedge between the privacy concept and reproductive rights.[29] They have sought to recast questions about whether abortion or contraception choices ought to be preempted by government as questions about liberty rather than about privacy. Their basic argument has a philosophical and a jurisprudential variant. The philosophical variant takes as its focus the requirements of conceptual clarity; the jurisprudential version relies on the requirements and constraints of constitutional adjudication in American law.

The philosophical variant contends that the government is limiting liberty when it takes away free choice respecting reproduction and with it women's control of their bodies and lives. Liberty, it is often observed, has a positive and a negative interpretation.[30] Negative liberty is non-interference; freedom from direct restraints, constraints, or coercion. Demonstrators in a rally protesting world hunger exercise negative liberty to the extent they are left alone by officials and members of the general public. And women possess an aspect of negative liberty to the extent that they are left alone by government and others in the procurement of abortion and contraception. Positive liberty, on the other hand, is freedom from indirect constraints. It is freedom from want, relative to basic needs whose satisfaction is presupposed by egalitarian conceptions of liberty. The argument that the liberty of women on welfare is impaired by the exclusion of abortion and contraception from the package of medical and health benefits made available by state and federal government relies upon the positive interpretation of liberty.[31] Lack of access to abortion and contraception means that the cycle of poverty will be perpetuated as the size and number of dependent families mount. It also means that poor women do not have the same opportunity for self-determination through family planning as do middle-class and affluent women, since their private choices are ineffective.[32] This is particularly troubling since children represent the greatest burden for poor women, who lack the economic bases of privacy in private life.

Liberty is conceptually distinct from privacy. This is the central message of the philosophical wedge-drivers. They are correct, I believe, on the basic point that privacy and liberty are distinct concepts. The concepts are distinct in the sense that certain conditions to which the expression "privacy" and its synonyms apply could not be aptly described by the term "liberty" or its synonyms and vice versa. As detailed in Chapter 1, "privacy" and expressions referring to paradigmatic forms of privacy, such as "seclusion", "solitude", "anonymity," and "confidentiality," are best defined in terms of inaccessibility to others. I do not offer a full-fledged philosophical definitional analysis of "liberty" here. Yet liberty, whether positive or negative, is invariably defined in terms of the absence of restraint, constraint, or coercion. While conditions of inaccessibility (privacy) are often marked by the absence of restraint, constraint, or coercion (liberty), this is not always the case. Thus, assuming the plausibility of the definitional understandings indicated, one must conclude that liberty is conceptually distinct from privacy.

The concept of decisional privacy has closer conceptual affinities to liberty than to paradigmatic senses of privacy. So too does the conception of family privacy elaborated later in this chapter. Both are best construed as aspects of liberty, understood as the absence of coercive interference. To refer to aspects of liberty that relate to reproduction and parenting as privacy simply because they relate to private life is to blur some of the conceptual boundaries suggested by everyday discourse and by careful attempts at philosophical definition. The occurence of "privacy" in the phrases "decisional privacy" and "family privacy" reflects a usage of "privacy" that is probably derivative of the public/private distinction, rather than of the concept of privacy as restricted access. Under this usage "privacy" refers to a particular aspect of liberty—namely, freedom from governmental interference with what is properly left to nongovernmental control. By extension, we have come to use the expressions "decisional privacy" and "family privacy" even when the outside interference in the private sphere is not strictly governmental.

The jurisprudential version of the attempt to drive a wedge between privacy and reproductive concerns is motivated by criticism of the Supreme Court's "right to privacy" analyses of contraception and abortion rights. It characterizes the analysis under which government is said, metaphorically, to enter the zone of constitutionally protected privacy when it preempts abortion and contraception choices as inaccurate and confusing. It depicts the Court as second-guessing legislative balances and reading vague substantive due process rights into the Constitution.[33] It construes laws preempting the choices of citizens as coercive and, consequently, as involving a denial of liberty. The proper test for deciding the constitutionality of coercive state abortion and contraception laws, it declares, is whether such laws abridge the Fourteenth Amendment proscription against deprivation of liberty without due process. The question becomes one of whether abortion laws are rationally related to legitimate state interests, which have been held by the Court to include promoting family life, regulating health care, and collecting statistical data on reproduction. The federal courts go too far, the legal wedge-drivers argue, when they grasp for a penumbral or fundamental Due Process right of privacy and rely on it as a strict, substantive test of the constitutionality of prohibitive abortion laws.

I propose an obvious response to both the philosophical and jurisprudential versions of the argument that the concept of privacy does not belong in discussions of reproductive concerns. Laws preempting decisionmaking admittedly constrain choice. They compel sexually active fertile women to give birth to unwanted children. They involve a denial of women's liberty. But they also involve a denial of privacy, for women lose privacy when they undertake motherhood. Assuming the most plausible account of what privacy centrally denotes (that is, degrees of inaccessibility), there is good reason for concluding that free choice (decisional privacy) and the right to it cannot be equated with paradigmatic privacy and the right to it. But, since coercive laws preempting free choice also result in significant deprivations of paradigmatic forms of privacy, discussion of privacy and whether the state may constitutionally impose privacy sacrifices on women has a place in legal discussion of reproductive rights. Since a loss of privacy is invariably implicated in reproductive rights cases, a federal court would be justified in appealing both to the concept of privacy and to the concept of liberty in explaining the rationale for outcomes that favor free choice for women. (This is not to say the federal courts have always made good use of the privacy concept in handing down opinions in reproductive rights cases.) The unresolved jurisprudential questions are questions of interpretation and judicial review. Does the Constitution in fact protect the reproductive liberties known popularly as decisional privacy? Does it embody substantive safeguards against the deprivations of seclusion, solitude, anonymity, or information that result from legislative constraints on the free choice of pregnant women? Are such safeguards fundamental in the constitutional sense?

While much is made of these philosophical and jurisprudential controversies in the scholarly literature, they are not of central import for understanding what is stake for women. For these controversies concern not so much what is at stake, but how what is at stake is to be labeled. What is of central import is clear recognition that decisional privacy, whether or not properly labeled "privacy," is important and promotes the existence of conditions that properly bear the privacy label. Seclusion, in particular solitudinous and anonymous forms of seclusion, is the clearest form of privacy afforded by free choice to sexually active fertile women.

Bodily Integrity and Self-determination

Bodily integrity and self-determination are both sometimes equated with privacy. By "self-determination" I mean autonomous determination of the course of one's life, especially one's private or family life. Like free choice, bodily integrity and self-determination cannot be straightforwardly identified with privacy. In the context of contraception and abortion, bodily integrity is not privacy. It is a possible consequence of private reproductive choices with implications for privacy. Bodily integrity for a woman means, inter alia, that if she elects otherwise, her physical person will not undergo a pregnancy and its characteristic physical strains and mortal risks.

The idea of bodily integrity is sometimes articulated in terms of self-ownership, owning one's own body and doing with it as one pleases. But this is a misleading way to put it, since human beings surely do not own their bodies, but *are* their bodies. Our claims to exclusive access to our bodies can be based directly on our being persons in the moral sense whose bodies should not be reduced to involuntary instruments of service for others' needs.[34] Hence, the concept of self-ownership is as superfluous as it is misleading. Moreover, arguments based on bodily ownership have no particular logical clout in abortion arguments. Conservatives on the abortion issue are free to assert that fetal rights include a right of the fetus to bodily integrity of its own. Pro-lifers can assert that fetuses have rights of self-ownership, too, if that is what the liberal is claiming for women in virtue of their humanity. Even pro-choice liberals may want to say that a pregnant woman's putative right of bodily integrity or self-ownership is not absolute in the later stages of pregnancy, because the viable fetus also has rights of bodily integrity and self-ownership.

This was, I think, what the Court in *Roe v. Wade* was getting at when it expressly rejected the notion argued by *amici* that the constitutional privacy right implies "one has an unlimited right to do with one's body as one pleases."[35] In response, the Court argued that the state has a legitimate (paternalistic) interest in safeguarding health and medical standards affecting maternal well-being. Moreover, the Court argued that the state's interest in protecting viable fetal life is legitimate and provides a reason to interfere with bodily integrity by prohibiting later-term abortions: "it is reasonable and appropriate for a state to decide that at some point in time another interest, that of potential human life, becomes significantly involved."[36]

Self-determination respecting childbearing is a condition enabling women to protect their health directly, and their privacy indirectly. By the final stages of pregnancy some of the risks to health have passed. For some women abortion at any stage of pregnancy is less likely to end in mortality than is childbirth. But risks to the privacy of the pregnant woman are as strong on the day of delivery as at the moment of conception.

Both bodily integrity and self-determination are forms of access control; they are privacy control mechanisms. Free choice makes these privacy control mechanisms operative and makes it more possible for women to achieve desired levels of privacy. Free choice signals sexual equality, too. It is likely that many women with powers of self-determination will choose lives that make the most of their educational, artistic, and professional potentials.

My discussion of "free choice" has so far revolved around a single point of clarification, namely, that although neither decisional privacy, nor free choice, nor bodily integrity, nor self-determination can be straightforwardly equated with privacy, each represents privacy planning and privacy control. They represent the ability to manipulate the quality and quantity of paradigmatic forms of privacy in one's life. I now want to turn to a consideration of what decisional privacy or free choice–based arguments, over and above paradigmatic privacy-based arguments, add to the case for permissive birth prevention policies.

Liberal Democracy

The prevailing ideal of government in the United States is the liberal democracy. It is democratic in its commitment to consensual government of citizens who meaningfully participate in their own governance. It is liberal in virtue of its commitment to individualism and neutral protection of individual rights. Democratic liberalism so described is capable of multiple interpretations. "Conservative," "liberal," and "libertarian" are names commonly used to designate adherents of influential interpretations of American democratic liberalism.

Many self-described conservatives are "pro-life." They reject abortion as a personal choice, and they reject permissive abortion laws. In addition, some conservatives are "pro-choice" rather than "pro-life." The pro-choice conservatives who rely on decisional privacy arguments rely essentially on the libertarian argument. The libertarian holds dear the principle that, to the extent the prevention of injury and the protection of property allow, government ought to refrain from limiting individuals' liberty. Reproductive liberty being no special case, the government should grant individual women the freedom to choose what they do to avoid and terminate pregnancies. On the libertarian view, abortion should be legally permissible up to the point at which it makes sense to ascribe individual rights to the unborn.

The argument for permissive birth prevention policies based on the importance of paradigmatic privacy asserts that seclusion and other paradigmatic forms of privacy are something all women need and ought not be deprived of. In contrast, the libertarian/conservative decisional privacy argument asserts that women should be free as individuals to choose to possess privacy (because, for example, they want it or think it best) or to choose to give privacy up (because, for example, they enjoy the idea of having and raising children). For the libertarian/conservative the importance of negative liberty rather than the importance of privacy is more fundamental to understanding why governmental interference with free abortion choice is wrong.

The liberal proponent of American democratic liberalism holds dear the ideal of liberty, but treats principles of equality and government neutrality as limiting individual and collective liberty. Ronald Dworkin has argued that a conception of equality requiring that government treat citizens with "equal respect and concern" is constitutive of liberal thinking. He has maintained that this conception is what distinguishes liberal thought from conservatism, libertarianism, collectivism, and other less similar political moralities.[37] Dworkin rejected a second liberal version of liberalism that takes equality to be an important but derivative value. On the rejected version, the principle of neutrality that the government ought not favor particular conceptions of the good life by which citizens live is regarded as constitutive.[38] For the "neutral principle" liberal, equal respect and concern is merely a device by means of which government can assure its own neutrality. This rejected form of liberalism, Dworkin contended, is "vulnerable to the charge that liberalism is a negative theory for an uncommitted people"—a theory for the wishy-washy.[39] Dworkin rejected "neutral principle" liberalism because it offers no effective argument against utilitarianism and other contemporary justifications for economic inequality.[40] It undervalues equality by treating it as just another preference.

The form of liberalism Dworkin embraced is grounded on a constitutive principle of equality requiring "equal respect and concern." It regards a principle of neutrality as a derivative principle, adopted to promote equality. Critics have typically gone after the "neutral principle" liberal, holding that neutrality is impossible and self-contradictory. Critics argue that a liberal conception of the good life is embodied in liberal policies as much as a non-liberal's conception of the good life is embodied in policies preferred by the non-liberal, who makes no pretense of neutrality. By arguing that equality is the fundamental substantive liberal principle and neutrality a derivative rule of thumb, Dworkin aimed to escape the criticisms leveled at the wishy-washy liberal. Dworkin has argued that neutrality as a derivative position is not self-contradictory. Nor is it a pointless impossible ideal. Approximating neutrality as among citizens with competing interests and values is a way government can strive to treat citizens as equality requires, with equal respect and concern, even if strict neutrality is impossible.

Dworkin has described the roots of the conception of equality as "equal respect and concern" as Kantian.[41] In his essay "Why Liberals Should Care About Equality," Dworkin gave an account of the liberal principle of equality and the nature of the constraint it imposes on interference by government. That account was both deontological and contractarian: government "must impose no sacrifice or constraint on any citizen in virtue of an argument that the citizen could not accept without abandoning his sense of equal worth."[42] This principle limiting citizen "sacrifice or constraint" is contractarian in its requirement that government be morally constrained by what a citizen could *accept* or *agree to*. It is deontological in its implication that a rational self-respecting person, one whose dignity is intact, is an end in itself. According to Dworkin, adherence to this principle of equality limiting state action entails (a) a principle of social justice that precludes enforcement of private morality, and (b) a principle of economic justice that precludes citizens having less than their equitable share of the resources available to all.[43]

The former entailment is the one that concerns us here. It would follow from the liberal principle of equality as articulated by Dworkin that government is precluded from impermissive restriction of reproductive liberties if these are matters of "private morality." For some liberals it has gone without saying that abortion and contraception fall within the realm of private morality. If private morality consists of rules of conduct governing what our culture has traditionally treated as falling within the private sphere and zone of privacy, this assumption is a reasonable one. Contraception and abortion do fall within the traditional "zone of privacy." They relate to the body, sexuality, marriage, family, and the home. All of these are closely tied to a person's sense of identity and individuality. Based on this analysis of private morality, many liberals readily conclude that restrictive birth prevention policies must be rejected, because government may not reach into the zone of privacy for purposes of interfering with private morality. As long as a person is acting within that zone, he or she ought to be off-limits to government and other unwanted third parties.

Opponents of permissive birth prevention policies would insist that even though matters of contraception and abortion fall within the private sphere of sex and family life, they are not matters of private morality. Abortion is a matter of public morality and legitimate governmental intervention because of the harm it represents for fetuses, they argue. In response, liberals have made two moves. They have claimed that "harm" to fetal life is of no moral consequence (because fetuses are not persons, or have no right to life, or have no rights that are not overcome by women's rights). They have also claimed that the lack of moral and philosophical certainty about the moral status of the fetus means government is not justified in constraining abortion choice. Roger Wertheimer's liberal pro-choice argument fits into this second mold.[44] He maintained that the moral status of the fetus has so far proven to be an irresoluble metaphysical question. Since the ideal of political freedom places the burden on government rationally to justify its coercive powers, as long as the state cannot establish that a fetus is a person or human being that counts, it must refrain from enacting a coercive law. For Wertheimer, metaphysical indeterminacy is what keeps abortion within the confines of private morality. But Wertheimer's argument is too timid. The point is not that the status of the fetus is an unresolved metaphysical question and government must keep its hands off until the philosophical truth be known. The point is that the truth pertains to a choice that is of a type individuals ought to decide for themselves even though fetal life may be extinguished as a consequence. Government must leave us alone in the making of the basic reproductive choice if it is to respect each of us as a person and an individual.

Even if reproductive liberties do not fall within private morality in the above sense, Dworkin's Kantian/contractarian account of governmental constraint provides a reason to accord women free choice. Imposing motherhood on women by denying them the right to decide whether to bear and rear children imposes a heavy burden of sacrifices and constraints in virtue of an argument a woman cannot accept without abandoning her sense of equal worth. Without abandoning their sense of equal worth, women cannot accept the pro-lifers' argument that the existence of an anonymous embryo or fetus is of greater value than full personhood, participation, and contribution by women.

While decisional privacy arguments are the preferred arguments for libertarians and liberals, paradigmatic privacy arguments are highly congenial to these interpretations of liberal democracy. Women may or may not make privacy-promoting reproductive choices where government is permissive. But if they do, they partake more fully of the bounties of individual liberty and public participation. Liberals and libertarians have a reason to encourage women to make paradigmatic privacy-enhancing choices and a reason to demand that government permit free choice by affording decisional privacy.

Indirect Constraints

It should go without saying that if in a liberal democracy privacy interests counsel against direct, blanket governmental constraints on birth prevention measures, such interests counsel as well against indirect, piecemeal constraints. Just as blanket prohibitions on abortion and contraception have implications for women's privacy, so too do regulatory schemes that impair freedom of choice. State regulations that make it unduly onerous for a woman to obtain an abortion and contraception impair decisional privacy and thereby affect her ultimate ability to obtain and exploit solitude and anonymity.

In the aftermath of *Roe v. Wade,* the legislatures of several states enacted laws to deter abortion through complex regulatory schemes. The effect, if not the intent, of abortion control legislation was to discourage abortion by making the decision to terminate pregnancy more burdensome, more expensive, and more time-consuming than it would otherwise be. Hence, while first trimester abortions were nominally available virtually on demand, the freedom to obtain an abortion was seriously hampered. The Supreme Court invalidated some forms of indirect constraint in *City of Akron v. Akron Center for Reproductive Health.*[45] Pennsylvania's egregious assault on abortion choice was cut back by the Supreme Court in the *Thornburgh* case which, as stated earlier, declared provisions of the Pennsylvania Abortion Control Act unconstitutional.[46] Since *Roe v. Wade,* states have sought to control abortion through

1. restrictions on the advertisement of abortion services;
2. zoning restrictions on abortion facilities;
3. record-keeping and reporting requirements;
4. spousal and parental notification or consent requirements;
5. the requirement of pre-abortion "informed consent" counseling by a physician;
6. the requirement of mandatory pre-abortion waiting periods;
7. the requirement of the presence of a second physician during the abortion procedure;
8. the requirement that a method calculated to spare fetal life be employed in post-viability abortions, if possible without substantial risk to the mother;
9. the requirement that all tissue removed during an abortion be sent to a laboratory for analysis by a certified pathologist;
10. a requirement that insurance companies offer at a lower cost a

health insurance policy without coverage for elective abortion, other than for elective abortion precipitated by incest or rape;

11. legislating a state-wide information campaign to communicate an official state policy against abortion;

12. legislating criminal sanctions against physicians knowingly aborting viable fetuses; and

13. a requirement that all non-emergency abortions after the first trimester of pregnancy be performed in a hospital.

Aspects of devices (3), (5), (6), (7), (8), and (12) were found unconstitutional in *Akron* and *Thornburgh*.

One requirement held unconstitutional by the Third Circuit Court of Appeals in *Thornburgh,* but not at issue before the Supreme Court in the same case, provided that insurance companies make available insurance policies that exclude coverage of elective abortions other than in cases of rape or incest. The state conceded that "insurance costs for women who wish abortion may rise," and for this reason the court found that the double-policy requirement constrains free choice. It creates a plain monetary incentive for women of child-bearing years to place themselves in a position in which they could not afford to obtain an abortion. Any difference in the cost of premiums would be of greatest consequence to women of limited means. The women likely to opt out of abortion coverage would include older and infertile women, but also poorer women, whose pregnancies represent the greatest economic hardship. Choice is constrained in other key respects. Women on the fence about whether they would ever choose to have an abortion might be drawn to opt against abortion coverage to take advantage of a lower premium. Later faced with an unwanted pregnancy, they would be unable to choose abortion because they could not afford to pay for it out of their own pockets. As purchasers of medical insurance for employee benefit packages, employers would presumably have a choice of policy and would be likely to opt for the less expensive one, thereby making up female employees' minds for them about whether to seek an abortion.

But while the constitutionally problematic insurance rule constrains choice, it serves ends with initial appeal. In the absence of the two policy system, women who would never have an abortion are compelled to subsidize others' abortions by payment of a higher premium. This cost-spreading is arguably per se unfair. The burden of paying for abortion is not placed exclusively on those most likely to have them. Nevertheless, the abortion control-oriented insurance rule unfairly singles out abortion. There are innumerable other medical procedures whose costs are likewise spread among those who would or could never undergo such procedures. Abortion is singled out in furtherance of a state policy to discourage abortion by making it economically less accessible. Is there a difference between abortion and other medical treatments that makes a difference? Many women regard abortion as murder and a sin. Compelling insurance firms to offer a policy that does not cover abortion spares women whose moral convictions oppose abortion from having to subsidize the abortions of others. Seen in this light, the two-policy requirement looks like an attempt to achieve liberal neutrality. It creates a system in which women can be more faithful to their own conceptions of what is right and wrong. But even if the intent were neutral, and in Pennsylvania it was not, the outcome is not neutral, since the effect is to discourage purchase of policies that keep abortion a live option.

The decisional privacy argument against state information campaigns designed to discourage abortion is not an obvious one. The basic thrust of the argument is that dissemination of information stressing abortions' risks and alternatives would influence women to opt against abortion. Influencing through dissemination of ideas and information is the "American way," highly consistent with ideals defended by democratic theorists. What, then, is troubling about abortion information dissemination by government or by health-care providers at the insistence of government? Official government disapproval of abortion, a medical procedure which has been held to be within women's constitutional rights, may lead women to abandon their considered judgments about what is best for them. As the "swine flu" vaccination fiasco attested, men and women rely even to their detriment on poorly researched governmental pronouncements about what is in their best interests. Even when dead wrong, government recommendations in the health area have an air of special legitimacy.

One can think of areas in which it would be highly desirable to have governmental information campaigns. Campaigns against alcohol and smoking excesses, for example. But, notice the difference between these and abortion. If a woman takes governmental advice against smoking and drinking, the worst outcome is that she will have become a teetotaling non-smoker. If a biased litany of risks and alternatives is presented by government and on that basis pregnant women opt against abortion, the consequences for the quality and character of their lives are serious and unlimited.

Given the infrequency of second- and third-trimester abortions,[47] actual ethical conflicts involving the fate of viable fetuses are rare. Nonetheless, the most difficult abortion control laws to assess are those that aim at protecting *viable* fetal life, even against the wishes of pregnant women.[48] These statutory provisions shift the focus from women's decisional privacy to fetal survival. The Pennsylvania statute challenged in *Thornburgh* required that physicians employ the method of aborting viable fetuses that results in greater likelihood the fetus will be aborted alive unless, in the physician's good-faith judgment, that technique "would present a significantly greater medical risk to the life or health of the pregnant woman."[49] One objection to this requirement denies that there is a procedure that would not add risk to the woman that would decrease risk to a viable fetus. This is more or less the ground on the basis of which the Supreme Court invalidated the Pennsylvania provision.

Suppose there were a method to save fetuses without additional risk. If a child "born" as a result of this method were to be deemed the responsibility of its mother, as it presumably would be in the absence of a statute to the contrary, her purposes for seeking abortion would have been thwarted. Is part of the abortion right a right not to give birth to a living child? A right not only not to bear a child, but not to have a child conceived of one's body alive in the world? The privacy arguments relating to seclusion, solitude, and anonymity are not obviously arguments that justify killing a fetus or letting a fetus die, if the state will assume complete care of the child. While it may cause the noncustodial mother a loss of solace and unhappiness to know a child she begat has survived an abortion, its survival does not diminish paradigmatic forms of her privacy. Fetal survival does, arguably, render her decisional privacy ineffective.

Decisional privacy arguments can be used to defend the idea that women are entitled to have abortions that are fatal for the fetus. Steven Ross has argued that women's desire for fatal abortion can be an understandable concomitant of a conception of parenting that obliges us to bear and rear children, if at all, in a responsible, personal, attentive, loving way.[50] A woman who cannot do that might prefer that there be no child of hers in existence at all. A fetal death wish can be nobly motivated.

State laws prohibiting abortion techniques calculated to destroy fetal life create special dilemmas for women. So too do state laws that automatically deny a woman custody of a child "born" in the course of an abortion. Consider this statute enacted in Missouri:

> In every case where a live born infant results from an attempted abortion which was not performed to save the life or health of the mother, such infant shall be an abandoned ward of the state under the jurisdiction of the juvenile court wherein the abortion occurred, and the mother and father, if he consented to the abortion, of such infant shall have no parental rights or obligations whatsoever relating to such infant, as if the parental rights had been terminated.[51]

The guiding idea behind this statute is that once a woman seeks abortion, expressing thereby a fetal death wish, custody of a child surviving abortion passes from her. It goes to the state or the natural father if he did not share in the death wish by consenting to the abortion. This statute creates an ethical dilemma for women that negatively affects their freedom of choice. Fewer women will choose to abort if they know that the fetus might survive and that if it did, it would either be given up for adoption or left to the state. Thus, "There is clearly an inverse relationship between advancements in fetal sciences and the degree to which the right of privacy [i.e., decisional privacy] as it pertains to abortion may be exercised."[52]

Were techniques developed whereby even the youngest pre-embryos could be brought to term outside the women who conceived them, women might come to view pregnancy as a trap. In many instances a woman would wish not to be pregnant, but would be unwilling to have her pre-embryo, embryo or fetus "rescued" and be permitted to develop into a child who would be an unwanted ward of the state, or given away to unknown adoptive parents. In the words of Janet Benschof: "The increasing tendency to view the fetus as an independent patient or person occurs at the cost of reducing the woman to the status of little more than a maternal environment."[53]

INFORMATION NON-DISCLOSURE

Lack of informational privacy can eviscerate decisional privacy altogether. Secrecy and confidentiality about procurement of birth control information, contraception or abortion effectuate free choice in an number of respects, in a variety of circumstances.

It has been proposed that married women should be required to disclose abortion plans to their husbands, or, more strongly, obtain their consent. This is because husbands are presumed to be prospective fathers when their wives are pregnant. Laws requiring spousal notification or consent would compel disclosure of what could otherwise have been a secret a woman kept to herself, or shared in confidence with her health care provider or others. The Supreme Court has found spousal consent requirements unconstitutional.[54] It seems that since decisional privacy is a personal right, spousal notification requirements should be deemed, like spousal consent requirements, unconstitutional constraints on free choice. There are many legitimate reasons a woman might desire not to notify her spouse of a pregnancy and of her plans to terminate it. She might desire to choose not to communicate plans to abort:

> 1) where the husband is not the father of the fetus; for instance, where the fetus is the product of an extramarital affair; 2) where the wife has been a rape victim, has not disclosed the incident to her husband, and has subsequently become pregnant; 3) where the husband, because of

strong religious beliefs or moral precepts, would strenuously object; 4) where the husband is seriously ill or emotionally unstable and is unable to participate in the abortion decision; and 5) where the woman is a "battered wife" and fears that discussion concerning an abortion may precipitate physical violence.[55]

Spousal notification and consent requirements can discourage abortion by women who fear the consequences of information disclosure. So too can requirements that abortion facilities keep records and file reports subject to public disclosure. In the *Thornburgh* case the special relationship between record-keeping and reporting requirements and "free choice" was recognized by the Court. Fear of disclosure and harassment may work to discourage women from having abortions. While medical records are generally subject to disclosure to researchers, government statisticians, and insurance companies, it is important that information collection and disclosure practices mandated in the abortion context be designed to reflect the social reality that abortion patients need anonymity, secrecy, and confidentiality. Without them, free choice is seriously constrained.

The relationship between a woman and the facility from which she obtains an abortion is in some respects a consensual transaction between players in an economic setting.[56] Indeed, it may be inappropriate to characterize it as a "private relationship." It is not a "private relationship" in the sense in which, for example, marriage is. But this is not dispositive of the need to recognize rights of confidentiality in the abortion setting.

Minors have a constitutional right protecting access to contraceptives and contraception information.[57] Moreover, every minor has a constitutional right to go directly to court, without parental notification, to attempt to establish that she is a mature minor who must be permitted to obtain an abortion without parental consent.[58] Many argue that the state ought to protect family privacy values and teen welfare by requiring parental approval or notification of sex counseling, prescription of contraceptives, and abortion. Indeed, recent federal regulations sought to require parental notification when unemancipated teens are dispensed prescription birth control in federally funded clinics.[59]

There is a certain cogency to the argument that younger teens have a right to paternalistic protection, and that that protection is best got from their families:

Clinics provide abortions to girls not yet teenagers. A pregnant minor is likely to be confused and frightened. Unfortunately, absent parental consultation following parental notice, the pregnant minor is not likely to encounter concerned advice. Abortion clinics are unlikely to encourage the minor's decision to abort or in other ways act contrary to their financial interest . . . Parental notice statutes would lessen the impersonal nature of this system. . . . Notifying the minor's parents would [give] the physician access to information concerning the minor's capacity to decide, best interest, and medical history.[60]

If teens are permitted by law on decisional privacy grounds to obtain contraception and abortion without the knowledge or consent their parents, parents may feel the state is interfering with family privacy. In this context, family privacy signifies the freedom of parents to exercise their authority and judgment in accordance with their own values to promote the interests and well-being of themselves and their children. This is no trivial matter, since birth control devices such as the intrauterine device (IUD) have proven to involve risks to health and fertility that a teenager, even in consultation with a physician, cannot be expected always to assess fully.

The ability of parents to be genuinely helpful to teenagers desiring information and advice is open to question. Parental consent and notification requirements can discriminate against and burden mature minors:

> Abortions are sought by minor women because of the weighty and often adverse consequences of having a child. These range from interruption of the woman's education to early and unstable marriages. Economic effects of childbirth can be particularly severe when a minor drops out of high school and attempts to support herself and a child. Health consequences for minor women can also be harsh. Maternal mortality and non-fatal complications from premature births are higher with women under twenty than with adult women. Access to an abortion is therefore a vital option for pregnant minor women faced with such consequences. Access to an abortion free from parental interference can be just as vital. For some minor women parental notification will prevent them from obtaining an abortion . . . One study on the probable impact of parental notification estimates that 19,000 minor women would resort to self-induced or illegal abortions and that 18,000 more minor women would bear unwanted children, were parental notification required. In addition, another 5,000 minors would run away from home either to have the unwanted child or to obtain an illegal abortion. [The] infant death rate is higher for children born to women under twenty, and minor women are far more likely to have premature or low-birth weight babies.[61]

Paradigmatic privacy arguments are not irrelevant to the case for unconstrained birth control choice for teens. Young women have many of the same underlying interests in solitude, seclusion and anonymity that mature women have. There is more controversy, however, over whether they are entitled to use occasions of private seclusion as opportunities for sexual intercourse. If we start with the realistic assumption that even very young girls will have sex and become pregnant in the absence of accessible contraception and sex education, the decisional privacy arguments against state-imposed obstacles are clear. Abortion must be realistically accessible, too. Since teens are sometimes slower to discover and act on their pregnancies, access to abortion in the second and third trimesters has special importance. To be saddled with a child at a young age is to be saddled with responsibilities that limit opportunities for education and privacy called for by personhood, participation, and contribution in the adult world.

DECISIONAL PRIVACY REVISITED

Giving Birth

Free to choose, some women would prefer giving birth in an intimate setting to giving birth in an institution in which strangers take charge and to which strangers have wide access.[62] At least one percent of all births occurring in the United States occur at home. Being free to choose conditions of birth without governmental or other third-party interference can be styled as yet another aspect of decisional privacy. Although state and federal courts have not faced the issue squarely, home birth and midwifery raise "two basic constitutional claims—that home birth is encompassed within the . . . right of privacy, and that the right of privacy includes one's choice of an unlicensed birth attendant."[63] Here, too, the privacy implications of constraints on reproductive free choice are clear, even if the appropriateness of the "privacy" label is not. As in the abortion context, the possibility of a legitimate state interest in protecting the health of pregnant women and their offspring presents itself. Some studies indicate that home birth is between two and five times as likely to result in newborn mortality than hospital birth. Home birth advocates argue that planned, midwife-assisted home birth is not significantly more risky than hospital birth.

Women typically have been more directly concerned with achieving intimacy and privacy in hospital births through the elimination of superfluous supervision and technology than with doing away with physician and government interference. The private birthing issue has not been prominent in philosophical and legal discussions of reproductive liberties. It nevertheless merits brief mention here to clarify the senses in which privacy is at stake in the choice of childbirth settings.

One of the earliest reported American cases in which the plaintiff expressly alleged an invasion of privacy involved privacy of birth.

DeMay v. Roberts, an 1881 Michigan case, was brought by a Mrs. Roberts against a Dr. DeMay and a Mr. Scattergood. Dr. DeMay took Mr. Scattergood to the Roberts's tiny home when he went to deliver a child on what the court described as a "dark and stormy" night.[64] At the time, Roberts and her husband assumed Scattergood was a trained medical assistant. In fact he was an "unprofessional young unmarried man," brought along to carry Dr. DeMay's lantern. Scattergood remained at Roberts's house for the many hours of Mrs. Roberts's protracted labor and delivery. At one point during the night he helped Dr. DeMay and the attending midwife by taking Mrs. Roberts's hand to restrain her from "rocking herself and throwing her arms."

Mrs. Roberts won her lawsuit alleging deceit, assault, and invasion of privacy. In his opinion the judge declared:

> To the plaintiff the occasion was a most sacred one and no one had a right to intrude unless invited because of some real and pressing necessity which it is not pretended existed in this case. The plaintiff had a legal right to the privacy of her apartment at such a time, and the law secures to her this right by requiring others to observe it, and to abstain from its violation.[65]

In addition to the conception of childbirth as a "sacred" occasion, the DeMay case reflects its era's norms about women's privacy in general. These norms are apparent in another case of the same period unrelated to childbirth but also involving medical procedures. In *Gulf v. Butcher,* a case brought before the Supreme Court of Texas in 1892, the argument was noted that a court order compelling a woman who claimed to have been injured in a rail accident to be examined by a physician was "an intrusion upon her privacy and modesty and should never have been permitted or been availed of."[66] The *DeMay* court's choice of terms to describe Scattergood—"unprofessional young unmarried man"—says a great deal about the requirements of female modesty in the nineteenth century.

Contemporary arguments for the right to private childbirth rest on the ideals of freedom and control over privacy and intimacy rather than on the need for modesty or respect for the sacred character of birth. The familiar principle implicit in commonly heard arguments is that individuals should be free to achieve desired self-regarding and family ends. Free choice is constrained only by the obligation that one commit no harms or cognizable offenses against others. Applied to childbirth, this principle seems to entail that if a woman wants a private birth for any reason—including but not limited to modesty or a sense that childbirth is sacred—then the power should lie with her, prima facie, to have precisely that. Maternal health, public health, and the well-being of the newborn justify some unwanted third-party regulatory interference with the choice of procedures and setting of childbirth. But women's freedom mandates that any such interference be strictly limited to what is demonstrably necessary for health and safety.

Consider the account one woman gave of her reasons for desiring to give birth at home rather than in a hospital:

> What were the other reasons? It had something very basic to do with control, power, and authority. At home, I would have them, in the hospital they would be handed over to the institution. I heard arguments for home rather than hospital birth that spoke about privacy. For me it was less a question of privacy and more a question of authority. At home nobody was coming in the door whom I did not choose to come in.[67]

Physical privacy was *one* of this woman's concerns. Being inaccessible to unwanted others was one of her reasons for preferring home birth. In her own mind, however, physical privacy was not the deepest reason to reject hospital delivery. She was concerned about physical privacy but also the *de jure* authority and power to have her choice of privacy respected. To put it differently, she wanted privacy in two senses: both seclusion from unwanted others *and* decisional privacy, the right to freely decide birth conditions without unwarranted interference.

Heading Families

With the birth of a child a multitude of parental obligations begin. Notable among them are obligations of maintenance, education, and health care. Freedom to decide for oneself how such obligations will be discharged is a key aspect of what is sometimes referred to as "family privacy." This conception of family privacy was referred to earlier in connection with the costs and benefits of a requirement that teens obtain consent or be required to notify parents prior to receiving birth control aids. Another conception of family privacy is enjoyment of a secluded home life with spouse, children, or kin. This is the aggregate family privacy feminist Charlotte Perkins Gilman condemned as antithetical to individual forms of personal privacy. I want to focus on the former conception of family privacy: decisional family privacy.

The claim of moral entitlement to be free from third-party, and especially governmental, interference in the discharge of familial obligations is commonly advanced as a claim of a right to family privacy. A moral right of family privacy is deemed to be a right of family members to be free from uninvited, unwarranted interference with the rearing, education, discipline, health, and custody decisions, made by family members (usually adults) on behalf of members of the same family (usually infants, children, teenagers, the elderly, or the infirm). Increasingly, women are becoming family heads as a consequence of conscious design, divorce, separation, and desertion. Female heads of household increased 84 percent between 1970 and 1986. Since women are more and more likely to be heads of households, concern for the right to family privacy in many cases boils down to concern for women's right to decisional privacy.

The decisional brand of family privacy is appealing, but it is also troubling. It is appealing because the idea of the family itself has substantial appeal. Like individual privacy, family privacy can function to promote the development of meaningful, intimate familial relationships. In general, it can allow individual family members the opportunity to make autonomous choices regarding how their personal lives will be ordered, and assure opportunities for unfettered, unobserved enjoyment of those lives. It can function to provide a context in which young persons develop responsibility and judgment requisite for meaningful social participation. Parental autonomy afforded by family privacy gives parents their due liberty and at the same time benefits children by maximizing their chances for normal development.[68] As argued by Goldstein, Freud, and Solnit in *Before the Best Interests of the Child,* to ensure timely development of children's capacities for physical closeness, emotional attachment, identification, and self-reliance, the state must recognize a trio of interlocking family integrity rights: a right to family privacy; a parental right to be presumed to have the "capacity, authority, and responsibility to do what is 'good' for one's children and what is 'best' for the entire family"; and a right of children to autonomous parents.

It has been widely argued that the state has a considerable interest in protecting the family. Alan F. Westin argued in *Privacy and Freedom* that family autonomy to permit preferred modes of education, religion, and home life is a basic commitment of liberal democratic societies.[69] It is one of the respects in which liberal democracy acknowledges the interests persons have in a life apart from the state. The axiom of American life that families achieve ends in virtue of which the government has an interest in protecting families has a corollary. Neither the state nor its agents, nor any other institution adequately achieves the same ends. Thus, although the interest the state is presumed to have in protecting the family might be thought to justify broad regulatory intervention, there is widespread contrary belief that the state's own ends are best served by a "hands-off" family policy.[70]

Yet, the notion of family privacy is a problematic, potentially dangerous one. It is problematic whether it practically vests in men alone, women alone, or is shared among family members. If a moral right of family privacy is ascribed a family unit, who is entitled to exercise that right? Who is the spokesperson for the family's interest? What if family members disagree about the desirability of governmental intervention? Of private third-party involvement? Family privacy is a troubling concept because

1. in traditional families, family privacy can amount to male domination of the women and children;
2. in child abuse or neglect cases and in child custody contexts where parents are at odds, family privacy policies can may stand in the way of efficient, essential state intervention on behalf of a child;
3. for teenagers mature enough to make up their own minds about, for example, religion, education, contraception, and abortion, family privacy can amount to parental tyranny;
4. family privacy can be a tool of discrimination when judicially interpreted so as to protect only the interests of traditional families to the exclusion, for example, of families headed by homosexual and unmarried persons; and
5. emphasis on family privacy, if at the expense of individual decisional privacy, "obfuscates privacy's deeper meaning."[71]

All of these concerns arise out of concern for the implications of family privacy for individual rights and freedoms.

Family violence is one of the contexts in which the risks attendant to application of the family privacy concept become apparent.[72] Family privacy cloaks even physical brutality in a protective mantle. Interfamilial violence has been treated as a "personal" and "private" affair, with the result, critics claim, that the law enforcement response to battered women's pleas for help has been to discount them. The "hands-off" notion of family privacy has played a role in denying spouses the rights enjoyed by other crime victims.

The risks attendant to application of the concept of family privacy come into sharper focus in cases involving the allocation of authority between teenagers and their parents. The right to family privacy can be interpreted as giving parents the authority to make choices as to their teen-aged children's education. But mature teenagers living at home are arguably justified in the desire to enlist state protection for some of their own preferences regarding their education. For example, they should be able to exercise the choice of a public over a private parochial school.

Teen-age sex and pregnancy raise problems for both the conceptualization and application of the right to family privacy. Teen-age pregnancy and parenthood is a national crisis. According to a recently completed two-year study of the National Research Council, a congressionally chartered research arm of the National Academy of Sciences, a 15-year-old American girl is at least five times more likely to give birth than girls her own age in other countries. Teen mothers and their babies are at high risk for medical complications; teen parents have severely limited career opportunities and are more likely to become dependent upon public assistance. In 1985 the economic burden for maintaining teen families was an estimated $16.6 billion in outlays for Aid to Dependent Children, Medicaid, and Food Stamps. Everyone agrees teen pregnancy is a problem. Opinions will vary about how much parental involvement is warranted in the resolution of an unemancipated minor's pregnancy. The age of the teenager, the circumstances of conception, disagreement among grandparents-to-be, economic resources, and drug problems can affect our views as to the best resolution of particular teenage pregnancies. But it is clear that the idea of the right to family privacy cannot have a central role in shaping policy in this area. Where society's prescriptive norms respecting the timing of procreation have been violated, the individuation of families for purposes of ascribing family privacy rights is complicated by the processes by which families are naturally perpetuated. The pregnant teen may believe that she and her unborn child, or she, the child, and its father are a family apart. The grandparents-to-be may believe their minor children are inside the proper sphere of their family authority, despite sexual activity and pregnancy. The problem with family privacy in the teen pregnancy context is that as youth approach adulthood and, biologically speaking, begin families of their own, the justification of parental authority becomes progressively less clear.

Tragic Choices

The problem with applying the concept of decisional family privacy in the context of non-treatment of newborns with severe birth defects is quite different. In this context the family privacy concept shields parents in the exercise of powers of life and death. It allows parents to make decisions regarding medical treatment, surgery, and feeding that effectively hasten their childrens' deaths. This is not to suggest that parents are heartless when it comes to newborns. Quite the opposite is suggested by the fact that aggressive infant life-saving treatment has rapidly become one of the most dramatic examples of high-technology medicine, with annual expenditures of $2 billion.[73] Still, the question remains whether the family privacy concept has too broad a sweep.

In 1982, in the first highly publicized "Baby Doe" case, an Indiana infant with Down's syndrome and a blocked esophagus died of starvation when its parents declined to authorize corrective surgery or extra-oral feeding.[74] A "Baby Jane Doe" born in 1983 at St. Charles Hospital in Port Jefferson, New York, with spina bifida, microcephaly hydrocephalus, and other serious abnormalities faced possible death following parental refusal to consent to surgical procedures some believed would be necessary to prolong the infant's life.[75] Congenital abnormalities are present in approximately 4 percent of all children born annually in the United States. Severe birth defects raise acutely the question whether medical treatments needed to sustain life should be ordered over parental refusal. The legal rights of parents who decide to let their defective neonates go untreated and perhaps die is unsettled. The New York Court of Appeals, however, has indicated a willingness to view such decisions as a privilege implied by family privacy.

Indiana child neglect laws were utilized unsuccessfully in an attempt to judicially override Baby Doe's parents' decision. (Baby Doe died before an emergency appeal could be brought before the U.S. Supreme Court.) Like similar statutes in other states, Indiana's child abuse and neglect laws authorized state investigation and intervention on behalf of children who are or will soon be at risk of serious injury. Intervention on behalf of a neglected child can result in medical treatments or surgery being ordered over parental objections. It can also result in a loss of parental custody of a neglected child.

Baby Doe was born in 1982, too soon for its parents to have to concern themselves with the reach of the federal Child Abuse Amendments of 1984. The Amendments were enacted in the wake of the highly publicized Baby Doe and Baby Jane Doe cases. Under the Amendments, in order to qualify for federal child abuse and neglect prevention funds the states are required to implement infant nontreatment programs and procedures. States must assure that infants faced with nontreatment have access to protective services; that hospitals have personnel charged with handling and reporting instances of nontreatment; and that state protective services be permitted to pursue legal remedies to prevent the withholding of "medically indicated treatment from disabled infants with life-threatening conditions."[76] The nontreatment decision of Baby Doe's parents may have escaped challenge by operation of the exceptions to the Child Abuse Amendments. Food, water, or medication may be withheld when an infant is irreversibly comatose; when doing so would merely prolong dying; when the treatment would not improve or cure the infant's life-threatening condition; or when virtual futility makes treatment inhumane under the circumstances. Treatment of Baby Doe might well have been deemed virtually futile and inhumane under the circumstances. Indeed, it has been suggested that "the new federal statute is not likely to be very effective in ensuring lifesaving treatment is provided to newborns [since] several of its key terms are open to interpretations that could limit protection severely."[77] Moreover it appears that the federal law does not require that states report nontreatment decisions or follow federal guidelines in deciding whether to order treatment. The present ambiguous state of affairs is likely to please neither infant advocates nor parental rights advocates.

Federal law prohibiting discrimination against the handicapped was unsuccessfully utilized as a basis for intervention in the Baby Jane Doe case. In March 1983, responding to a Presidential directive prompted by the Indiana Baby Doe case, the Department of Health and Human Services (DHHS) promulgated new rules pursuant to Section 504 of the Rehabilitation Act of 1973. The new rules prohibited federally assisted hospitals from discriminatorily withholding food or life-saving treatments from infants handicapped by birth defects. University Hospital, where Baby Jane Doe was transferred shortly after birth, refused the DHHS's repeated requests for copies of the infant's medical records. The DHHS argued it was entitled to investigate whether Baby Jane Doe was being discriminated against on the basis of handicaps in violation of federal law. In an action brought by the DHHS, the Federal District Court and the Second Circuit Court of Appeals concluded that there was no discrimination within the meaning on Section 504.[78] In a related case, *Bowen v. American Hospital Ass'n* (1986), the Supreme Court reached the same conclusion; since the hospital's non-treatment was based on a bona fide, reasonable medical decision and since parental consent was applied non-discriminatorily as a prerequisite of surgery, there was no basis for federal government interference in the case. The informational privacy and family decisional privacy interests of Baby Jane Doe and her parents played no overt determinative role in the outcome of the federal case.[79]

On another front, the New York Court of Appeals, New York's highest state court, sustained the reversal of an order sought on behalf of Baby Jane Doe by Vermont lawyer Lawrence Washburn through a guardian *ad litem*. The order would have required University Hospital to perform corrective spinal surgery. Stressing that strangers to the "family circle" were challenging "the most private and most precious responsibility vested in the parents for the care and nurture of their children,"[80] the state court held that the petitioner had failed to follow established agency procedures for investigation of alleged child abuse prior to bringing suit.

Like abortion decisions, parental decisions in neonate non-treatment cases are life-and-death decisions. Their outcomes determine whether new life will be given further opportunity for growth and development. In practice some parents opt for non-treatment solely to spare the newborn a painful, futile, or grotesque existence. It should not be difficult to sympathize with any desire parents may have to spare themselves the emotional and financial hardship of rearing a severely diseased, handicapped, or mentally retarded child. In neonatal care cases there will sometimes be a unity of interest between parent and offspring. The quality of life for both parent and child would be tragically low were measures authorized that would prolong a newborn's life.

Where it exists, moral ambivalence about the exercise of the family privacy decision-making privilege may stem from the feeling that, fundamentally, it is parental self-interest or economic expediency rather than love or humanity that dictates the decision to accelerate death in Baby Doe cases. Here, as in the abortion context, it may be tempting to some to view the central question as whether pursuing self-interest and economic savings at the expense of off-spring ought to be sanctioned. Putting the question in these terms loads the dice against parents, and especially against women as the primary direct caretakers of children.

The lives of some "defective" neonates are terrible and brief. With surgery some live on. What does responsibly mothering severely handicapped children mean for women's progress toward greater personhood, social participation, and contributions beyond the family? The arguments for decisional privacy appealed to in defense of contraception and abortion apply with even greater force here, in relation to family decisionmaking. The sacrifice of independence and individual privacy represented by caring for a normal child increases severalfold when the child demands the additional attention that, for example, a child with Down's Syndrome will demand. (Children with Down's Syndrome can be severely retarded. As infants they commonly have heart disease and intestinal obstructions that require corrective surgery.)

While the privacy sacrifices of mothering mentally and physically handicapped children are greater, it is arguable that the privacy arguments for parental authority to order non-treatment must inevitably be weaker. For parents claim a right of infanticide. Parents claim a right not only to prevent pregnancy or abort, but also to allow another fully born human being to die.

In favor of the parents' right to decide, it is sometimes argued that it is in a newborn's best interest that its parents, rather than less concerned doctors, hospitals, or state authorities, decide its fate. There is doubtless truth to this argument, but I offer another alongside it. As a matter of self-determination, in view of the weighty consequences uniquely for them, it is fitting that parents in our society claim and be permitted to exercise the right to elect non-treatment of newborn children. If, like the goddess Athena in the Greek myth, all human young sprang fully grown from their fathers' heads, robust and armed to fight life's battles on their own, these powerful parental rights to make tragic self-protective choices could be avoided.

CONCLUSION

Typical discussions of privacy in connection with contraception and abortion suffer a common flaw. They focus exclusively on questions of decisional privacy. Decisional privacy is an aspect of liberty: freedom to choose without unjustified coercion or restraint. Decisional privacy is centrally at stake in the choice among competing contraception and abortion policies. Other reproductive rights concerns also implicate decisional privacy. For example, decisional privacy is importantly at stake where the issue is the permissibility of nonconsensual sterilization, the enforcement of surrogate mothering contracts, or the ability of the state to prosecute women for conduct during pregnancy that poses health risks for the unborn.[81]

My discussion of birth control shifted the focus from decisional privacy to privacy in paradigmatic restricted-access senses. This chapter stressed that the right to decide whether to beget a child has implications for paradigmatic forms of privacy. Decisionmaking about the conditions of childbirth and neonatal care also have important implications for paradigmatic forms of privacy.

The argument for reproductive liberties is not only that the exercise of free choice belongs to women as a requirement of moral justice. It is also that the privacy called for by moral concern for the quality of individual and group life depends upon the ability of women to determine when and if they have children. Women need privacy and ought to exploit opportunities for meaningful individual privacy in the private sphere. These opportunities depend, inter alia, upon the abrogation of patterns of dependence, marriage, and childcare in virtue of which a woman's time and fate belong to others. To have a private life that is her own, a woman must have powers of effective decisionmaking respecting contraception, abortion, childbirth, and childcare.

CHAPTER 5

Privacy in Public

WOMEN FACE SPECIAL OBSTACLES to privacy within the private sphere of home life, sexuality, and the family. But women face special obstacles to the enjoyment of privacy in the public sphere as well. This chapter examines the nature of some of those obstacles, their legal status, and the morality of intentional intrusions upon women's privacy in the the public sphere.

First, I consider women's privacy in public places. Places that are open or exposed to the public at large and places that are owned by public authorities are, in different senses, public places. In talking about public places, I have in mind places open or exposed to the public, whether they are publicly or privately owned. Privacy-invading forms of sexual harassment have been among women's most common problems in public places. Second, I consider women's privacy in connection with some of their important public roles and relationships. Women have been particularly vulnerable to privacy problems in roles and relationships away from home and beyond the family as workers, students, and even as church members.

PRIVACY IN PUBLIC PLACES

The concept of privacy in public is no contradiction. Our homes are where opportunities for individual forms of personal privacy can be most reliably anticipated. It is also possible to speak meaningfully of personal privacy outside the home in connection with, for example, shops, parks, museums, airports, and city streets. Discourse about privacy in public is not limited to the private areas of public places. The users of the toilet facilities of a municipal park have cognizable privacy interests,[1] and so do the users of its hiking trials, golf course, and swimming pool. Privacy in public, like privacy in private, can be

123

defined as the inaccessibility of persons, their mental states, and information about them to the senses and surveillance devices of others. Seclusion, achieved through physical distancing, and anonymity, achieved through limited attention paid, are the forms of inaccessibility that significantly constitute privacy in public.

A high degree of privacy cannot be counted on in public places. The solitude, solace, and intimacy afforded by privacy may be difficult to achieve amid the hubbub of commercial and community life. In a society of any size and modernity, no one can reasonably expect total freedom from the observation and approach of others. Economic interdependence, public safety, law enforcement, democratic politics, and social concern require uninvited attention paying and contact.

It can be both more difficult to achieve privacy in public places and less reasonable to expect it. Nevertheless, important forms and levels of privacy ought not be intentionally interfered with in public places. Some such interferences are mere annoyances; others are so serious that they raise moral and legal concern. Seclusion is wrongfully disturbed when close physical proximity to another is uninvited and unexcused. It is not, for example, a wrongful interference with seclusion deliberately to touch or crowd others on a New York City subway at rush hour. It is wrongful interference with seclusion deliberately to touch or crowd others in a near-empty subway car where there are ample places to sit or stand at a distance. Similarly, anonymity is wrongfully disturbed if uninvited attention is paid or drawn to another person without justification. A person wearing a clown suit and green wig cannot complain if others gawk. A popular television actress cannot complain if others stare when she strolls city streets without having taken steps to conceal her identity. A presidential candidate cannot complain if journalists trail him at his own bidding.

The moral imperatives underlying the recognition of the importance of privacy were set forth in Chapter 2. These same imperatives also represent constraints on the extent to which persons who have ventured into public places may be made the object of uninvited attention. Interference with privacy outside the home harms the feelings and sensibilities. It impedes individual tasks and purposes. Serious intrusions reflect disregard for moral personality.

The concept of a right to privacy is aptly applied to claims for privacy in public places. The expression "public place" is often used to designate areas owned and maintained by public authorities for the use of the general public. Designation of a location as a "public place" in this sense does not imply a total absence of constraints on conduct, however harmful or offensive to others. On the contrary, liberty and privacy-respecting constraints on conduct make it possible for a person to use public places owned by government for their intended governmental, commercial, and recreational purposes. The concept of a public place presupposes privacy norms. These norms are the basis of claims to a right to privacy for individuals while they are in exposed areas where the public at large has a right to be.

Unreasonable Intrusion

The importance of privacy in public places has not been entirely lost on American courts. The invasion of privacy tort recognized by a growing number of states includes a right against intrusions upon seclusion. Courts have occasionally allowed plaintiffs to recover damages for intrusions upon their reasonable expectations of seclusion in public places. For example, in 1983 a Michigan court held that a skating rink owner who installed see-through panels in the ceiling of the women's restroom was liable for invasion of privacy.[2] Yet, an absolute legal right to privacy in public places has never been recognized. In a 1956 Wisconsin case, no invasion of privacy was found even though a bar owner had photographed a woman while she was in the restroom and circulated the pictures among bar patrons.[3] Because of a strong public policy interest in the deterrence and detection of theft, a shopper observed while disrobing in a clothing retailer's fitting room is not guaranteed legal success when suing for privacy invasion.[4]

Freedom from intrusion while in areas of public places designated for dressing, trying on clothing, and toilet use is (to an extent) protected by privacy rights. But what of public areas of public places—are intrusions there legally protected, too? Intrusions that are minor embarrassments are not protected. According to a Kansas court, a man asked by a waitress at a pharmacy lunch counter whether he intended to pay for his coffee has not suffered legal injury.[5] Placing a person under close surveillance may not subject the intruder to liability for invasion of privacy. A Maryland court ruled against a union official who sought to bring unreasonable intrusion claims after he discovered he had been watched closely by opponents hoping to collect incriminating evidence of an extra-marital sexual affair. The court stressed that the plaintiff had not been aware of the surveillance at the time and that he had been watched while he was on public streets and hence "not then in seclusion."[6]

A Pennsylvanian was similarly unsuccessful in 1963 when she brought a lawsuit alleging invasion of privacy in thoroughly public places. An insurance company hired private detectives to follow claimant Isobel Forster as she walked and drove about town. The detectives were instructed to take motion pictures of Forster for use as evidence of a fraudulent disability claim. During the investigation, Forster noticed she was being followed closely by an unknown man with a camera. This made her "extremely nervous and upset, causing her frequent nightmares and hallucinations which required medical treatment." Denying Forster a right to recover, the court remarked that: "Although we sympathize with the plight of appellant, the social value resulting from investigations of personal injury claims and the absence of any willfulness . . . require us to deny redress in this case."[7]

A number of courts have held that the legal rights against tortious intrusion upon seclusion and harassment apply to protect and compensate those who suffer wrongful losses of seclusion and anonymity in public places. For example, In 1959, Shirley Bennett successfully brought a lawsuit in which she claimed that her privacy had been invaded in a public place. Her problem began when she visited a self-service retail establishment. She examined a purse and some skirts before deciding against a purchase. She then left the store. Thereafter:

> Twenty feet from the entrance she was overtaken by the Assistant Manager of the shop, who was red-faced and angry and in his shirtsleeves. He put his hand on her shoulder, put himself in position to block her path and ordered her to take off her coat, which, being frightened, she did. He then said: "What about your pockets?" and reached into two pockets on the sides of her dress. Not finding anything, he took her purse from her hand, pulled her things out of it, peered into it, replaced the things, gave it back to her, mumbled something, and ran back into the store. Passersby stopped to watch, to [her] great distress and humiliation.[8]

The Pennsylvania Supreme Court held in Bennett's favor: "The gist of privacy is the sense of seclusion, the wish to be obscure and alone. . . . The angry performance of [the store Manager] was an unreasonable and serious interference with [her] desire for anonymity and an intrusion beyond the limits of decency."[9] The court explained that a lawsuit for invasion of privacy redresses "the sense of personal outrage" a person feels when, notwithstanding other legal injuries, public modes of seclusion and anonymity are disturbed.

Judge Bok's illustrative example of justifiable outrage at a loss of privacy in a public place is instructive: "If a modest young girl should be set upon by ruffians who did not touch her but by threats compelled her to undress, give them her clothes, and flee naked through the streets, it could not be doubted that her privacy had been invaded as well as her clothes stolen."[10] Why was the young girl in the hypothetical made modest? The implication the Judge invited is that an immodest woman would not have good reason to be outraged. Yet, surely anyone in our society, male or female, modest or immodest, would be justified in feelings of personal outrage if compelled by a gang to disrobe in a public street. In contrast, the football fan who knowingly unzipped his trousers and posed for *Sports Illustrated* was scarcely justified in feeling outraged when the embarrassing photograph was published.[11]

In 1973, a New York federal district court awarded relief for privacy-invading harassment in public to Jacqueline Onassis, widow of President John F. Kennedy and wealthy Greek shipping magnate Aristotle Onassis.[12] Onassis and her children had been stalked and photographed by paparazzo Frank Galella. The court issued an order restricting Galella to a distance of at least twenty-five feet and prohibiting him from touching, blocking, endangering, harassing, alarming, or frightening the family.

Who is it that typically invades the privacy of others in public places? In the *Bennett* and *Onassis* cases it was a merchant's employee and a professional photographer, respectively, individuals with an economic interest in privacy invasion. Indeed, in recognition of their economic interests, merchants are legally privileged in many states to detain anyone reasonably suspected of shoplifting.[13] Similarly, in recognition of their economic interests and the public interest in news, journalists and photographers are legally permitted a high degree of intrusion into the lives of public figures, officials, and other newsworthy persons.[14] But merchants and photographers are not the most common privacy intruders. Ordinary men and women have a tolerant attitude toward the commonplace public intrusions they deem potentially beneficial to themselves or other members of the community. Persons seeking charitable contributions, taking opinion polls, soliciting signatures for political petitions, or selling crafts or trinkets are generally welcome. Drug dealers, prostitutes, petty thieves, and pranksters are generally not.

The consequences of unwanted intrusion can be serious. Unwanted intrusion can lead to momentary offense and short-lived negative emotions. But it can also lead to persisting emotional distress and patterns of panic. Frequent intrusion can negatively affect attitudes about particular neighborhoods. It can lead to prejudice against other persons of the same sex or ethnic group as the frequent intruders. It can make one regret and even resist leaving home. Regardless of the consequences of the intrusions, we feel we can do little as individuals even about the egregious intrusions suffered in public places. We fear dangerous altercation, we wish to avoid embarrassment, and we haven't the time or money to seek police or legal protection. Jacqueline Onassis was "fortunate" enough to be wealthy and suffer similar intrusions over a period of time perpetrated by the same readily identifiable individual.

Her fame rather than her gender prompted Gallela to harass Onassis. (Although, since her notoriety stemmed from her media image as a chic First Lady and alluring eligible widow, her attractiveness to Galella as a subject for his pictures was not unrelated to her sex.) Apparently Gallela did not subject Onassis to another kind of harassment to which ordinary women are routinely subject: privacy-invading sexual harassment.[15] Not all harassment is sexual harassment; not all sexual harassment qualifies as an invasion of privacy. Nonetheless, one of the most common and significant privacy losses women suffer away from home is privacy-invading sexual harassment.

Sexual Harassment as Privacy Invasion

Four forms of sexual harassment commonly experienced by women of all ages in public places are also invasions of privacy. They go by many names, but I will refer to them as "leering," "insulting," "prying," and "offensive touching." These four types of harassment constitute losses of the form of privacy known as anonymity. In the broad sense utilized here, anonymity is limited attention paid a person, as well as undisclosed identity. Offensive touching and leering also invade privacy: they interfere with seclusion. They breach otherwise applicable norms regarding distancing and observation.

It goes without saying that men and women are noticed in public places. Leering at a woman is more than noticing her; it is more than tracing the contours of her face or figure with the eyes. In the sense intended, leering is a mode of evaluative observation. It draws attention to the observer and to what he observes. Leering can involve deliberately moving into close physical proximity to the target of evaluation, even briefly trailing her. It can be flamboyant, accompanied by bold gestures and exaggerated facial expressions. Flamboyant leering communicates to the target and to third parties that a sexual evaluation is taking place. Flamboyant leering may even inspire third parties to join in with leering of their own. Flamboyant leering is often intended to draw the attention of its target. Aware that she is being sexually appraised, a woman may respond with annoyance, embarrassment, humiliation, anger, and even fear.

These same responses can result from the insulting that sometimes accompanies leering. The intent of an insult may be to "compliment" by conveying a favorable evaluation: If I got into bed with you I'd never get out! I know your husband is a happy man! I bet you'd like to fuck![16] On the other hand, the intent of a verbal sexual insult may be to anger, humiliate, or offend: Bitch! Whore! You're ugly! Do you like me, or do you only like to suck white cocks?! I'd like to get into your pants, beautiful! It is possible that insults are sometimes intended neither to compliment nor to offend, but simply erupt as expressions of hostility or rage. The use of sexual profanity can make an offensive, hurtful sexual insult even more so.

Prying is a third form of privacy-invading sexual harassment. Information is nominally sought: Do you live around here? What's your name? Can I go with you, baby? Are you married? What's your phone number? The real purpose of prying may be to express approval or to offend. Offensive touching is the final form of privacy-invading sexual harassment. Here the intruder pats, pinches, strokes, kisses, or rubs. The breasts or buttocks may be touched, an arm, hand-bag, or scarf clung to.

Many women have first-hand familiarity with leering, insulting, prying, and offensive touching, but the experience may be less than universal. Rare in some communities, it is a frequent, daily occurrence in others. It is difficult to say where privacy-invading sexual harassment most often occurs. It can occur on suburban streets and at county fairs. The "cat-calling" for which construction workers are famous is by no means limited to big cities. Sexual harassment in public places may be more common in larger cities where there is a high degree of anonymity and little accountability. The problem of sexual harassment of women on city streets is exacerbated by poverty and the lack of meaningful economic opportunity, which give rise to a chronically unemployed male population with little better to do than bide time on corners and rattle passersby.

Why Sexual Harassment Is a Moral Problem

The public realm is very much a place of private tasks. It is a realm to enter to alleviate or escape the stresses of home life or employment. It is a realm into which individuals go with their heads full of quintessentially private thoughts. These may be musings, ideas, half-baked ideas, wistful remembrances, embarrassing thoughts, secrets, and confidences. A woman walking her dog may want to be left alone because she is deliberating a moral choice or is deep in self-assessment. A woman walking to work or strolling at lunchtime may want to be alone and anonymous because she is planning a project or solving a problem. Flamboyant leering, insulting, prying, and offensive touching break the flow of thought and distract a women's attention, utterly without legitimate purpose, from her own concerns. Private tasks and repose are replaced with what can be more than fleeting feelings of anger, annoyance, embarrassment, humiliation, and fear.

Since the public realm includes municipal, state, and federal facilities financed by women's tax contributions, women subjected to street harassment also feel that they are being treated unfairly. It is unfair that they should be less comfortable in public places than men are.

Some public places, such as parks, gardens, and libraries, are set aside as places of repose and relaxation. Yet sexual harassment, like crime, makes the public realm inhospitable to women. In the 1980s women all over the country marched by candlelight to "take back the night," but in some communities, they do not even have the day.

A letter to the editor printed October 23, 1983, in *Equal Times*, a Boston-area newspaper, perceptively sums up the way many women feel about privacy-invading sexual harassment in public places:

> I . . . feel angry toward men who openly demonstrate their "approval" of me on the streets. [T]hose who say "ignore it its harmless" are sadly misled. Not only is it *not* harmless, it is symptomatic of a very serious disease within society, wherein sex divisions are emphasized and culti-vated to the advantage of men.
>
> Whistling, jeering and commenting may all seem harmless enough. After all, we women walk away physically intact. But it is like a small sore on the surface of the skin which, to the sensitive observer, signifies the presence of a grave illness lurking within the body.
>
> The argument for equality could carry this issue in both directions: that men should stop this behavior, or that women should start it. But in either case, this obvious . . . illustration of inequality needs to be faced, combatted and settled.
>
> And to the argument that men's sexual comments to us on the streets are merely veiled compliments, I say to the contrary. So often do I detect a note of hostility, anger, even hopeless rage, that I almost want to apologize for being female! It is harassment, not praise.

As the author of the letter notes, although harassment may seem harmless because "women walk away intact," it is not harmless. Nor is it morally tolerable conduct, on any plausible conception of what morality requires.

A morality that places a premium on equality and respect for persons must condemn privacy-invading sexual harassment. Doubt-less there are some who view sexual harassment of women on the streets as something less than cause for moral concern. The argument could be made that while privacy invading sexual harassment is vulgar behavior and bad behavior, it is not serious enough to be condemned as immoral. "The leering, intruding, prying, and insult-ing behavior you describe," the argument would go, "is vulgar, and mischievous; but it is not, strictly speaking, immoral, for immoralities are grave harms."[17]

Vulgar conduct and mischief are immoral to the extent that they treat persons like mere objects rather than as thinking, feeling indi-viduals of dignity and equal worth:

Some actions such as commenting loudly on a woman's figure as she passes are both morally wrong and vulgar, but the two ranges do not coincide. It is probably significant that a large number of cases where vulgarity and moral wrong coincide involve the degradation of a person ... [C]ommenting on a woman's figure is typical. To treat a person as just so much flesh is morally wrong, but it can be done with varying degrees of vulgarity. "Dig the jugs on the chick" is considerably more vulgar than "That young lady is very well-endowed." It would seem that the moral offense is increased by the vulgarity, although from a strictly ethical standpoint treating a person as a thing should be unjustified no matter how it is done.[18]

Not every form of vulgarity and mischief is immoral. Drinking Kool-Ade from a jelly jar at the opera is not immoral. But some vulgarity is immoral, namely, vulgarity which violates the Kantian precept that persons be treated as ends in themselves and never solely as means. Privacy-invading sexual harassment treats women as objects of ridicule and thus as inferiors.

A morality that places a premium on conduct that promotes individual happiness and psychological well-being must condemn privacy-invading sexual harassment. Sexual harassment burdens women with mental distress and a panoply of negative emotions that can undermine their ability to enjoy themselves and be effective in the public sphere. As psychologists have confirmed, drawing and paying attention to a person can lead her to experience self-awareness. Self-awareness—that is, consciousness of one's own physical traits, mental states, conditions, status, or effect on others, is generally a good thing. Many enjoyable, useful, and harmless private activities such as "introspection, diary-writing, day-dreaming, meditation, and looking into a mirror" increase self-awareness.[19] The self-awareness created by privacy-invading sexual harassment is a cause of social anxiety. "Social anxiety" is a term used by Arnold Buss to refer to the negative effects of certain experiences, perceptions, and expectations that occur in the presence of others. Embarrassment and shame are two leading forms of social anxiety. Underlying these effects is "an intense awareness of one's self as a social object."[20] For a victim of sexual harassment whose face, body, and gender subject her to lewd attention, there is an intense awareness of self as a *mere* social object. She is a mere sexual object: not a person worthy of respect as a unique subject of experience, but a mere object for others; not an individual with feelings and sensibilities that matter, but an instance of a type that counts for naught.

Women who are made to be conscious of themselves as objects through sexual harassment recognize that because they are women they do not enjoy the same privacy in public places that men on the whole do. Some women will understand that this is yet another sense in which there is not yet social equality for women. Fearful, resentful, and distressed, women may come to accept deprivations of public privacy as a way of life. But acceptance has a cost that can be measured by its cumulative effects on the victimized women, and on the quality of social life of their communities. One evident effect of continual invasion is that women come to believe they have no claim to even a minimal level of privacy in public. They simply accept that they venture into public places as "fair game." Some women become debilitated by anxiety about being alone in public and making use of public facilities. Some women stay at home.

Social scientists have theorized that social anxiety and an expectation of harm make women even more vulnerable to aggressive sexual harassment and actual sexual violence:

> The potential for anxiety people carry with them increases their vulnerability to implicit and explicit threats of danger in their environment. . . . Threats accepted as legitimate by those who receive them, by targets of threats are unquestionably more effective than threats that do not bear any aura of legitimacy.[21]

Women who feel threatened by privacy-invading sexual harassment may also feel a kind of frustrated aggression toward male strangers they perceive as having the upper hand and as egregiously violating conventions of physical distancing and courtesy. This can lead to a perpetuation of the hostility and mistrust many women feel toward men. Feeling crowded, women who are approached or followed by strangers may find that their cognitive clarity is affected, as aggression and other antisocial responses are stimulated.[22]

Viewed individually, the moral harm of some instances of privacy-invading sexual harassment is *de minimis;* yet, the moral wrongness of intrusive acts is compounded by their frequency. Sitting uninvited next to a woman on a park bench, asking for her name, or leering at her would be a minor immorality but for the fact that women frequently experience just this type of offense. The appropriateness of an act of intrusion must be assessed from the point of view of the cumulative impact of similar such intrusions.

It is ironic that, in communities like uptown Manhattan in New York, sexual harassment of women on the street is so exceedingly common that one is tempted to describe it as an accepted and acceptable part of the culture rather than as a harmful immorality. The indigenous women may appear to the casual observer to have become immune to it, even to encourage it. Is sexual harassment in some communities ethically acceptable (that is, beyond ethical criticism) because the subjective experience of the indigenous peoples is not one of offense or outrage? It is hard to conclude with confidence that frequent harassment should be written off as part of any human culture, much less any contemporary American community. We must consider whether women in communities where leering, insulting, prying, and offensive touching are commonplace grow up with attitudes about their social worth that belie an initial impression that sexual harassment as a social phenomenon is not a moral problem. We must consider whether women might appear free of offense and outrage as a strategy for self-control and adaptation.

Flirtation, Ambiguity, and Mistake

Some degree of privacy intrusion should escape moral condemnation as harmless flirtation. We could not meet members of the opposite sex via chance encounters if, for fear of harassment and invasion of privacy, we always kept puritanical distances from one another. Nothing I have said is intended to suggest that a man or woman should never draw attention to himself or herself or a stranger as a means of initiating an encounter. Some evening spots and social organizations exist for that very purpose. The privacy-diminishing intrusions that are to be condemned as morally disrespectful and harmful have little to do with genuine personal interest in the women who are victimized. Such behaviors are more readily explained as products of boredom, one-upmanship, hostility, and misogyny aimed at getting attention, shocking, and offending. This would explain why men who insultingly proposition women for sex continue to do so despite records of repeated failure.

As a group, women spend millions of dollars annually on cosmetics and fashions. Many women want to be attractive to others and to be noticed. To some extent, making oneself attractive in accordance with the fashion of the times is necessary to land a job, impress clients, attract a mate, and be treated politely.[23] It cannot be supposed that women are obliged to neglect hygiene, dress unattractively, or stay at home to avoid being harassed.

Social scientists have shed light on the truths behind some of the cultural truisms that bear on the harassment of women. The first is the truism that a man is more likely to approach a woman he finds attractive than is a woman to approach a man she finds attractive. The second is the truism that a man is more likely than a women to be mistaken about whether an overture would be welcome. Studies of nonverbal behavior suggest that men's comparatively greater willingness to initiate contact occurs because the presence of a woman is more relaxing to both men and women than the presence of a man. The more relaxing (less threatening) response evoked by women is no doubt due in part to the prevalence in society of images of women as "weak, childish, dependent, domestic . . . and subordinate."[24]

In some respects, men are more forward, in general, than women. The greater forwardness of men may also relate to a lesser ability to interpret nonverbal cues. Studies show that men are less able than women to "take a hint."[25] Males of all ages lack the ability of females of all ages to interpret nonverbal cues. A possible explanation for the difference is that for men the body "has sexual connotations that distract [them] from the judging task."[26] Both men and women are at times the victims of ambiguity, which is found in both verbal and nonverbal behavior. Still, what needs to be explained is why ambiguity may lead a man to act with confidence where a woman would have held back. It may be that "persons with a sense of control and thus of self-confidence, regard ambiguity as permission to act and expect their actions to lead to desired outcomes."[27]

Remedies

It is worth noting that American law recognizes several classes of civil injury and misdemeanor relevant to sexual harassment.[28] Verbal abuse has the status of a misdemeanor in some states. Highly offensive intrusion upon seclusion is actionable as an invasion of privacy in many states. "Intentional infliction of emotional distress" through outrageous conduct is another legal cause of action that could be applied to severe cases of sexual harassment in public places. In fact, privacy plaintiffs frequently also allege intentional infliction of emotional distress. An obstacle to pressing privacy invasion and emotional distress claims in court is that victory requires proof that the defendant's conduct was "highly offensive" or "outrageous" by the standards of the community—the very community whose treatment of women we want to improve. Where sexual harassment in a public place consists either of (a) deliberate harmful or offensive touching or (b) intentional conduct creating fear of imminent harm or offense, claims for civil assault and battery can be brought.

Relying upon the foregoing remedies to combat typical instances of sexual harassment in public places appears to be impractical. Prosecutions or citations under the criminal laws require either that police be on the scene to catch offenders in the act, or that victims be willing and able to identify offenders. A private lawsuit for money damages or injunctive relief would have little chance of success if the plaintiff's emotional injuries were not demonstrably severe. Moreover, bringing a lawsuit at all is only a theoretical possibility where the identity and location of the intruder are unknown, and where the victim of harassment lacks the time and resources needed to sustain a legal battle.

Unless they can also promote heightened moral awareness and social change, legal sanctions are not a promising route for addressing the problem of privacy-invading sexual harassment in public places. Laws against street harassment will be mainly symbolic until the conditions of inequality that breed disrespect and hostility are eliminated. Not only *sexual* inequality is at issue. Anecdotal evidence suggests that one of the causes of street harassment among inner-city blacks is that chronically unemployed and underemployed men resent working women who have successfully reaped the benefits of the civil rights and women's movements. It is unlikely that legal remedies of the sort just enumerated would be effective to deter the daily indignities black women suffer in our cities. Black women, least of all, can afford to make litigation against street harassers a priority in their lives.

Consciousness-raising is sometimes proposed as a remedy for sexual harassment. The hope is that through it "people can be made to experience as problematic events or situations which they previously accepted without complaint."[29] Whether alternative methods of dispute resolution, such as those afforded by neighborhood justice centers, could provide effective relief is a question to consider.[30] It is doubtful that the aggrieved and the accused could often be brought together for conciliation. The unusual case of persistent, habitual street harassment by particular individuals known to others in a well-defined community could perhaps be successfully brought before a neighborhood forum. Community programs, however, would encounter many of the same resource limitations encountered by more traditional legal remedies.

I suspect urban women of all races have sensed with frustration the irony of their predicament as frequent victims of harassment. The irony is this, that while privacy-invading sexual harassment is the immorality of individuals, it is immorality that could be more easily corrected by reassessing national employment policies than by assessing individual fault on a case-by-case basis.

PUBLIC DISPLAY OF PORNOGRAPHY

Graphic images of female genitalia are commonplace in erotic magazines and films but are rarely seen on public display. Artistic depictions viewed in museums and galleries are the exceptions. The fashion dolls with which little girls play have breasts without nipples and no external sex organs. This is perhaps a reflection of Westin's observation that "virtually all societies have rules for the concealment of the female genitalia, and restrictions on the time and manner of exposure."[31] The American rule respecting adult women's genitalia would seem to mandate public concealment and permit private disclosure to limited adult audiences.

Contemporary American society has few rules of concealment barring exposure of the external female anatomy other than the genitalia. Attitudes about acceptable nongenital nudity are complex and contradictory. Public breast-feeding and topless sunbathing are not widely acceptable practices in the United States. Ideals of feminine modesty strictly limit what professional women may wear in the workplace, but women may appear all but naked in popular magazines and on network television.

Pornographic depictions of nude and semi-nude women are widely displayed on newsstands and in bookstores. Many women are deeply offended by the pornographic images of women found in public places. Some women are even embarrassed and humiliated by pornographic images of other women. These reactions have led to the intriguing argument that public display of pornographic depictions of women ought to be prohibited—even if pornography itself is not prohibited—because it invades women's privacy. The privacy of the women who model for pornographers is not directly at issue; rather it is the privacy of women who, as a group or class, inadvertently view publicly displayed pornography. Members of the class are forced to view pornography on public display, and this is alleged to violate their privacy.[32] Moreover, as a consequence (it is supposed) of public display of pornographic images of women, members of the class are sexually harassed in public places in ways that invade their privacy.

What is "pornography"? When is a depiction of a woman pornographic? The suggestive origin of the word is the Greek words for "writing" and "prostitute."[33] Anthropologist Margaret Mead was quoted as defining pornography benignly as erotica, involving the attempt to "stimulate sex feelings independent of the the presence of another loved and chosen human being."[34] Definitions that build disapproval into the very concept are more common. Pornography has been described as "sexual obscenity—the exposure to public view of intimate bodily acts severed from social, affectional and moral consideration that make human relationships human."[35] Sexual obscenity has been characterized as "making public that which is private [by] intrusion upon intimate physical processes and acts or physical-emotional states" and as "a degradation of the human dimensions of life to a sub-human or merely physical level."[36]

Feminists commonly distinguish between sensuous erotic materials and lewd, licentious, pornographic ones. In this vein Eva F. Kittay has suggested that pornography can be distinguished from erotica in that "pornography deals in the representation of violence, degradation, or humiliation of some persons (most frequently female) for the sexual gratification of other persons (almost exclusively male)." On her characterization of pornography, depiction of exposed genitalia and explicit sexual behavior are neither necessary nor sufficient indicia of the pornographic.

> The infamous *Hustler* cover [of the naked torso of a woman being fed into a meat grinder], the photographs of clothed women bound and gagged, an album cover with a woman's buttocks stamped "prime meat" . . . all show neither explicit genitalia nor explicit sexual acts yet are more clearly pornographic than the photographs of nude prostitutes taken by the photographer Belloque. And this, notably, in spite of the etymology of the word "pornography", which is a depiction of prostitutes.[37]

On the broad understanding advanced by Kittay and others, it is quite possible that pornography would have to include at least some depictions of women that appear far outside the adult bookshop, "men's entertainment" magazines, and X-rated video arenas. It could include, for example, the Rolling Stones billboard that perched atop Sunset Strip in Los Angeles in 1976. It depicted a woman in a mini-dress, arms tied above her head, legs bound and tied to stakes driven into the ground. The woman's legs were spread apart and a picture of the Rolling Stones rock group hovered between her thighs. A caption read, "I'm 'Black and Blue' from The Rolling Stones—and I love it!" (The billboard was removed after an organization called Women Against Violence Against Women protested to Atlantic Records.) Depictions of violence against women on record jackets in the 1970s included an Ohio Players' album, "Pleasure," which depicted a nude woman in chains. A decade ago the prevalence of images of violence against women led a *Time* magazine writer to observe that:

> Despite the rise of feminism—or perhaps because of it—images of women being physically abused are becoming increasing common. In record-album photos, fashion and men's magazine layouts, and even a few department-store windows and billboards, women are shown bound, gagged, beaten, whipped, chained or as victims of murder or gang rape.[38]

Two objections to much of what is described as pornography are especially noteworthy. The first is that existing forms of pornography contribute to inequality, discrimination, and disrespect for women.[39] Pornography fosters degrading, false, and hateful beliefs about women's wants, needs, and proper social roles. Some proponents of this general view maintain that morally acceptable pornography depicting nudity and sexual intimacy is possible, but that existing male-entertainment publications do not pass moral muster.[40] They depict women as inferiors, as belonging in ancillary social roles, and as being harmed. According to some, another problem with contemporary pornography is that it disrespects women by ignoring women's actual preferences for lovemaking. Other proponents view pornography depicting females as inherently disrespectful to women. They argue that it would be objectionable even if what is depicted were loving couples having straightforward genital intercourse and having all of their needs acknowledged and satisfied.

The second important general objection is that pornography actually contributes to violence against women.[41] In 1986, the Attorney General's Commission on Pornography reached the conclusion that violent pornography "bears a causal relationship to both sexual violence and to sex discrimination." It also offered the tentative finding that non-violent material that is degrading in its portrayal of sex can also lead to violence.[42] The 1970 Presidential Commission Report on Obscenity and Pornography concluded that there was no empirical basis for tying pornography to antisocial behavior. Some experts view the question of a causal link between pornography and violence as unsettled. Whether pornography contributes to actual physical violence against women was raised in connection with the New Bedford pool table rape in 1983. A Massachusetts woman was gang-raped on a pool table by four men in a crowded neighborhood bar. "Coincidences" surrounding the rape strongly suggested that the rapists were influenced by what they may have seen and read in "adult" materials: "Shortly before the attack a local porno theatre reportedly ran a film showing a woman having sex on a pool table. And the January 1983 issue of *Hustler* magazine featured a photo layout of a waitress-model being wrestled to a pool table, stripped and raped by four men."[43]

Public display of materials defined by lawmakers as "obscenity" is unlawful in many cities and states. Notwithstanding the constitutional right to view obscenity in the privacy of one's own home established by the Supreme Court in *Stanley v. Georgia*, lawmakers and courts have concluded that obscenity is harmful and indecent enough to prohibit its sale, transport, distribution or public display. In 1984, Ruth Marsh, while acting as a sales clerk, sold magazines entitled "Redi-Whipt" and "Cat Fight" to undercover Pittsburgh Police officers. She was criminally prosecuted under the Pennsylvania Obscenity Statute. The statute prohibits both the sale of obscenity and the display of obscenity visible from a public thoroughfare.

Not all arguably pornographic images that may offend women meet legal definitions of obscenity.[44] At the present time some arguably pornographic depictions of women are lawfully displayed. The question of whether the sale and manufacture of pornography or sexual obscenity, however defined, ought to be prohibited is quite distinct from the question of central concern here. My central question is whether an argument against public display can be based on the notion that display of pornography or obscenity is an invasion of women's privacy.

Consider this line of argument. It is in women's better interest that less attention (of certain lewd types) be paid them. Privacy-invading sexual harassment is one type of such attention. It is degrading and distressing. If we can show that public display of pornography aggravates the problem of privacy-invading sexual harassment, then we can causally associate public display with the lost privacy of women as a class. We can say that the anonymity interests of women as a group argue against the public display of sexually explicit publications. Men's-entertainment magazines call attention to what in our society are still (if ambivalently and inconsistently) regarded as private parts of the bodies: the sex organs, women's breasts and buttocks. The configuration of the female body is no secret to adults of either sex. Nevertheless, public display of pornography not only sells magazines but, we are supposing for the moment, contributes to the degrading, offensive syndrome of sexual harassment whereby women in public places are subject to comments about their bodies and sexuality by strangers.[45]

There are problems with this line of argument. We know that male-entertainment magazines are widely circulated at newsstands. Of the 10,366,817 copies of *Playboy* and *Penthouse* sold in 1984, roughly half were sold at newsstands, half through subscriptions. Even assuming that the open display of *Playboy, Penthouse, Hustler, Club* and similar magazines is a cause of privacy-invading street harassment, it may be impossible adequately to assess its causal impact. We know that the sale and rental of adult videos is lucrative business. We also know that sexual harassment on the street is a problem. But we do not know how much the former phenomena contribute to the latter.

Pornographic materials are displayed by merchants so that more copies will be sold. Without a clearer causal link between display and harassment, laws forcing merchants to hide covers designed to stimulate interest would be an arbitrary impediment to magazine sales. The economic rights of individual magazine owners and distributors should not be diminished lightly. Nor should state and local law casually abridge the constitutionally protected rights of free speech, liberty, and due process that may be at stake.

In *Ernonik v. City of Jacksonville*, 422 U.S. 205 (1975), the Supreme Court characterized the privacy interests of persons on the public streets as limited, too limited to justify censorship of otherwise protected free speech. The case involved the manager of a drive-in cinema who was prosecuted under a Jacksonville ordinance which declared it unlawful to feature a motion picture containing images of "the human male or female bare buttocks, human female bare breasts, or human bare pubic areas" that were "visible from any public street or public place." Films depicting nudity playing at the drive-in theatre were easily viewed from public cites. Invalidating the ordinance as an unconstitutional limitation on lawful free speech, the Court maintained that persons offended by nudity on the drive-in screen could simply avert their eyes. In an earlier case, *Redrup v. New York*, 386 U.S. 767 (1967), involving display of sexually oriented books and magazines, the Court relied upon the same principles applied in *Erzoznik*. It argued that no legally cognizable invasion of privacy occurs where pornography is in public view unless the manner of display is "so obtrusive as to make it impossible for an unwilling person to avoid exposure to it."

Perhaps women offended by public displays of pornography should simply avert their eyes, as the high Court suggests. But the Court's First Amendment free speech argument for eye-averting is only as morally compelling as the lack of evidence that public display of pornography has the causal tie to privacy-invading sexual harassment and violence feminists have alleged.

The empirically certain point is that many a woman who inadvertently views pornography on public display feels embarrassed and humiliated. As she identifies with the woman depicted on the magazine cover or video packaging, the other woman's immodesty and degradation become her own; she is also exposed and demeaned; she feels a loss of her own privacy, though, in fact she has lost none. On the other hand, some women are unaffected by public displays of pornographic images of other women. They do not identify at all, or they identify approvingly. Women freely engage in the consumption, sale, and creation of pornography. Hence, to say public display invades the privacy of women as a class unrealistically assumes a uniformity of sensibility and taste among women. Of course, opponents of pornography sometimes make the paternalistic argument that pornography and its display should be prohibited because they injure women's interests, whether most women realize it or not.

It is unlikely that general legal prohibition of the display of pornography, other than sexual obscenity, will ever be the rule in this country. This fact makes it no less important to understand that a woman's sense of modesty can be offended even when her own privacy is not violated. It is also important to understand that pornography offends many women's sense of public decency as well as their sense of personal modesty. Unless one takes the illiberal view of James Fitzpatrick Stephens that anything which is deemed by some to be an affront to human decency is also an actionable violation of privacy,[46] these feelings are not dispositive of whether privacy is diminished and, if so, whether the offending displays ought to be prohibited.

ROLES AND RELATIONSHIPS IN THE PUBLIC SPHERE

Virtually any human relationship can give rise to the problems of lost and inadequate privacy. Relationships with government, employers, educational institutions, insurance companies, banks, credit bureaus, health facilities, and even churches and social organizations require yielding information and permitting others to store, share, and collect it. A distinction is sometimes made between personal information and business or financial information relating to individuals. Nonetheless, any information disclosure relating to financial matters can potentially injure sensibilities, feelings, and reputation.

Are women more likely than men to suffer informational and other privacy losses in their relationships within the public sphere? This is an empirical question whose answer is apparent in some contexts, unclear in others. It is clear that women have suffered greater privacy losses than men due to sexual harassment in the workplace.[47] It is unclear that women are any more likely than men to be subjected to employer polygraph testing or coercive drug and alcohol testing. Some limited evidence suggests that polygraph examiners hired by employers to screen job applicants and reduce theft reserve their most abusive questions for female subjects.[48] It is not clear that gender is a significant variable in unwanted privacy losses connected with the insurance industry. And while it is obvious that abortion record keeping and disclosure affects women's informational privacy more directly than it affects men's, it would be surprising to learn that female hospital patients are more likely than male hospital patients to suffer privacy losses as a result of nonconsensual uses of medical records. (Some investigators believe that women confined to health-care institutions do suffer greater abuse than comparably situated men.)[49]

Where women have been more likely than male counterparts to suffer lost or inadequate privacy, the explanation has generally included one or more of the following causal factors, each of which is discussed separately below: (a) women are perceived as subservient and may in fact have roles as inferiors or ancillaries; (b) women are deemed safe targets because there are ineffective moral, institutional, or legal sanctions to serve as deterrents; (c) women are presumed to be limited by private obligations; and (d) women are held to higher standards of private conduct. Lost and inadequate privacy resulting from these four causes can have serious consequences. Emotional distress and injury to self-esteem may follow egregious invasions of privacy premised on female inferiority. Substantial career and economic losses may accrue as well, as where a woman is denied employment because of her marital status or sexual unavailability.

Inferiors and Ancillaries

Women have been more likely than men to experience privacy-invading sexual harassment on the job. Studies of sexual harassment in the workplace reveal the difference sex can make in determining whose privacy is most often invaded in the workplace.[50] In the absence of formal studies, differences can be predicted. Women are more vulnerable to privacy-invading sexual harassment. Their typically subservient worker status and their inferior social status combine to make and keep them vulnerable. A number of writers have recounted the experiences of working women and students who have had to face sexually oriented prying and demands for personal information as forms and companions to sexual harassment.[51] In *Phillips v. Smalley Maintenance Services,* a Florida woman alleging invasion of privacy testified that her boss regularly called her into his office to ask what she thought about various sexual positions.[52] Workers have even reported the use of binoculars and telescopes by male co-workers seeking to stare at their breasts through the crevices of their blouses. Co-workers without supervisory standing over a woman have reportedly sought to use the confines of the office as a context in which to capture women's attention through conduct that amounts to harassment.

While women are the moral equals of men, their employment patterns and social roles reinforce notions of subservience. Women often have ancillary roles in the workplace that place them on the bottom of the hierarchy rather than in positions of leadership. More than 93 percent of all dental hygienists, secretaries, receptionists, practical nurses, registered nurses, domestic servants, typists, and teacher's aids are women.[53] Ancillaries are employed for the use and convenience of their superiors. It is ironic that although secretaries are entrusted with the secrets and confidences of their employers, their workspaces are often open, public areas, and their desktops and work products are accessible to wandering eyes. Sexual services may be among those sought by a boss accustomed to thinking of a female employee as "there for him."

Privacy-invading sexual advances are not the only kind of privacy loss women experience by virtue of their status as inferiors and ancillaries. *Bodewig v. K-Mart* is a striking illustration.[54] In this case a shy young female cash register clerk was ordered by a 32-year-old male retail manager to disrobe in the store's public restroom to allow the female assistant manager to investigate an irate customer's claim that the clerk had stolen twenty dollars. The manager acceded to the customer's demand for a strip search even though his own search of the clerk's clothing and a register tally failed to turn up the money, and even though the customer admitted not knowing how much money she had brought with her into the store. The manager also invited the customer to watch the strip search. The search ended when the customer indicated the otherwise naked clerk need not remove her panties because she could see through them. Here a low-level employee's privacy was readily sacrificed to further the presumed business interest of her employer. Further, it was sacrificed in a reckless, thoughtless manner that reflected a lack of concern for the employee's sensibilities and integrity.

The ancillary status women have in the workplace does not end when they enter professional careers. In large law firms, for example, women have not yet come to be frequently represented among the partners but usually work as associate attorneys under male partners.[55] Professional women may thus be subject to the same problems faced by ancillary women in nonprofessional careers. Female college and university students are also vulnerable to privacy-invading harassment and other privacy problems by virtue of their analogous status as ancillaries and inferiors. In colleges and universities, undergraduate women and female graduate students are viewed as institutional and intellectual inferiors. Viewing female students as inferiors can result in attractive young coeds being urged to trade sex for grades. Female graduate students may be pressed to trade sex for grades, for teaching assistantships, for thesis supervision, and for job recommendations.

Absence of Sanction

Women lose privacy because others perceive that no significant negative sanctions or significant risks are associated with intrusion. The absence of risk relates closely to women's being perceived as inferiors. Women who have the power to hire and fire and women who are known to be capable of utilizing systems of redress cannot be easily viewed as inferiors. Were women closer in physical strength and social standing to men, they might be more intimidating and thereby repel intrusions. Men know that making a pass at a woman is unlikely to result in physical violence. Consequently, differences in size, bodily strength and attitudes about physical retaliation can be exploited to the advantage of the unscrupulous.

Moral, institutional, and legal sanctions possibly serve as deterrents to privacy invasions, but institutional antiharassment guidelines have seldom provided for stiff, enforceable penalties. Employee and student groups at Harvard University and elsewhere have sought to clarify the meaning of harassment and give teeth to the sanctions. Legal remedies to harassment include actions brought under Title VII of the Civil Rights Act of 1964 and civil suits for invasion of privacy or for infliction of emotional distress. Nonetheless, problems of proving that particular acts of harassment are "highly offensive" or "outrageous" and the personal costs of litigation make legal sanctions only part of the answer. Small-scale consciousness raising (really moral education), personnel training programs in the workplace, public discussion, and media publicity are further strategies.

The absence of adequate legal sanction exists, in part, because state law does not always impose civil liability for misconduct women deem to be outrageously offensive invasions of privacy and sources of grave emotional distress. For example, about twenty-five years ago a Kentucky woman attempted to recover damages from her landlord for invasion of privacy stemming from an uninvited visit to her hospital bedside. Although he was aware that she was about to give birth, landlord Albert Murphy entered her hospital room and, in the presence of other persons, informed her that he had locked her husband and children out of their home because they were "filthy and dirty." Plaintiff Virginia Pangallo maintained that Murphy's outrageous conduct was an invasion of privacy, caused mental anguish and nervous shock, and prolonged her hospitalization.[56] The lawsuit was dismissed on the ground that Kentucky state law did not recognize a cause of action for invasion of privacy by oral publication.

Another example illustrates the same point. In a 1985 Florida case, a woman alleged that she had been wrongfully terminated from her job and that her male employer had attempted to induce her to join him in a sexual liason. She brought a complaint in state court charging wrongful discharge, invasion of privacy, and infliction of emotional distress. The court held that the employer had a right to terminate Brenda Ponton "at will." It held that the employer's words of seduction did not come within the "zone of conduct permitting a determination that Ponton's right of privacy was unlawfully invaded," and that the employer's conduct was "condemnable by civilized standards" but was not "so outrageous in character, and so extreme in degree, as to go beyond all possible bounds of decency."[57] The court also rejected outright Ponton's claims that policies underlying Florida and federal civil rights laws should "serve as a basis for a common law cause of action where a female's rejection of sexual advances is the motivation underlying her termination from employment."[58]

Phillips v. Smalley Maintenance (1983) was good news for women who view sexual harassment at work as an invasion of privacy. The case could serve as a valuable precedent. In *Phillips,* an Alabama court held that sexual harassment by an employer is a common law invasion of privacy. The defendant employer sought to avoid liability on the ground that his alleged attempts to extract sexual information and sex from a married female employee failed. The employer also argued that plaintiff Phillips was hired as a temporary and that the completion of the job for which she had been hired rather than the absence of sexual intercourse between them was the reason she was terminated. The court found that sexually oriented prying and pressuring in the workplace can be an intrusion into seclusion even if no sexual information is obtained and no sexual contact actually occurs. Phillip's allegations of verbal and physical harassment that created a hostile environment were thus held to be a sufficient basis for bringing a civil suit for invasion of privacy against her employer.

Title VII of the Civil Rights Act of 1964 created the Equal Employment Opportunity Commission (EEOC). The EEOC has administrative authority to receive, investigate and resolve complaints of discrimination in the terms or conditions of employment on the basis of race, color, religion, sex or national origin by certain private employers, labor organizations, and employment agencies engaged in or related to industries affecting interstate commerce. Women who believe they are victims of discrimination and wish to sue under Title VII in federal court are required by law to first take their complaints to the EEOC for attempted agency resolution. Although Title VII appears to have had a favorable effect on improving employment opportunities for women,[59] the EEOC has not always been responsive to claims of privacy-invading sexual harassment in the workplace made by woman who allege no economic harm.

In 1986 the Supreme Court interpreted Title VII as providing a basis for relief for such women. In *Meritor Savings Bank v. Vinson*, 477 U.S. ___, 106 S. Ct. 2399 (1986), Mechelle Vinson alleged that she was sexually harassed by Vice President Sidney Taylor, her job supervisor at the Meritor Savings Bank. The alleged harassment included public fondling, pressure to have sexual intercourse, to which she acceded "40 or 50 times," and rape. The Court held for the first time that the creation of a "hostile environment" by virtue of sexual harassment, even where there is no "tangible" or "economic" harm, is actionable sex discrimination under Title VII. The Court rejected the argument that employers are automatically immune from liability for sexual harassment by supervisory employees if they have grievance procedures and policies against sexual discrimination. But, the Court also rejected the rule that, regardless of the circumstances, employers are absolutely liable for the sexual harassment of supervisors. The need to prove employer fault in supervisor harassment cases increases the already great legal burden of plaintiffs. Still, the *Meritor* case is a gain for women. It creates a federal sanction that may significantly deter privacy-invading harassment in the workplace.

Limited by Private Obligations

Women may suffer losses of informational privacy because they are presumed to be limited by private obligations arising out of traditional feminine roles. When applying for a job, for example, a woman may be expected to answer prying questions about marriage and family, questions not put to her male counterparts. Questions about marital status, spousal attitudes about work and travel, and child-bearing and child-rearing plans are deemed relevant. Women, even successful young women who are applying for high-paying professional positions, are believed to place personal relationships first. Indeed, many do. But it is presumed women lack independence, and that their commitments to employers are highly contingent upon their husband's wishes as well as subject to biological imperatives.

In quite a different vein, potential creditors may seek personal information that is then used against a woman because they assume her sex and roles make her an unworthy credit risk. Federal legislation has made these practices largely unlawful.[60]

A High Standard of Conduct

Women may lose privacy because they are held to a higher standard of personal conduct than are men. A 1984 case involving an Oklahoma woman who belonged to a fundamentalist Christian church is illustrative. Marian Guinn confessed in confidence to her pastor a sexual affair of which he disapproved. When the pastor publicized her "fornication" to the entire congregation as part of her penance, she brought a lawsuit.[61] While her church undoubtedly had high standards of chastity for men and women, the actions of her minister suggest a view that redressing female sexual sin is of special import. Religious paternalism could be the best explanation of why church leaders demanded Guinn's public penance. But their treatment of her smacks of the nineteenth-century conception of women as having a special obligation to lead morally exemplary lives. As mothers and moral educators of children, women must exert a proper influence or precipitate the ruin of civilization.[62] The treatment of Guinn smacks too of the notion that immodest, unchaste women have no reasonable expectation of privacy and every expectation of exposure and rebuke.

EXCLUSION AND GROUP PRIVACY

The final topic I want to consider in relation to the public sphere is group privacy.[63] Organized and ad hoc women's groups have flourished. Women's civic, charitable, political, and professional organizations; their collectives; their social clubs; their consciousness-raising groups; and their coffee klatches have forged personal bonds based on friendship, mutual assistance, and common interest. More often than not, women have been able to meet in seclusion. They have also been able to set exclusive membership criteria or enjoy de facto exclusions of men and women of dissimilar interests, beliefs, social classes, and ethnicities. Because group seclusion and exclusivity are relatively easy to come by in American society, the privacy problems of women's groups have been of limited magnitude.

Yet, forming and participating in groups of their own with serious purposes has not always been easy for women. Involvement in groups presupposes not only interest, but also autonomy, leisure time, and mobility. Women's interest in extrafamilial activity is easily undermined if they are overburdened with domestic responsibility, if their mates are unsupportive, and if they lack safe, affordable means of transportation. Women who would like to belong to a women's organization but who hold down jobs face additional barriers. A drop in the fertility rate to 2.1 children per American woman might suggest that women have more time than they did thirty years ago to devote to social and civic groups. But the fact that women now constitue about half of the workforce means otherwise. Women's charities began to report volunteer "brain drain" in the 1970s as more and more women with leadership potential and organizational skills turned to paid careers.

Women today are seeking admission to men-only activities and organizations from which they have been traditionally barred.[64] Women have been barred from admission to fraternal clubs, such as the Elks and Lions; civic clubs, such as the Rotary Club, Kiwanis Club, and Jaycees; athletic clubs, such as the Alexandria, Virginia, Old Dominion Boat Club; eating clubs, such as New York's Century Association and Princeton's eating clubs; and professional and hobby groups, such as the exclusive New York Hortist Club, which admitted its first female horticulturalist in 1987. Ambitious women perceive that a key to success in business and the professions is gaining entry to the world of men. Michael Kinsley, the syndicated columnist and editor of the *New Republic,* is among those who have argued that eliminating men-only clubs is not a worthy goal for the women's movement, even if some business transpires in them.

The reverse phenomenon of men seeking admission to women's organizations has not occurred frequently.[65] To some extent this is because men do not perceive entry to women's groups as advantageous. Men are eligible for membership in the more influential women's groups such as the League of Women Voters, which has sponsored nationally televised debates between presidential candidates. In the 1960s and 1970s women's political and professional organizations sometimes suffered bitter division over the question whether men should be excluded from meetings and sponsored events. Radical feminists frequently opposed the presence of males on the ground that they introduced competition, sexual distraction, and repression into otherwise egalitarian, purposeful gatherings. Liberal feminists argued that exclusion of men was sexist in reverse, and wrong. Compromisers sometimes suggested that men be admitted but not permitted to speak. In any event, more often than not, women concerned with matters of principle, not men desiring admission, led to the debates.

Women's group privacy problem could actually be termed a *reverse* group privacy problem: exclusion from private, men-only activities and organizations. The concept of sexually segregated activities and organizations has deep cultural roots and is by no means limited to American and Western societies. John M. Roberts and Thomas Gregor highlighted the "most dramatically defined rule of privacy" among the Mehinacu Indians of Brazil:

> The men's house is a small building in the center of the village. This building functions simultaneously as a temple and a social club. During most of the day there are a number of men inside, chatting, telling jokes, working on their bows and arrows, or playing a set of sacred flutes stored within. Admission to the men's house, or even setting eyes on the sacred flutes, is absolutely forbidden to the women of the tribe. Should they intrude, the punishment is well-defined; gang rape by all the men of the community.[66]

The sanction is so frightening that women not only obey the prohibition, but avert their eyes when passing the men's house. As a consequence "the men are provided a well-defended private area for carrying on masculine activities."[67]

American law has helped to preserve a kind of "men's house" in our society—a system of organizations with more than mere social purposes from which women are excluded. The Supreme Court has interpreted the First Amendment right of free association to apply permissibly, allowing persons to meet or assemble with others; but it has also interpreted it as a right to exclude:

> It is the constitutional right of every person to close his home or club to any person or to choose his intimates and business partners solely on the basis of personal prejudices.[68]

> The associational rights which our system honors permit all white, all black, all brown, and all yellow clubs to be formed. They also permit all Catholic, all Jewish, or all agnostic clubs to be established. Government may not tell a man or woman who his or her associates must be. The individual can be as selective as he desires.[69]

The courts have announced that the right to associate with persons of one's own choosing is protected by the constitutional right to privacy embodied in the penumbra of the Bill of Rights. More than a hundred years ago, the Ninth Amendment, which reserves certain basic unenumerated rights to citizens, was held to protect the "social right" of individuals to form truly private organizations that refuse membership based on sexual, racial, and political criteria.[70]

The Thirteenth and Fourteenth Amendments, the Civil Rights Act of 1964, and other federal civil rights legislation limit discrimination in places otherwise open to the general public. Nonetheless, the Public Accommodations Act of the Civil Rights Act of 1964 expressly excepts "private clubs" or "other establishments not in fact open to the public" from the definition of "places of public accommodation."[71] Private organizations that are not acting in tandem with or functioning as public entities, and that are not in fact open on an indiscriminate basis to the public, may exclude on the basis of race, color, creed, sex, or national origin.

Should federal law be changed? Should local law be amended to fill the gap? In *Roberts v. United States Jaycees*, 468 U.S. 609 (1984), the Supreme Court held that the Minnesota Department of Human Rights Act, which prohibited discrimination in places of public accommodation on the basis of sex, could bar the exclusion of women from membership in U.S. Jaycees chapters located within the state. The Court stressed that constitutional rights of private association and free expression protect intimate, personal groups from government interference. The Jaycees are subject to state anti-discrimination laws because membership is neither small nor selective, and because a large number of non-members of both sexes regularly participate in the Jaycees' activities. Lower courts in Massachusetts, Alaska and Minnesota have similarly held the Jaycees to be public rather than private under local anti-discrimination laws by virtue of the organization's lack of selectivity and exclusivity. In *Board of Directors of Rotary International v. Rotary Club of Duarte*, No. 86-421, May 4, 1987, the Supreme Court held that California's ban against sex discrimination could be applied to prevent Rotary International from revoking the charter of one of its 19,000 clubs after the affiliate admitted three women as members. An undivided Court emphasized the lack of selectivity and exclusivity of the Rotary Clubs, which have 900,000 members in 157 countries; it also emphasized that the public service goals of the Rotary Clubs would be enhanced rather than harmed by permitting otherwise qualified female members.

New York City amended its public accommodations laws in 1984. Explaining the intent of legislation aimed at redefining most "private clubs" as places of public accommodation, then City Counsel President Carol Bellamy stated that the legislation would close a legal loophole. The exception for "distinctly private" clubs enabled traditionally private clubs—which she maintained were actually public meeting places providing as many or more non-members as members access to contacts valuable for professional success—to "mock the intent" of the city's anti-discrimination law.[72]

The New York Club Association, representing 125 organizations, challenged the amended public accommodations law in state court after the city's Commission on Human Rights issued complaints based on the new law against the all-male Century Association, Union League, and University Club. Under the amended law "An institution, club or place of accommodation shall not be considered in its nature distinctly private if it has more than four hundred members, provides regular meal service and regularly receives payment for dues, fees, use of space, facilities, services, meals or beverages directly or indirectly from or on behalf of nonmembers for furtherance of trade or business."[73] On February 17, 1987, New York State's highest court unanimously upheld the validity of 1984 amendments. Unless the U.S. Supreme Court hears an appeal and decides otherwise, New York City clubs which lost their protected status as "distinctly private" by operation of the amended law may no longer lawfully refuse to accept female members.

The important rationale behind the move to amend public accommodation laws to treat organizations like New York's downtown eating clubs as places of public accommodation has been summarized by Catherine M. Goodwin:

> A widely held legal tenet is that separate is inherently unequal. To the extent that club membership results in tangible professional benefits, such as enhanced professional status, mobility and contacts, would-be members are denied economic and employment interests. Historically, public policy has protected the equality interests that are derived from federal and state constitutions. Currently, there is an increasing awareness of the need to protect free access to commerce and the pursuit of a profession.
>
> The injury to an excluded individual is symbolic and psychological as well as tangible. Those denied full participation in certain parts of society suffer a decreased sense of self worth. In addition, society as a whole inevitably suffers from arbitrary class-based discrimination due to reinforced social stereotypes and impeded social change. Although religion and morals are matters of individual conscience, law has become the dominant collective expression of social ideals.[74]

Clarence Ruddy, who chaired the Conference of Private Organizations, an informal coalition of national private membership organizations, has presented the opposing viewpoint. Ruddy argued that proposals calling for amendment of Title II of the Civil Rights Act of 1964 to reclassify private clubs as places of public accommodation threaten freedom of association and the right to privacy and speech protected by the First and Ninth Amendments. He maintained that the Supreme Court has definitively interpreted freedom of association to mean freedom to associate for economic as well as social purposes with persons of one's own choosing and has held that civil rights do not override social rights. He argued that the legislative history of the Civil Rights Act supports maintenance of the Act's express private club exceptions; and that source of income, that is, whether a club's income derives from members or business patronage, is an unprecedented criteria for identifying bona fide private organizations.[75]

As an ethical matter, the possibility must be confronted that some organized single-sex activities and associations serve beneficial as well as individually and socially desirable ends. There is every reason to believe they do. Nonetheless, in ways that disadvantage women, the social and the economic are poorly demarcated in some men's organizations. Tradition has conjoined men's purely social rights with economic superiority. A "men's house" with dual purposes has been created. If women cannot achieve complete economic parity without changes in civil rights laws designed to dismantle the temple of male society and privilege, then legal reform is a just response. Tradition and social rights make an unpersuasive argument for obstructing the legal reform that would dismantle the men's house in the name of greater economic justice.

Of course, the distinctions between business and leisure, dealmakers and friends, are not exact. But the demand of justice for women shifts the burden to men who crave opportunities for single-sex companionship to develop modes of group privacy that more greatly approximate the severance of privacy and privilege. This shift of burden is not an unfair one, for the possibilities for innovation in social life are unbounded.

CONCLUSION

In both the public sphere and the private sphere, women experience privacy losses that are unique to their gender. At work, at school, wherever women go, they are especially subject to privacy losses. This, I have suggested, is because they are so often perceived as inferiors and ancillaries, because of the absence of effective negative sanctions, because they are presumed to be limited by private obligations, and because they are held to a high standard of personal conduct.

Harassment on the streets is a daily privacy problem for some urban women. They are subjected to leering, insulting, prying, and offensive touching that interferes with their desire to be let alone and anonymous. Public display of pornography does not directly invade women's privacy because it does not make women, as a group, more accessible to others. But, public display of pornography can have disturbing effects. Some women who view nude and semi-nude pornographic images of women become angry and frightened. Some experience sympathetic feelings of immodesty and degradation. It is conceivable that public display of female pornography feeds disrespect for women and contributes to privacy-invading street harassment and violence. Given the very close relationship between privacy, on the one hand, and personhood, well-being, and fitness for participation and contribution, on the other, the privacy-related effects of pornography and harassment are morally serious problems. It is unclear that these moral problems have legal solutions. The difficulty of crafting the subtle and qualitative legislation needed, combined with the cost of enforcement, has led some civil libertarians and feminists to favor non-legal, educative solutions to the problems of public display of pornography and street harassment.

For purposes of contrast, I presented the men-only club issue as a "reverse privacy" problem for women. Should men be allowed realms of private association from which women are excluded? Should women give men social breathing space free of female attention? I argued that they should, if an important condition is met. Men's social organizations have no just claim to exclude on the basis of sex if they also function as centers of commercial privilege. The mixing of social and economic functions turns innocuous social segregation into real inequality for women.

In discussing women's privacy in public, this chapter has focused on public places and on public roles and relationships. Not fully discussed are the problems of privacy women can experience in their public roles and relationships with government. To an extent, that was at issue in earlier discussions of governmental interference with reproductive liberties. And since government is a major employer of women, it was implicitly at issue in this chapter in discussions of privacy losses at work. In Chapter 6 our topic is women's privacy and decisional privacy when they have a non-employment relationship with government that places them in the hands of the law as criminal suspects, criminals, and crime victims.

CHAPTER 6

Privacy in the Hands of the Law

I N NUMEROUS RESPECTS routine law enforcement, criminal prosecution, and imprisonment entail sharply diminished personal privacy. Even so, some unnecessary privacy losses occur. The moral dimensions of privacy deprivation in the justice system are slowly gaining the recognition they deserve. This chapter considers moral aspects of privacy losses experienced by women when they are in the hands of the law variously as crime victims, suspected and accused criminals, and convicted offenders. Specifically, I focus on the privacy problems of three disparate groups of women: female rape victims, arrested and incarcerated women, and women who prostitute.

The characteristic privacy losses of rape victims stem from unwanted media publicity, information disclosure in public prosecutorial records and proceedings, and self-disclosure in the court room. Print and broadcast media that abide by rape victim anonymity policies show regard for the special privacy needs of victims of sexual crime. Both procedural fairness for criminal defendants and the integrity of the criminal justice system demand frank courtroom testimony as a condition of the accused's conviction and punishment. But respect for the privacy of the victim of rape demands constraints on the admissibility of evidence lacking in relevance or probative value concerning her character and sexual history.

Like rape victims, women taken into custody as criminal suspects, accused criminals awaiting trial, and convicted offenders are subject to unwanted media publicity and information disclosure through public records and court proceedings. Convicted offenders face a life of surveillance substantially lacking in freedom of action and associa-

153

tion. While in the hands of the law, women may be sexually harassed, their personal ties may be irreparably broken, the discharge of family obligations may be permanently interrupted, and sexual and reproductive choices may be thwarted. In this chapter I distinguish three distinct, competing conceptions of how much privacy and privacy-related liberty is due to women behind bars in view of countervailing punitive goals and practical constraints.

Prostitution places women who engage in it on the wrong side of the law and thus potentially in the custody of police and jailers. For this reason the female prostitute is subject to all of the privacy and privacy-related problems of women arrested, detained, and jailed for other crimes. She faces unwanted publicity, information disclosure through public records and proceedings, sexual harassment, fractured personal ties, and curtailed sexual and reproductive self-determination. In addition, the illegal status of prostitution can itself be viewed as a privacy problem, namely, breach of the sexual privacy principle that freely consenting adults have a moral right to engage in sexual conduct without unreasonable governmental interference.

NEED TO KNOW, RIGHT TO KNOW

Individuals experience privacy losses when they or facts about them are in the hands of the criminal justice system as a result of investigation, arrest, prosecution, incarceration, record-keeping, and data-sharing. Respect for individual privacy in criminal justice has recently taken a step forward in the important area of record-keeping.[1] The privacy (and accuracy) of criminal record information is an important concern because of the stigmatizing effects of arrest for suspicion of crime, criminal prosecution, and incarceration. A criminal history relating to the "women's crime" of prostitution is especially stigmatizing inasmuch as commercial sex and its vendors are held in particularly low esteem. Inaccessibility of criminal history information may be needed to assure that those suspected or guilty of misconduct in the past are not wrongfully denied peace of mind, social approval, or employment in the future.

In the early 1970s Congress amended the Omnibus Crime Control and Safe Streets Act of 1968 to require that criminal history record information held by state and local criminal justice agencies receiving federal support be kept confidential and be used only for law enforcement and other lawful purposes. Between 1974 and 1984 almost every state enacted legislation and operational policies designed to safeguard the privacy of criminal histories. These measures "have been critical to the establishment of standards for data quality, dissemination, security, access by record subjects, and audits of criminal history record information."[2] Former police discretion to release criminal history data to anyone claiming a "need to know" is now strictly limited on both security and personal privacy grounds.[3] Many states seal or purge records of unprosecuted arrests and prosecutions ending in acquittal. Some states also seal or purge records of first-time and misdemeanor offenders who complete specified treatment or supervisory programs, or who can demonstrate rehabilitation. Notwithstanding these developments, criminal history record information is becoming increasingly available outside the criminal justice system under open records or freedom of information statutes covering some types of criminal information: "special access rights are increasingly accorded to governmental agencies with security missions and licensing boards and some private employers screening applicants for sensitive positions, such as those involving public safety, supervision of children or custody of valuable property."[4] It is open to debate just how the "special access rights" of agencies and individuals outside the justice system undercut the privacy protection goals of recent access-limiting state and federal legislation.

While criminal records are subject to more official privacy safeguards today than they were a generation ago, the same is not true of civil or criminal court proceedings. The popular sentiment that "the public has a right to know" is also the law.[5] Hence court filings, hearings, and trials are usually open to media and the general public.

The sealing of transcripts and the closing of proceedings to accommodate special privacy needs has sometimes sparked controversy. For example, in October 1985 a mental patient newly released from King's County Hospital, where she had been diagnosed as a potentially dangerous person, pushed Catherine Costello off a New York City subway platform. Mary Ventura's arbitrary act of violence resulted in critical injuries for Costello. Commenting not at all on any interest Ventura may have had in the confidentiality of her medical problems, *The New York Times* argued on its editorial pages that the sealed transcripts of the hearing in which she had been adjudicated fit for release should be opened to the public: "New Yorkers need to know whether this tragedy could have been avoided, and if so, who was responsible."[6]

In criminal cases, judicial proceedings are usually open to the public even when the accused offender would prefer that they be closed. The notoriety of the New Bedford barroom attack in which four men raped a 21-year-old mother of two on a pool table stemmed in part from the live telecast of the trial. The Sixth Amendment constitutional guarantee that criminal defendants "shall enjoy the right to a speedy and public trial" derives from a traditional Anglo-American common law policy favoring public proceedings. This policy developed as a check on judicial power and as a deterrent to perjury by witnesses. The express wording of the Sixth Amendment right to public trial provision can be read as implying that defendants may waive their right to public trial.[7] Federal courts, however, give the amendment a different interpretation, holding that the right to public trial cannot be waived. They maintain that public trials are for the protection of the integrity of the justice system and the public as much as for the benefit of the criminal defendant.[8]

RAPE VICTIM PUBLICITY AND SELF-DISCLOSURE

For better or for worse, the parties in civil and criminal proceedings experience unwanted privacy losses; but they are not alone. Witnesses are subject to privacy losses as well. As previously noted, a policy assumption of open proceedings is that witnesses are less likely to perjure themselves if they are made to testify in a forum open to the community. In the prosecution of rape cases, where the alleged victim of crime often must testify for the prosecution or see her accused assailant go scot free, witness privacy has proven to be a major difficulty.

Rape victims are spared one round of publicity and its consequences where local print, broadcast, and other media are faithful to rape victim anonymity policies. These policies protect the feelings and sensibilities of sexually brutalized women by withholding their names when reporting the newsworthy crimes they have suffered. Victim anonymity policies have been criticized as "gallantry" premised on the false notion that a woman who has been raped has been disgraced.[9] They have also been criticized as playing into out-moded conceptions of women as creatures of special modesty. However, we do not have to assume that sexual brutality brings disgrace to its victims in order to support rape victim anonymity policies. Nor do we have to assume that female modesty should be accorded special protection.

We need only suppose that information non-disclosure gives rape victims a shield against media sensationalism and public abuse. Rape victims are sometimes viewed as unchaste or disgraced. Old attitudes die hard. Anonymity shields women from the social consequences of public identities as sexual victims. A further justification of rape victim anonymity policies is that rape is experienced as a grave indignity of a type that can be worsened by public knowledge. Other misfortunes innocent people suffer also can be worsened by publication. Losing a job may be such a misfortune. Rape is like other misfortunes, but is in some respects unique. Rape is an act of physical violence which by its very nature is an affront to privacy. It represents forcible exposure of aspects of oneself that are protected by conventions of limited access. These conventions are normally adhered to out of regard for well-being and respect for personal privacy. To publicize a rape victim's identity is, in effect, to augment her wrongful exposure through additional unwanted exposure.

Female victims of rape whose feelings and sensibilities are injured by publicity are not alone. Warren and Brandeis launched the right to privacy in American tort law on the theory that the "inviolate personality" of the reasonable person is assaulted by mass media publicity of family affairs and social gatherings.[10] Consider how much more the "inviolate personality" of a reasonable person is assaulted by mass media publicity of her own self as victim of a grave, inherently privacy-invading crime. It seems clear upon consideration that having one's feelings and sensibilities injured by publicity of this type has very little to do with peculiarly feminine modesty.

Victim anonymity will not normally interfere with the essential news and public service functions of the media. In typical cases, as long as the rape itself is publicized, along with information about the location and methods of the crime, the news needs of the general public are satisfied.[11] The public does not need to know the victim's identity to protect themselves and to help police apprehend suspects. Policies of victim anonymity may even work to encourage more women to be willing to report and help prosecute their rapes, for it reduces the personal price women pay for seeking prosecution.

A policy of victim anonymity is ineffective to the degree that it is not uniformly adhered to by all the media reporting a given rape. In July 1986, the city's first conjugal rape case was tried in Pittsburgh, Pennsylvania. A husband was convicted of raping his wife and teen-aged daughter. *The Pittsburgh Post-Gazette*, the city's general circulation morning paper, adhered to its policy of not printing the rape victims' names. The popular afternoon newspaper, *The Pittsburgh Free Press*, fully disclosed the victims' identities. In addition, throughout the trial, print and broadcast media identified the name and address of the accused offender in their news stories. This was tantamount to identification of the victims, since they shared a name and a previous home address with the accused. Conjugal rape and family rape thus present unique problems for rape victim anonymity, which the Pittsburgh case well illustrated.

American courts have held that media are not legally required to withhold rape victim identity. This is not only because laws requiring anonymity are deemed to clash with First Amendment freedom of press guarantees, but also because victim identity is (typically) a matter of public record, and because the occurrence of crime is newsworthy. In March 1975, the Supreme Court overturned a Georgia statute that forbade the publication of the names of victims of rape.[12] The family of 17-year-old rape and murder victim Cynthia Cohn brought suit for invasion of privacy in violation of the statute after Atlanta Station WSB-TV twice broadcast details of the crimes, illustrated by Cynthia's high school yearbook photograph. Following the broadcasts, members of the Cohn family were subjected to cruel and tasteless harassment for which they believed WSB-TV was liable. The station argued that it was not liable for invasion of privacy since Cynthia's name had been obtained by one of its reporters from indictments publicly available at the trial of the six youths prosecuted in connection with her rape and death. Justice Byron White, who wrote the Court's majority opinion, agreed. He maintained that "even the prevailing law of invasion of privacy recognizes that the interests in privacy fade when information involved already appears on the public record."[13] Lower-court cases in which female victims of crime have alleged invasion of privacy against the media have gone further, holding that the media enjoys a privilege in virtue of which they are immune from liability for invasion of privacy when they publicize matters of a private nature in which the public has a legitimate interest. A Florida court relied on this rationale in 1982 when it denied recovery for invasion of privacy to a woman who sued owners of a newspaper that published a photograph of her in the nude, clutching a dish towel in front of her body. The photograph accompanied a story relating that she had been rescued by police after her ex-husband kidnapped her at gun point, took her to their previous home, forced her to disrobe, and then fired a pistol.[14]

A rape victim spared privacy losses in the hands of the media may still face privacy losses as a complainant and witness in the courtroom. She may testify voluntarily out of a desire to cooperate with prosecutors for personal vindication, but she does so at a cost to her privacy. For example, she cannot demand that records of proceedings in which personal aspects of her past sex life are scrutinized be sealed to protect her privacy.[15] Twenty years ago it would not have been uncommon for a criminal defense attorney's inquiries to probe past sexual conduct of the victim with "at best a tenuous connection to the offense for which the defendant is being tried."[16] In support of the Privacy Protection for Rape Victims Act of 1978, now Rule 412 of the Federal Rules of Evidence,[17] it was argued in Congress that evidentiary rules should not permit defense lawyers "great latitude" in bringing out intimate details about a rape victim's life where the evidence serves "no real purpose and only results in embarrassment to the rape victim and unwarranted public intrusion into her private life."[18]

By virtue of Rule 412 and the similar evidentiary rules of forty-eight states, proof of unchastity is no longer automatically admissible.[19] At least four distinct approaches to providing privacy protection to rape complainants have been identified.[20] Under Rule 412, in criminal rape and sexual assault cases, reputation or opinion evidence about the "past sexual behavior" of the alleged victim is never admissible. Under Rule 412, evidence of the complainant's past sexual conduct may be admitted only to prove that the complainant consented to sexual intercourse, or that the accused was not the source of semen or injury. But, Rule 412 requires that prior to admitting evidence of past sexual behavior for these purposes, the attorney for the accused present a written offer of proof to the presiding judge. *In camera* the judge must determine whether the "evidence which the accused seeks to offer is relevant and . . . the probative value of the evidence outweighs the danger of unfair prejudice."[21] The federal approach of Rule 412 has been followed by five states: Connecticut, Hawaii, Iowa, New York, and Oregon.

What kinds of evidence has Rule 412 been used to exclude? In *Doe v. United States,* it was held to prohibit evidence of the complainant's general reputation on the army post where the accused resided, her alleged habit of calling out to soldiers in their barracks and meeting them at a post snack bar, and a former landlord's experiences with her putatively promiscuous behavior.[22] Deemed admissible in the same case was, on the other hand, evidence of telephone conversations between the victim and accused and evidence of the accused's state of mind in view of what he knew of the victim's reputation and what she had said to him in their phone conversations. In *United States v. Nez,* admission of evidence of the circumstances surrounding two prior unprosecuted rapes was denied a defendant who admitted having had sexual intercourse with the complainant.[23] In *United States v. One Feather,* Rule 412 was utilized to preclude inquiry into when and where the complainant, who testified that she was the divorced mother of an infant son, had been married.[24]

Rape victim shield laws, as Federal Rule 412 and similar state rules have been termed, "create a presumption that the sexual history of a rape victim will never be admissible, except when compelled by due process because of overwhelming probative value."[25] This shift of presumption may facilitate enforcement of the criminal law, because victims have less cause to dread testifying against the accused. Nevertheless, the shift of presumption has led to the criticism that:

> some rape victim shield laws violate the Sixth Amendment right to defend oneself. In an attempt to protect the sensibilities of rape victims, the defendant's right to present evidence to the jury is infringed. [T]he rights of defendants charged with rape are no less important or protected than the rights of defendants accused of other crimes. To the

extent that a defendant is categorically prevented from offering types of evidence that other criminal defendants may offer, his Sixth amendment rights are violated.[26]

The argument contained in this passage pits "mere" sensibilities against constitutional due process and the right to a fair trial. In the battle so conceived, there can be no doubt of the victor.

But the sensibilities of the rape victims constitute a more formidable foe than first appearances might suggest. Rape victim protections are sometimes criticized as protecting "mere sensibilities" in the form of outmoded conceptions of female modesty. Nonetheless, rape victim shield laws protect the legitimate gender-neutral sensibility that private life ought to be beyond arbitrary public scrutiny.[27] Protecting sensibilities is the basis of the modern legal rights of privacy enjoyed by both sexes. As noted earlier, the purpose of the common law right to privacy recognized in most states is to protect "inviolate personality" by guarding feelings and sensibilities.[28] The purposes of the constitutional right to privacy are less clear, having been subject to varying and inconsistent interpretations by the Supreme Court.[29] As applied in numerous cases, constitutional protection of privacy has focused on the right to the privacy of intimate relationships, interpreted as freedom from governmental interference and coercion. As a matter of principle, a right that affords women freedom from coercive birth control and abortion policies, which allows them to marry persons of their own choice and to rear children in accordance with their own values, would also seem to be a right that protects against nonconsensual extraction in court of intimacies of personal life that have no demonstrated bearing on the proceedings.

Enlarged by moral conceptions of privacy due to individuals, privacy rights surely bar harassment by defense counsel that subjects women's personal morals to a level and type of scrutiny calculated to discredit and demean them and to distort the truth. The sensibilities at stake for a rape victim are more than lost modesty. Her self-esteem, sense of dignity, and sense of self-worth are at stake. If her virtue is placed on trial in lieu of the accused's conduct, her sense that she and others like her are entitled to retribution through the criminal justice system may be irreparably shattered.

Notwithstanding women's privacy, an important question of fairness to the criminal defendant is involved. A basic principle of fairness and of due process as a fairness constraint is that like cases ought to be treated alike. Rape defendants ought to be treated like other criminal defendants to the extent that their alleged crime and the requirements of a procedurally fair trial are alike. Yet evidence of reputation poses a problem in rape and sexual assault trials that it does not pose elsewhere. Absent rape victim shield laws, rape and sexual assault defendants have a built-in advantage over the prosecution. They can exploit the special vulnerability of complainants that stems from the social meanings of rape. Women who are raped are commonly suspected of provocation and immoralities. Jury susceptibility to double standards and innuendos of female promiscuity tilt the outcomes of rape cases toward the defendants. More than other criminal defendants, the rape defendant can easily turn his or her own trial into a trial of the virtue and morality of the alleged victim. For this reason courts have rightly utilized rules like Rule 412 and the policies they represent to exclude prejudicial evidence of past sexual conduct and alleged lewd behavior.[30]

At least a dozen state courts have held that rape victim shield laws do not violate the accused's constitutional rights of due process or to a fair trial.[31] According to Harriett Galvin:

> rape-shield laws were meant to exclude irrelevant prejudicial evidence that does nothing but taint the fact-finding process. Because the defendant has no constitutional right to introduce irrelevant, prejudicial evidence, and because the policies underlying rape-shield legislation will be served by rejecting only the irrelevant and out-dated uses of sexual conduct evidence, the interests of both "sides" are symmetrical and need not be "balanced" in the institutional sense.[32]

Since no criminal defendant is entitled to introduce irrelevant evidence, there is no Sixth or Fourteenth Amendment constitutional argument against rape shield legislation.

It is important to avoid falling prey to the nineteenth-century notion that women are altogether unfit to serve as witnesses due to emotional and moral frailty. The rape victim shield is not a privilege of easy treatment; it is a ban on irrelevance. It is a device that corrects an imbalance in the adversary system that undercuts even frank, composed, unembarrassed testimony.

The prevasiveness of rape victim shield laws does not mean that social attitudes about women and sexuality are no longer a problem in the courtroom. Some American courts are still required to instruct the juries in rape and sexual assault cases to the effect that:

> You must keep in mind that a charge such as that made against the defendant in this case is one which, generally speaking, is easily made, and once made, difficult to disprove even where the defendant is innocent.

> From the nature of the case, the complaining witness and the defendant would usually be the only witnesses to the actual act or acts constituting the crime. Therefore, you are instructed that the law requires that you examine the testimony of the prosecuting witness with caution.

> If, after hearing all of the testimony, you determine that the testimony

of the prosecuting witness is unreliable, improbable, fairly impeached or discredited, all of which creates reasonable doubt in your mind as to the defendant's guilt, you must find the defendant not guilty.[33]

Mandatory cautionary jury instructions such as the above "have come under increasing attack."[34] Their potential for prejudice is great. Unfortunately, some jurors will earlier have been exposed to myths about the emotional and moral frailties of women. In particular, they will have heard the myth that provocation, seduction, or other victim fault is the frequent cause of rape. Jurors who try to keep an open mind in weighing the evidence could be swayed by a judge's cautionary fabrication instruction at the close of evidence. The instruction is susceptible of the interpretation that women who complain of rape automatically merit suspicion and distrust. It could be interpreted to assert that accused rapists are invariably at an unfair disadvantage because women can easily fabricate charges. Nevertheless, there is no evidence either that women are prone to fake rape or that it is easy for women to fake rape and endure the role of chief witness for the prosecution.

WOMEN ON THE WRONG SIDE OF THE LAW

Regardless of the position one takes on the evidentiary rights of the accused in rape cases, it is not difficult to feel compassion for the rape victim who is deprived of privacy at high cost when heinous acts and circumstances thrust her into the hands of the law. In contrast, it can be difficult indeed to muster compassion for women in the hands of the law who are themselves criminal wrongdoers. But as the remainder of this chapter is intended to make plain, the privacy and decisional privacy losses of women on the wrong side of the law also sometimes merit public concern. One such instance is when the state imposes privacy intrusions that eat way the foundations of self-respect and undermine the rehabilitative function of punishment. A second instance is when unjust prostitution laws result in police harassment, arrest, detention, and punishment that diminish privacy.

Behind Bars

Sex and social roles create unique privacy and privacy-related problems for women in the custody of police and correctional institutions.[35] Women convicted of crimes and serving sentences share some of the same privacy problems as women who have merely been arrested and women who are detained and awaiting trial.[36] Other privacy problems arise only because women have committed serious crimes and are serving lengthy sentences. That many arrestees and

detainees will never be found culpable of a crime heightens the sense
that they should not be lightly deprived of important forms of
privacy. In 1985 Samantha Hodges, a 16-year-old Brooklyn resident,
filed a $1.175 million law suit against the City of New York after she
was undressed and strip-searched by a male police officer in a jail cell
in contravention of policies and regulations. While awaiting a friend
at a pizzaria, Hodges had been arrested on a disorderly conduct
charge that was never explained and later dropped.[37]

A female inmate at Riker's Island was recently quoted in a popular
women's magazine. Her poignant complaint was about privacy:
"Three or four times a week the guards will strip you, expecting to
find drugs or razors. It eats up your privacy." The central question
raised by the recognition that incarcerated women have morally
legitimate privacy claims is this one: how much privacy do women in
jail or prison have a right to? The complexity of the question is
greatest when we include within the ambit of "privacy" not only
limitations on the accessibility of the person and personal information, but freedom from governmental interference in the zone of
privacy constituted by sexual intimacy, reproductive choice, and the
discharge of familial duties.

Three competing principles serve as general answers to the question of how much privacy is due incarcerated women. They are
implicit in what has been written for and against prison privacy
reform. The first, the "no privacy" principle, answers that incarcerated women are not entitled to any privacy or private life. The
second, the "no affirmative privacy deprivation" principle, answers
that incarcerated women are entitled to be free from deprivations of
privacy and interferences with private life not justified by goals of
punishment, protection, deterrence, and rehabilitation. The third,
the "privacy maximization" principle, answers that women in custody
are not only entitled to be free of unjustified deprivations and
interferences, but they are also entitled to privileges and facilities
needed to enhance privacy and extramural marital, familial, and
other interpersonal relationships.

The "No Privacy" Principle

Punishment, along with the protection of society, the deterrence of
crime, and the rehabilitation of offenders, is a major goal of criminal
incarceration. Incarceration is deemed punitive because it entails
severely limiting freedom of action and with it, freedom of association. Limitation of these freedoms is brought about by confinement
within cells and fenced compounds. It is also effected through surveillance, property searches, and bodily examinations designed to prevent escape, promote discipline, and ensure safety. It is generally

accepted in the United States that imprisonment is a morally legitimate—if not imperative—response to serious crime. It is also generally accepted that certain conditions, such as extreme overcrowding, can turn an otherwise morally acceptable jail or prison into an inhumane, unacceptable one.

Is deprivation of privacy one of the conditions that can make jail or prison conditions morally unacceptable? The "no privacy" principle answers that it is not. The "no privacy" principle has a degree of initial appeal. Deprivation of substantial amounts of privacy is inherent in the act of imprisonment and is thus justified by the same principles and considerations that justify incarceration itself. Additional initial appeal comes from the conception of moral forfeiture whereby wrongdoers forfeit all rights, including their right to privacy, when they breach the social contract by committing illegal acts. The view in the United States once was that inmates shed their privacy rights at the jailhouse door, but this is no longer the official view. The Supreme Court has held that prisoners "are not beyond the reach of the Constitution" and must be "accorded those rights not fundamentally inconsistent with imprisonment itself or incompatible with the objectives of incarceration."[38]

Thoroughgoing respect for individuals requires rejection of the "no privacy" principle. Just as it would be impermissibly degrading and cruel to deny a prisoner all freedom of movement and choice, it would similarly be degrading and cruel to deny an arrestee, detainee, or convict all expectations of privacy and private choice. Even though privacy deprivation is not commonly heralded as a punitive goal of punishment,[39] prisoners behind bars are likely to feel punished as much by needless loss of privacy and private choice as by their loss of freedom. This is borne out by prisoner lawsuits claiming that particular deprivations of privacy are "cruel and unusual" punishment within the meaning of the Eighth Amendment.[40] Brought under the Fourth Amendment's unlawful search and seizure strictures and under the due process clause of the Fifth Amendment, privacy deprivation claims have been successful to the extent courts have been willing to meaningfully depart from the traditional "no privacy" view.

In recent years, a wide array of actions taken by authorities have been criticized on moral grounds as constituting or implicating wrongful deprivations of privacy and private choice. These privacy-diminishing actions have included observation of bathing and toilet use, mail screening, forced feeding, behavioral modification, denial of state-funded abortion, unannounced cell searches, "double-bunking," body and personal property searches, dress and appearance codes, public executions, and denial of conjugal visitation.[41] A common ground of criticism is that punitive goals and administrative needs do not justify specific governmental privacy deprivation or interference with decisional privacy. It is also argued that privacy deprivations suffered by detainees held pending trial because they cannot afford bail or were adjudged poor bail risks are especially difficult to justify since they have not been found guilty of crimes meriting punishment.

The question of women's privacy in prisons has been raised chiefly in the context of two clusters of concern. With regard to both clusters, it is argued that if certain basic privacies are not respected, incarceration is morally degrading, unjust, and should be unlawful. Questions about the adequacy of women's privacy have been raised, first, in the context of concern for a degree of seclusion and bodily integrity. It is argued that respect for privacy requires that a woman behind bars have opportunities for solitude and be free from leering eyes, eavesdropping ears, probing hands, and harassment. The second context in which the question of the adequacy of women's privacy has been raised is in connection with whether prisoners are entitled to state-funded abortion, marital sex, and parenting. As in other contexts, women's interests in bodily integrity, self-determination, and freedom from governmental interference in reproductive and parental decision making have been advocated under a privacy rubric.

Should Prisons Maximize Privacy?

Respect for individuals and their privacy at minimum requires rejection of the "no privacy" principle. The alternative "no affirmative privacy deprivation" principle would require that, once a person is taken into custody, neither officials nor those under their supervision and control be permitted gratuitously to invade personal privacy or to usurp private choice.

Practical administrative and institutional rationales for diminishing privacy include the rationale that prisoner privacy threatens security. Unannounced cell searches and body searches may be the only effective means of achieving safety and discipline.[42] The right to privacy must yield to the right of fellow inmates, prison guards, and visitors to be safe from serious bodily harm that could result were weapons, drugs, or implements of escape to fall into the hands of prisoners. Another practical rationale for diminishing privacy is a limited public fisc. But if the concept of a moral right of privacy is the backbone of claims to greater privacy in prison, then practical and economic arguments against privacy and privacy-related privileges and amenities are less strong than they first seem. On the influential conception advanced by Ronald Dworkin, moral and constitutional rights override considerations of utility.[43] Rather than force dehumanizing deprivations of privacy on prisoners, the state must incur costs necessary to bring conditions of life behind bars into line with fundamental rights.

Accomplishing incarceration itself, protecting the safety of inmates and personnel, and coping with limited institutional financial resources are potentially legitimate reasons for diminishing privacy. Reasons for diminishing personal privacy can include paternalistic protection of the inmate herself. Paternalism denotes interference with the conduct of another with their best interest in mind.[44] Rights-based liberalism countermands paternalistic interferences with freedom except in cases of mental or physical incapacity. Paternalistic deprivation of privacy that will prevent a distraught prisoner from committing suicide, for instance, would typically be justified.

One form of privacy deprivation that would obviously be countermanded by the "no affirmative privacy deprivation" principle is privacy-invading sexual harassment of female prisoners by male guards. Sexual harassment that invades privacy is apparently a significant problem facing women in prisons staffed by male guards:

> Sexual harassment [defined as any unwanted sexual attention a woman experiences . . . ranging from leering, pinching, patting, verbal comments, and subtle pressure for sexual activity, to attempted rape and rape] of female inmates by male guards permeates American prisons because the imbalance of power between the guard and the prisoner allows and encourages it to exist. . . . Women are forced to endure invasions of their bodily privacy ranging from being viewed in the nude to being forced to submit to body cavity searches in the presence of, and in emergencies by, male guards. At times they engage in "voluntary" relations with the guards—bartering sex for psychological and physical freedom. If a staff member requests sexual favors, it may be perceived by the inmate as a demand. Thus, even so-called "voluntary" sexual activity must be viewed as coercive. Women prisoners are also victims of sexual abuse and rape.[45]

Privacy-invading sexual harassment would have to be eliminated under the "no affirmative privacy deprivation" principle. This does not entail that only women should serve as guards in women's prisons. Equal employment opportunity arguments oppose basing qualifications for prison guard jobs on the sex of the applicant. Yet, if prison security is impossible without direct surveillance of prisoners bathing and performing other personal tasks, there is a privacy argument to be made that sex is a bona fide job qualification. Likewise there is an equal employment argument that prisons ought to be redesigned so that sex will not remain a bona fide job requirement.

The "no affirmative privacy deprivation" principle does not require that incarcerated women be accorded abortions at governmental expense, intramural infant care facilities, extended access to their children, or conjugal visitation during which sexual intercourse is permitted. The "privacy maximization" principle would imply that some or all of these positive entitlements should be available to incarcerated women.

In what has been written urging reform in the treatment of women's privacy behind bars, there is a discernible tension between the "no affirmative privacy deprivation" principle and the "privacy maximization" principle. The "privacy maximization" principle requires that prison life and facilities be designed, to the extent possible, to promote prisoner privacy and to preserve the sexual and familial bonds of private life. Adoption of this principle would indicate a belief that while the goals of incarceration require serious diminution of freedom, it is inhumane to deny prisoners access to private ties constitutive of their identities and closely linked to personal satisfaction and self-respect. Like the "no unjustified privacy deprivation" principle, the "privacy maximization" principle opposes arbitrary diminution of privacy where the goals of incarceration could be accomplished at a lesser privacy cost. But it requires more than bare non-interference with privacy and privacy-related liberties; it requires that jails and prisons go a step further. For example, they must seek to determine and accommodate the interests of incarcerated women in mothering their children and sustaining their marriages. The privacy maximization concept may be a utopian ideal in view of limited public resources for prisons. Nonetheless, if retention of family ties and self-determination are fundamental rights, it may be that incarceration on terms approximating the "privacy maximization" principle is the only morally acceptable form of incarceration.

Conjugal visitation has been permitted in a few American prisons in Mississippi and California.[46] Although denial of visitation during which prison inmates and spouses meet privately and have sexual relations may serve the goals of retribution, deterrence, and protection, it may frustrate the goal of rehabilitation:

> The deprivation of heterosexual conduct has been shown to have psychologically destructive effects on the inmate and his marriage. Conjugal visits would mitigate these negative effects and thereby facilitate rehabilitation.
>
> ... If rehabilitation remains the favored goal, as it now seems to be, the benefits of conjugal visiting should tip the scale in the prisoner's favor.
>
> ... [T]he implementation of a conjugal visitation program makes sense because the rehabilitative benefits of such a program can be gained at

little expense to the goals of retribution and deterrence. Prisons will remain unpleasant places even if conjugal visiting is allowed several times a month.[47]

It has been suggested that prisoners have a right to conjugal visitation because they are entitled to rehabilitative treatment, and also because the right to marital privacy requires it. According to the latter argument, wrong-doing by one spouse does not mean the non-imprisoned spouse should suffer a loss of sexual companionship. Thus, the argument goes, the state must do what it can to create the conditions within which married prisoners may meet on an intimate basis with their spouses.

Analogous "family privacy" arguments claim that women behind bars should be able to visit with their children and, in the case of infants, keep their children within the prison for nurture and bonding. Children, it is urged, need families and access to parents. Mutual access of mother and child is rightly denied only where long-term imprisonment entails permanent loss of legal child custody, where a mother has a history of child abuse or neglect, or where a mother has been convicted of a violent crime under circumstances that do not rule out a likelihood of recidivism.

Assessing these arguments is difficult indeed. A great deal more is at stake in prison policy than privacy and private choice. Adoption of the "privacy maximization" principle can be grounded on arguments that are prisoner-centered, prisoner spouse-centered, prisoner child-centered, institution-centered, or society-centered. The argument that separation of a prisoner from the intimacies of marriage and family life is inhumane deprivation of private life is prisoner-centered. Unless one believes that incarceration ought to be as harsh and disruptive as possible, prisoner-centered arguments for the "privacy maximization" principle cannot be dismissed out of hand. Adoption of the "privacy maximization" principle could be motivated wholly by the spouse- or child-centered argument that the rights and needs of the spouse and children of the incarcerated require intimate access. "Privacy maximization" could be grounded on institution- or society-centered arguments, for example, that there would be less problematic homosexuality and sexual assault if marital and familial ties were not forcibly severed, and that society's rehabilitative and economic ends would be promoted if incarcerated prisoners could preserve close familial ties that would serve as a basis of motivation and support after release or parole.

The close ties between opportunities for personal privacy and values of personhood, social participation, and contribution emphasized in earlier chapters argue in favor of selecting the "privacy maximization" principle over the "no affirmative privacy deprivation" principle. This would entail prison conditions designed to allow for the highest degree of respect for individual seclusion, anonymity, and information non-disclosure, as well as decisional privacy respecting abortion and childbirth. Whether this ought to mean public abortion funding for poor women behind bars is a question of some interest. Does having custody of a poor woman whose decisional privacy and bodily integrity it must respect mean a state must pay for any otherwise lawful abortion she might elect to have? I am prepared to argue that it does, since her access to many private sources of money are cut off in virtue of incarceration.

For advocates of traditional marriage and family life the value of families and marriage rather than the value of privacy and decisional privacy as such may provide the strongest arguments for conjugal visitation and prisoner parenting privileges. The concepts of a right of family privacy and marital privacy link the value of marriage and families to the value of privacy and decisional privacy. The family privacy and marital privacy concepts embody the belief that families and marriages have special importance relative to basic human needs that warrant a hands-off policy by government. Consistent family and marital privacy policies would seem to require that states be guided by the "privacy maximization" principle. It requires efforts to preserve marital and family ties, signaling a deep commitment to their continued existence across the broadest spectrum of society. The weaker "no affirmative deprivation" principle can be interpreted as sanctioning official indifference to the implications of incarceration for private life.

PUBLIC WOMEN

Prostitution is the commercial exchange of sexual stimulation for pay. As used here, "prostitution" could describe the work not only of the impoverished street-walker and stylish escort or call-girl, but also of the exotic dancer, stripper, peep-show or sex-show performer, sex-shop masseuse, and pornographic film actress. The purpose of opting for a conception of prostitution broad enough to embrace all these sex-related fields is not to extend lines of opprobrium. It is rather to highlight what women in these fields have in common: they earn their living by sexually stimulating others.

Although the lives of many prostitutes do not in fact fit the pattern, it is widely believed that prostitution necessarily removes women from the private roles of wife, mother, and homemaker. Some of the women earning a living as prostitutes spend many of their working hours soliciting alongside public thoroughfares, and in bars, hotel lobbies, and other places open to the public. Sexual contact may take place virtually in public places, such as in the marginal seclusion of an automobile. Women in prostitution are thus, in a sense, public women. They are "set forth in public" and "exposed for sale" in keeping with the etymological origins of the stigmatizing label of "prostitute."

But it is a mistake to associate women in prostitution too closely with the public realm. Their sexual services fix them firmly within the privacy and private lives of individual clients who may demand anonymity, confidentiality, and seclusion. Moreover, the bedrooms, hotel rooms, sex shops and other closed quarters in which they often perform their services are private places protected by laws and conventions that limit unwanted access.

Anti-prostitution Laws

The conception of women who prostitute as belonging to the public realm is reinforced by laws that make their conduct a matter of public regulation and proscription. Historians report that curious restrictions have been imposed on women in prostitution from antiquity to modern times. Prostitutes have been required by law to live in the care of church officials in special houses away from the center of town; they have been required to wear cloaks of a specified color to assure that they not be mistaken for *good* women.[48]

Today prostitution is criminalized, restricted, or regulated by state statute in all of the United States.[49] Even in Nevada, where many forms of prostitution are not crimes under state law in the absence of prohibitive local ordinances, women in prostitution are subject to health and licensing requirements from which other sexually active women are exempt.[50] Legal obstacles to prostitution take at least five generic forms: (a) status laws, (b) illicit or commercial sex act laws, (c) commercial sex promotion laws, (d) public conduct laws, and (e) regulatory and zoning requirements.

Status laws provide that it is a crime simply to be or live the life of a prostitute; or to be a street-walker, dissolute person, or vagrant, where these are defined to include prostitutes.[51] Illicit or commercial sex act laws require actual sexual contact or sexual intercourse to trigger criminal penalties. Illicit sex laws expressly criminalize prostitution, illicit sex, fornication, lewdness, or adultery.[52] Commercial sex laws expressly criminalize engaging in sex or indiscriminate or illicit sex for money, a fee, for hire, or as a business.[53] Commercial sex promotion laws criminalize pimping,[54] pandering,[55] or occupying or operating a house of ill fame or for prostitution.[56] Public conduct laws proscribe engaging in prostitution-related negotiation and solicitation. Hence loitering, camping, or traveling for the purpose of prostitution;[57] beckoning, stopping, or interfering with motor vehicles for the purpose of prostitution;[58] and soliciting or acquiescing to solicitation of sex for pay in public have all been subject to criminal prohibition.[59] Finally, statutes may require prostitutes and brothels to comply with health, licensing, advertising, and zoning regulations.[60]

One argument against legal prohibition of commercial sex and the collateral activities that make commercial sex possible starts from this premise. Prostitution is merely a business, no more harmful than many socially sanctioned and legally permitted businesses. Prostitution, the argument continues, should be seen as just another service industry. Anti-prostitution laws are an unreasonable limitation on economic rights.

No economic right to engage in prostitution is currently recognized in the United States. It could be supposed that the privacy of the home would shield commercial sex at home from criminal prosecution. A Hawaii court has held otherwise.[61] Public policies prohibiting commercial activity in the home are not unique to the commercial sex context. New England's home knitting industry has been prohibited under federal law.[62] While a lucrative source of income for women workers who prefer to work at home, home knitting has been opposed as an exploitative use of female labor.

One might also suppose that an economic right to prostitute follows from women's owning their own bodies and being thus entitled in a market society to profit therefrom. The troublesome starting point of this argument is its assumption that the relationship of women to their bodies is one of ownership. Women are their bodies, they do not own them. Moreover, even if women did own their bodies it would not follow that commercial activities that were immoral and unavoidably harmful should be deemed lawful. Few commercial ventures have been criticized as being as socially harmful and deeply immoral as prostitution. Were Judge Surkow's rationale in the New Jersey Baby "M" case followed, surrogate mothering contracts would be upheld, not because women own their bodies and have a right to commercially profit from their use, but because the contracts fall short of slavery and baby selling, and because the constitutional right of privacy implies permission to bind oneself to contracts to create families in novel ways.

Prostitution as an economic right has received less attention than prostitution as an economic necessity. Earlier in this century a New Yorker called Rose Haggerty earned four cents per dozen hemming shirts. She turned to prostitution to keep her children and family together.[63] A common argument against anti-prostitution laws today is that prostitution is the only way many poor women can earn a living wage to care for themselves and their families: "Women turn to

prostitution because we have no pay for our work at home, low pay
for outside work, and if we're on welfare, we and our children can
barely survive. Prostitution is welfare the state doesn't pay."[64] Defending the rights of women in prostitution in a like vein, U.S. Prostitute's
Collective spokeswoman Margaret Prescod asserted that prostitution
"is not about sex, its about money."[65] It is argued that ending wage
discrimination and enacting "comparable worth" laws would alleviate
the economic need for prostitution and make it less attractive as an
occupation.

A third argument against many of today's prostitution laws is that
they are unfair. It is alleged that their enforcement is sporadic and
arbitrary. Prostitutes are arrested through entrapment, which permits police officers to enjoy sex with targeted women with impunity. It
is alleged that antiprostitution laws are enforced against poor street-
walkers, while affluent, sophisticated call-girls and barroom prostitutes are left alone. The fact that the customers of prostitutes do not
normally suffer the same legal sanctions as prostitutes themselves is
unfair. It is further alleged that prostitutes are unfairly distinguished
from dependent wives and girlfriends. Prostitutes do on a non-
monogamous basis only what other women do: they trade sex for
economic support.

A fourth, often-cited argument against anti-prostitution laws is that
their enforcement is impracticable. Social scientists have argued that
enforcement has been obstructed because the biological and social
factors that sustain the practice have not been eliminated. Sex is not
freely available due to conventions of monogamy and chastity. Men
are more promiscuous than women. Women are socially and economically discriminated against. Men make prostitution illegal, but nonetheless patronize prostitutes.

Which brings us to a fifth argument against anti-prostitution laws:
they are hypocritical because society in fact condones prostitution. It
is difficult to read a history of prostitution, whatever its moral
posture, without concluding that for all the tarring, dunking, tortur-
ing, imprisonment, and humiliation of prostitutes, Western society
has in fact condoned prostitution.[66]

Some of the above grounds for opposing anti-prostitution laws
have been presented by legal scholars and in constitutional court cases
alongside distinctly constitutional arguments against anti-prostitution
laws.[67] Status laws have been attacked with limited success in court on
the ground that they are unconstitutionally vague and violate the due
process clause of the Fourteenth Amendment. Attacks on public
conduct laws on the ground that they violate First Amendment free
speech guarantees have had limited success.[68] Regulatory requirements have been attacked on Fourteenth Amendment equal protec-

tion grounds. Sex act and commercial sex prohibition laws have been constitutionally challenged on equal protection grounds, but also on the theory that punishments meted out for prostitution are "cruel and unusual"—disproportionate—given the victimless nature of the crime. Key for our purposes, all categories of anti-prostitution laws have been attacked on grounds that constitutional privacy is violated.[69] These attacks have met with negligible success. Notwithstanding the lack of courtroom success for legal privacy arguments, is there a moral privacy case to be made against anti-prostitution laws? Numerous state and federal courts have denied that the constitutional privacy right recognized in landmark contraception, abortion, and sexual privacy cases starting with *Griswold* applies to commercial sex.

The Privacy Case for Prostitution

In one sense of the term, not much of a privacy case can be made for prostitution. An individual with a keen taste for personal privacy would be very unhappy indeed working as a street-walker or in a sex shop where continual exposure to others, sexual harassment, and risk of arrest and public court appearances were the order of business. It is doubtful that a privacy loving woman with a choice would choose most forms of prostitution. Nor could one who highly valued privacy and understood its importance relative to morally significant ends recommend it to another about whom one cared.

From the point of view of political morality, however, there is a decisional privacy case to be made for repealing laws that punish and prohibitively regulate prostitution-related offenses. Whether to engage in prostitution or not ought to be a matter of private choice. This conclusion follows from the sexual privacy principle that freely consenting adults have a moral right to engage in sexual conduct in private without governmental interference. The principle gives primacy to the self-regarding preferences of competent adults. Since enforcement of prohibitive sex laws entails losses of physical privacy to enforcement officials, the sexual privacy principle protects nondecisional forms of privacy as well. The sexual privacy principle is implicit in American law as a limitation on state interference with heterosexual adult couples who have sex in the seclusion of their own homes, but the principle has not been fully realized in American law. We are still a country in which a married couple can be prosecuted for oral sex in their own bedroom, and a homosexual can be charged with consensual sodomy in his own home.[70] This is because courts sometimes construe the right to sexual privacy as a right to traditional nuclear family life.

One objection to subsuming prostitution under the sexual privacy principle asserts that its commercial character takes it out of the realm of private morality and places it in the realm of commerce. Yet, there is no non-question-begging argument for locating prostitution so wholly within the realm of commerce that concerns for privacy and private choice for prostitutes and their customers lose their moral pull. Fundamental liberties of free speech are thought to constrain state regulation and control of the pornography industry. By analogy, privacy and privacy-related liberties are reasonably deemed to constrain regulation and control of the prostitution industry.

From the point of view of a prostitute's customer, prostitution is the functional equivalent of noncommercial recreational sex between consenting adults. This observation adds weight to the argument that the moral privacy rights implicated by the one are implicated by the other. From the point of view of the prostitute herself, prostitution is work. It is quite distinct from both loving intimacy and noncommercial recreational sex. But it is work that essentially involves her body, the seat of her identity. She is wrongly saddled with governmental interference of a sort that implies she is unworthy of bodily integrity and selective disclosure because she demands payment for sex. For these reasons, I conclude that most prohibitive prostitution laws do not pass moral muster. Tax laws and labor protections ought to apply to prostitution income, since they represent no unwarranted special privacy burden. Certain health regulations designed to prevent the spread of communicable disease might also be in order, but discrimination is always a risk. Nevada's law requiring physicians and others to report the venereal disease of any "common prostitute" but not others who are infected smacks of unjust discrimination.[71] Unannounced health inspection would represent unwarranted special burdens. Whereas public health concerns argue in favor of unannounced inspections of meat packing plants, the personal privacy interests of prostitutes and their customers argue against unannounced inspections of brothels where sex acts may be taking place.

A second objection to subsuming prostitution under the sexual privacy principle is that it is either a grave cause of social ills, inherently immoral, or both. The idea behind this two-pronged objection is that, while the sexual privacy principle is generally sound, prostitution is an exception to the sexual principle. Many generally tolerant individuals who reject the view, eloquently argued by Patrick Devlin,[72] that prostitution should be stamped out as an offense to public standards of morality, see the "social ills" argument as having genuine moral force. Recent work by activists, social scientists, and lawyers has made it abundantly clear that women in prostitution are due fairer treatment. In many cases, they are due greater sympathy and respect than they have been historically accorded in the United States. Yet, the liberalization of sexual mores in the 1960s and 1970s apparently did little to alter the widely held belief that prostitution, "the women's crime," is also immoral.

Liberals and libertarians sometimes describe prostitution as a "victimless" crime. Nevertheless, prostitution is cited as a causal factor in crimes and social ills that do have victims. Prostitution is widely thought to encourage illegal conduct, such as assault, battery, theft, violation of obscenity laws, and drug trafficking.[73] It is thought to support organized crime. It is thought to encourage the kidnap and exploitation of children and teen-age runaways, to lead to violence against women, and to perpetuate women's social inequality. Prostitution is thought to be a significant factor in the spread of sexually transmitted diseases.

The link between prostitution and some of the above social evils is uncertain and poorly understood. Consider the relationship of prostitution and drugs. The link between prostitution and drug use was critically examined in a 1979 study conducted by Paul Goldstein in which he examined the role of drug use in becoming a prostitute and patterns of drug use among different classes of prostitutes. The study concluded that only a few of the subjects who were not prostitutes but who were addicted to heroine turned to prostitution to finance their drug habit. Second, for many prostitution milieus, such as massage parlors, brothels, and call-girl circuits, drug use was a deterrent to entry since addicted women were considered unreliable, criminal, and unattractive to customers. Goldstein discovered that the presence of illegal drugs in establishments devoted to prostitution was believed to increase the likelihood of arrests and of convictions in the case of police raids. He found that pimps did not welcome heroine-addicted street-walkers, whom they believed to be less profitable because they were careless about their appearance and more likely to become police informants. One of Goldstein's most interesting conclusions was that:

> many of the specific relationships between drug use and prostitution [are] not unique to the occupation of prostitution. [M]any of the explanations that physicians give for their drug use are remarkable [sic] similar to those given by prostitutes, for example overwork, poor self-concept, the euphoric or depressing effect of the drug, insomnia, guilt, despair, monotony and pressure.[74]

The relationship between prostitution and the incidence of sexually transmitted diseases is tenuous and speculative. Prostitutes who spoke on a panel at the 15th Annual Conference on Women and the Law in Los Angeles in 1984 insisted that they had never had a sexually transmitted disease and that their standards of sexual hygiene were especially high because of the nature of their work. The incidence of venereal disease among high school students reportedly exceeds its incidence among street-walkers. Recently, concern has turned to the role of prostitution in transmitting acquired immune deficiency syndrome, commonly known as AIDS. The link between the spread of AIDS and prostitution is still unclear. Anti-prostitution laws, which have failed to eliminate prostitution, could not be expected to check the spread of the deadly AIDS virus. The availability of low-cost confidential health examinations and public education about "safe sex" are promising methods of curbing the spread of AIDS by prostitutes and their customers.

The view that prostitution is a social evil because it perpetuates female inequality is empirically based, but not subject to straightforward corroboration. This may explain why feminists are divided over the prostitution question. Some feminists insist that prostitution is a symptom and perpetuation of male domination, and that it is imperative to take effective steps to eliminate it. Women's role in promoting prostitution is recognized as part of what must be eliminated. In 1986 two New York women were convicted of bringing 50 Taiwanese women into the United States to work in a family brothel enterprise operating in four states. Other feminists insist that prostitution is an acceptable economic option for women and demand that opponents "call off their old tired ethics."[75]

Moral arguments against prostitution not based on causal ties to social ills are most difficult to assess. Judeo-Christian religious morality opposes prostitution because it is fornication or adultery. It is inconsistent with Holy Scriptures, institutional traditions, and conceptions of female duty and chastity. From secular ethical viewpoints, prostitution is a degenerate, even unnatural form of sexuality. It degrades human dignity and demeans those who participate in it. An important moral argument advanced by some feminists is that prostitutes are used by men in total disregard for their status as equal persons deserving respect and concern.[76] That prostitutes are paid for their labors does not, on this argument, erase the fact that they are being exploited. Prostitutes who believe they are acting autonomously and are in control of their lives are merely active, willing participants in their own degradation.

What does it mean to degrade a person, to use her? On Immanuel Kant's influential account it would mean to treat her solely as a means and not as an end in herself. It would mean to treat her as a thing, an object for one's own purposes and ends. It could be argued that sex for pay is inherently degrading. I prefer to think that whether prostitution is degradation in this sense depends ultimately on precisely what it is that prostitutes and their customers do, and with what attitudes they do what they do. Graphic accounts of experiences with prostitutes suggest that those who participate in prostitution as vendor and customer engage in activities that can be described only as mutual degradation.[77] On the other hand, women in prostitution, like Sydney Biddle Barrows, the "Mayflower Madam," sometimes depict the business as mutually beneficial and consistent with personal integrity.[78]

It is by no means clear where commonly made moral objections leave the case for repealing anti-prostitution laws. Should prostitution be an exception to the sexual privacy principle? The "social ills" argument is only as persuasive as the empirical evidence that prohibiting prostitution is the only practicable means for eliminating public problems linked to it. The arguments based on the precepts of particular religions can have very limited force if what we are considering is constraints a liberal society may justly impose through its laws. If prostitution is something women do not freely choose but have had thrust upon them by conditions of sexual and economic inequality, arguments that prostitution is demeaning and perpetuates sexual inequality have considerable force within a liberal framework. Arguments of this type potentially undercut the case for shielding prostitution under the sexual privacy principle.

But what if some men and women do freely choose mutually morally degrading, commercial sex? And what if it has no relevant connection with social ills such as drugs, disease, and crime? Should the government act paternalistically, through its laws and law enforcement policies, to spare individuals the degradation they choose?

John Stuart Mill's liberal conception of when state paternalism is impermissible has been influential. Paternalistic intervention is not permissible where adults of sound mind and ordinary intelligence act against their best interest but do not seriously injure others or themselves. According to Mill, the "strongest of all arguments" against the interference of the public is a utilitarian one: when the public interferes with purely personal conduct the odds are that it interferes wrongly and in the wrong place.[79] Mill may not have identified the strongest argument one might make for his maxim "that the individual is not accountable to society for his actions in so far as these concern the interests of no person but himself." But there is cause for skepticism about the value of public interference with self-regarding conduct.

Should government act to impose conventional morality on prostitutes and their customers? Ronald Dworkin has defended a contractarian principle, considered in Chapter 4 in connection with abortion choice, that a government which accords each individual equal respect may not impose sacrifice and constraints in virtue of an argument that a citizen could not accept without abandoning his sense of equal worth. Professional prostitutes and their customers will not share the perception that they morally degrade themselves any more than the participants in noncommercial consensual adult recreational sex. Hence, they could not accept a moral degradation argument for prohibiting prostitution without abandoning their sense of equal worth. From their point of view anti-prostitution laws treat them unfairly and discriminatorily. This is an argument that sex for pay is protected from outright prohibition and prohibitive regulation.

Prostitution and the Good Life

Women in prostitution and their advocates sometimes defend prostitution as an acceptable vocation, consistent with self-esteem, and undeserving of moral criticism. To be sure, women in prostitution have not deserved the hypocritical moral criticism to which they have been subject. Let us assume *arguendo* that prostitution merits no moral criticism, hypocritical or otherwise. Would it follow that prostitution is a good vocation, just as worthy from every point of view as being, for example, a nurse, school teacher, accountant, or auto mechanic?

I think not. A good vocation is one that provides income, but also contributes something of more than fleeting value. Prostitution's contribution to participants and society has uncertain and possibly negligible value. Female prostitution may function to provide a sexual outlet for men who cannot attract mates, family men for whom marriage is temporarily or permanently sexless, and men whose sexual frustrations might lead to anti-social conduct. Nevertheless, by spending their days sexually stimulating others (and perhaps themselves), women in prostitution forego participation in vocational experiences of indubitably greater and longer-lasting value.

American women can aspire to more than a minimally acceptable vocation. Even if making prostitution one's life work were acceptable, sex between strangers simply is not important enough to warrant choosing it. And while prostitution may be consistent with self-esteem, self-esteem is a matter of degree. I suspect the self-esteem of street-walkers is lower than that of women who earn a living in many other careers. As educational and job opportunities for women of all races improve, prostitution becomes a poorer and poorer solution to women's economic difficulties.

In summation, the problem with female prostitution is that it is a waste of women's talents and resources. It is not something women who have a choice about the matter ought to choose for themselves. In an early film by director Woody Allen, homes were equipped with a mechanical pleasure closet called the "orgasmatron." In Allen's world of the future, sexual satisfaction could be obtained by walking into the orgasmatron and closing its door. There are no orgasmatrons in the real world, but there are prostitutes. At best, a life lived as a prostitute is a life lived in an orgasmatron. At worst, it is a life lived *as* an orgasmatron. Clients come, then clients go. To put it this way is not to condemn the women who have turned to prostitution in desperation to earn a living wage, feed children, and keep families together. It is rather to press upon those who defend prostitution, as a legitimate, wrongly criminalized vocational choice for themselves and others, a certain stark conception of the essential character of their selection. It is not a selection of the good life.

Conclusion

I N THE PREVIOUS CHAPTER and throughout this book I have touched upon a number of distinct contexts in which women's desires for privacy can be thwarted. Privacy, in its paradigmatic sense, is restricted access. Restricted access in the senses of seclusion, solitude, and anonymity is the desire of women trapped at home with children, women about to give birth in a room filled with technicians, women who crave intimacy, women harassed by intruders in the streets, women sexually hounded at work, and women strip-searched in prisons. Restricted access in the sense of confidentiality, secrecy and reserve is the desire of women who reveal themselves in diaries, women who are victims of rape, women who want control over information about their reproductive choices, and women who seek to avoid prejudicial disclosures about marriage and sexuality in the employment setting.

Privacy is also decisional privacy. Privacy in this sense is really an aspect of liberty: freedom from coercive interference. Decisional privacy is the desire of women who want to be free to obtain contraception and medically safe abortions. It is the desire of women who want to decide who will be present when they give birth, and who want to choose how to care for their handicapped newborns and how to raise their children. It is also the desire of women who want to be left alone in their choice to enjoy casual sex or exchange sex for pay.

The central normative message of this book has been that women in the United States must have significant opportunities for individual forms of personal privacy and private choice. These opportunities enhance traits associated with moral personhood. They make women more able to contribute up to the level of their capacities and participate as equals. To the extent that American women have a privacy problem, it is not simply the problem of acquiring the privacy

180

and decisional privacy they do not have; it is also the problem of getting rid of unwanted forms of privacy. The privacy entailed by outmoded conceptions of female modesty and chastity is just one example. Another example is confinement in nuclear family homes as traditional caretakers. A third example is lonely lives without intimate affiliation and personal commitment to others.

The relationship of women to privacy is a paradoxical, uneasy one. Women have forms of privacy they do not want. This leads to the rejection of privacy. Yet, there are forms of privacy women want and need very much. So, women are led to embrace privacy once again. But as this book has shown, the paradox is really no paradox at all, for the privacy given up is not the privacy sought.

How can policy-makers and individual actors be more responsive to women's special privacy problem of possessing too much of the wrong kinds of privacy? We can start by seeking to understand the legal, economic, and social bases of meaningful privacy and private choice. At the same time, conditions by virtue of which women face so much unwanted, pernicious privacy must be eliminated. Finally, the internal uneasiness many women experience with increased privacy and independent decisionmaking must be dispelled. The required changes cannot be expected to come about all at once. Fortunately, some of the most important changes have already occurred. Greater opportunities for privacy were opened up for women when they won basic reproductive liberty in the courtroom. Many women have been able to take advantage of their decisional privacy rights to abrogate motherhood or control family size, thereby creating private time and conditions of privacy at home. In addition, the women's movement, federal civil rights laws, the sexual revolution, and pervasive participation by women in government, business, and the arts have each helped to create new norms of female conduct. Women are no longer expected to make heterosexual chastity and modesty their special virtues. Women's privacy has already acquired new and better meanings.

Notes

CHAPTER 1

1. Cf. Stanley I. Benn, "Privacy, Freedom and Respect for Persons," in *Privacy: Nomos XIII*, ed. J. Roland Pennock and John W. Chapman (Atherton Press, 1971), p. 1.
2. John Rawls, *Theory of Justice* (Harvard Univ. Press, 1971), p. 62.
3. Ibid.
4. David A. J. Richards, *Toleration and the Constitution* (Oxford Univ. Press, 1986), p. 245.
5. Ibid.
6. In particular, see Jeffrey Reiman, "Privacy, Intimacy, and Personhood," *Philosophy and Public Affairs* 6 (1976): 26. Reiman's account of the value of privacy will be discussed in Chapter 2. Both Benn ("Privacy, Freedom and Respect") and Reiman ultimately ground respect for privacy in the notion of respect for persons. For a criticism of Benn's effort, see Stephen D. Hudson and Douglas N. Husak, "Benn on Privacy and Respect of Persons," *Australasian Journal of Philosophy* 57 (1979): 324–29. They argue that respect for persons is not the moral imperative behind respect for privacy; governments deny citizens some of the privacy they want precisely because they are persons. Benn has an obvious reply. Moral respect for persons requires more than treating me in some way that acknowledges my personhood. It requires treating me as a moral end rather than as an instrument of state objectives. Treating me as a moral end arguably requires that I be allowed to have the privacy I want unless my having it would directly harm others or unless I have consented to give it up. For a general analysis of the concept of respect and respect for persons as a fundamental ethical principle, see Stephen D. Hudson, "The Nature of Respect," *Social Theory and Practice* 6 (1980): 69–90. For a survey and analysis of philosophical uses of the concept of personhood, see Jenny Teichman, "The Definition of *Person*," *Philosophy* 60 (1985): 175–86.
7. See Alan F. Westin, *Privacy and Freedom* (Atheneum, 1967); Edward J. Bloustein, *Individual and Group Privacy* (Transaction Books, 1979); Ruth Gavison, "Privacy and the Limits of Law," *Yale Law Journal* 89 (1980): 421; and Boone C. Keith, "Privacy and Community," *Social Theory and Practice* 9 (1983): 1–30.

8. See Michael A. Weinstein, "The Use of Privacy in the Good Life," in *Privacy: Nomos XIII*, ed. J. Roland Pennock and John W. Chapman (Atherton Press: 1971), p. 88.

9. Analytical surveys of attempts by philosophers and legal scholars to define "privacy" include Gavison, "Privacy and the Limits of the Law"; Barbara Baum Levenbook, "Privacy," *American Philosophical Association Newsletter on Philosophy and Law* 14 (1982): 2; David M. O'Brien, *Privacy, Law and Public Policy* (Praeger, 1979); W. A. Parent, "Recent Work on the Conception of Privacy," *American Philosophical Quarterly* 20 (1983): 341 (hereinafter "Parent I"); Ferdinand Schoeman, "Privacy: Philosophical Dimensions," *American Philosophical Quarterly* 21 (1984): 199.

10. See R. Dixon, "The *Griswold* Penumbra: Constitutional Charter for an Expanded Right of Privacy?," *Michigan Law Review* 64 (1965): 197, 199 (few concepts more vague or less amenable to definition) (one of the warmest words in the literature of political and legal philosophy); Hyman Gross, "The Concept of Privacy," *New York University Law Review* 34 (1967): 34, 53 (the concept of privacy is infected with pernicious ambiguities); Richard A. Posner, "The Right of Privacy," *Georgia Law Review* 12 (1978): 393 (the concept of privacy is elusive and ill defined) (hereinafter Posner I); Edward Shils, "Privacy: Its Constitutional Vicissitudes," *Law and Contemporary Problems* 31 (1966): 281 (the idea of privacy is a vague one).

11. See, e.g., Judith Jarvis Thomson, "The Right to Privacy," *Philosophy and Public Affairs* 4 (1975): 295.

12. See, e.g., Tom Gerety, "Redefining Privacy," *Harvard Civil Rights–Civil Liberties Law Review* 12 (1977): 233; Richard Parker, "A Definition of Privacy," *Rutgers Law Review* 27 (1974): 275; Lubor C. Velecky, "The Concept of Privacy," in *Privacy*, ed. John B. Young (John Wiley & Sons, 1978), p. 13.

13. Shils, "Privacy," p. 281.

14. Charles Fried, *Right and Wrong* (Harvard Univ. Press, 1978), p. 138.

15. See, e.g., Gavison, "Privacy and the Limits"; W. A. Parent, "A New Definition of Privacy for the Law," *Law and Philosophy* 2 (1983): 305–38

16. Parker, "A Definition," p. 347.

17. W. A. Parent, "Privacy, Morality and the Law," *Philosophy and Public Affairs* 12 (1983): 269 (hereinafter "Parent II"); Parent I, p. 347.

18. Gavison, "Privacy and the Limits," p. 428.

19. Samuel Warren and Louis Brandeis, "The Right to Privacy," *Harvard Law Review* 4 (1890): 193.

20. Westin, *Privacy and Freedom*, p. 7. Westin's definition can be criticized as being not a definition of "privacy" at all. His definition characterizes privacy as a *claim* rather than a *condition* about which legal and moral claims can be made. As such, it is better viewed as an attempt to explicate the concept of the right to privacy (or the right to informational privacy) rather than the concept of privacy itself.

Westin further and more broadly defined privacy as "the voluntary and temporary withdrawal of a person from the general society through physical or psychological means, either in a state of solitude or small group intimacy or, when among larger groups, in a condition of anonymity or reserve" (ibid). This definition is better, but wrongly construes privacy as the product of *voluntary* acts. Plainly, not all states or conditions of privacy are the result of voluntary human conduct. Privacy can be thrust upon a person unwillingly, as when a married man or woman is abandoned by a spouse.

21. Richard A. Posner, "Privacy, Secrecy, and Reputation," *Buffalo Law Review* 28 (1979): 1, 5 (hereinafter Posner II).

22. Ibid., p. 3.

23. The expression "nominal definition" has not been utilized by privacy theorists, although it applies well to describe the kind of definitions many privacy theorists have advanced. As described by K. Adjukiewicz, "On Definitions," *Dialectics and Humanism* 11 (1984): 235, 244, a *"nominal definition of a expression W on the basis of a vocabulary S is a linguistic utterance allowing the translation of each sentence constructed by expressions from the vocabulary S and the expression W into a sentence constructed only of expressions from the vocabulary of S. . . . the simplest form of nominal definition are those in which a straight translation of the defined expression W into some expression constructed solely of expressions from vocabulary S is given."*

A fair amount has been written by philosophers and logicians about the task of definition. Cf. Raziel Abelson, "Definition," *Encyclopedia of Philosophy*, vol. 2 (Collier Macmillan, 1967), pp. 314–24. Ethicists and legal scholars interested in privacy have not penetrated this literature. Much of it is inconclusive and applies to concepts from logic, science, and mathematics. It is not obvious how the literature could be utilized to aid definitional projects in ethics and law.

24. Adjukiewicz, "On Definitions," p. 247. He points out that "if we say that expression A is a translation of expression B, we may either intend to say that these expressions have the same meaning or content, or we may be wanting to say only that they have the same extension" (ibid., p. 246). It is nominal definitions of extension rather than meaning or content that I have in mind and attribute to privacy theorists. In no case could it be supposed that the *definiens* offered by privacy theorists are intended to be interchangable with "privacy" in English sentences on account of sameness of meaning.

25. Velecky, "The Concept of Privacy," p. 18.

26. Gerety, "Redifining Privacy," pp. 234–35.

27. Parent I, pp. 344–46.

28. Velecky and Gerety did not attempt full-scale definitions meeting the criterion of adequacy in question. Parent (in Parent I) tried but failed, as extensively discussed below.

29. Gavison, "Privacy and the Limits," p. 428.

30. Sissela Bok, *Secrets* (Oxford Univ. Press, 1984), p. 10.

31. Dixon, "The *Griswold* Penumbra," p. 212.

32. Irwin Altman, "Privacy—A Conceptual Analysis," *Environment and Behavior* 8 (1976): 7,8 (hereinafter Altman I); Irwin Altman, "Privacy Regulation: Culturally Universal or Culturally Specific?," *The Journal of Social Issues* 33 (1977): 66, 67. Cf. his *Environment and Social Behavior* (Brooks/Cole Publishing Co., 1975).

33. O'Brien, *Privacy, Law*, p. 22.

34. Keith, "Privacy and Community," p. 6.

35. Roland Garrett, "The Nature of Privacy," *Philosophy Today* 18 (1974): 263, 264.

36. Ernest Van den Haag, "On Privacy," in *Privacy: Nomos XIII*, ed. J. Roland Pennock and John W. Chapman (Atherton Press, 1971), p. 149.

37. O'Brien, *Privacy, Law,* p. 22.
38. Carl D. Schneider, *Shame, Exposure, and Privacy* (Beacon Press, 1977), p. 41.
39. Altman I, p. 8.
40. W. A. Parent has criticized restricted-access theories of all three types. *See* Parent I, pp. 344–46, and Parent II, pp. 273–74. To my knowledge, no other theorists have devoted similar attention to the critique of restricted access definitions.
41. Cf. M. Masud and R. Khan, *The Privacy of the Self* (International Universities Press, 1974), an exploration of psychoanalytic themes relating to the accessible and inaccessible dimensions of the inner self.
42. See Garrett, "The Nature of Privacy," p. 275. See also O'Brien, *Privacy, Law,* p. 18. He explains "causal privacy refers to the limitations on causal access to an individual . . . interpretative privacy refers to the limitations on the accumulation and disclosure of information about an individual."
43. Ibid.
44. Westin, *Privacy and Freedom,* pp. 31–32.
45. Velecky, "Concept of Privacy," p. 18.
46. Parent I, p. 346.
47. Parent II, 271.
48. Parent I, p. 347.
49. Bok, *Secrets,* p. 10; Gavison, "Privacy and the Limits," p. 428.
50. Carol Warren and Barbara Laslett, "Privacy and Secrecy: A Conceptual Comparison," in *Secrecy: Cross Cultural Perspectives,* ed. Stanton Tefft (Human Sciences Press, 1980), pp. 25, 26–28.
51. Ibid., p. 26.
52. Ibid., p. 270.
53. Bok, *Secrets,* p. 11.
54. Carl Friedrich, "Secrecy Versus Privacy: The Democratic Dilemma," in *Privacy: Nomos XIII,* ed. J. Roland Pennock and John W. Chapman (Atherton Press, 1971), pp. 105, 119.
55. Charles Fried, "Privacy," *Yale Law Journal* 77 (1968): 475; Gerety, "Redifining Privacy"; Parker, "A Definition of Privacy"; Gross, "Concept of Privacy"; and Westin, *Privacy and Freedom.*
56. Parent I, pp. 344–45; and Parent II, pp. 272–73; Gavison, "Privacy and the Limits," pp. 425–28. Gavison and Parent rejected all definitions that equate privacy with forms of control, including (and for my purposes, especially) access control definitions.
57. Gavison, "Privacy and the Limits," pp. 427–28.
58. See O'Brien, *Privacy, Law,* pp. 25–29.
59. Parent I, p. 344.
60. Ibid., pp. 344–45.
61. Ibid., p. 346.
62. Ibid.
63. Gavison, "Privacy and the Limits," p. 436.
64. Richards, *Toleration and the Constitution.* Thus far, so too has the Supreme Court. *Cf. Whalen v. Roe,* 429 U.S. 589, 600 n. 26 (1977) (privacy interests at issue in Supreme Court cases relate to "marriage, procreation, contraception, family relationships, and child rearing and education").
65. J. Hart Ely, "The Wages of Crying Wolf: A Comment," *Yale Law Journal* 82 (1974): 920. Ely attacked the notion that the Court should be in the business of second-guessing majoritarian legislatures in reliance upon

idealized interpretations of the Bill of Rights. But he also puzzled over the conceptual cogency of describing governmental interference with freedom to live one's life as one chooses as "privacy" (see p. 932). For an excellent critique of both prongs of Ely's attack on constitutional privacy, see Richards, *Toleration and the Constitution*.

66. Parent II, pp. 282–88.

67. Cf. A. Allen, "Women and Their Privacy: What Is at Stake?" in *Beyond Domination*, ed. C. Gould (Rowman & Allanheld, 1984), pp. 233–39. I suggested that since decisional privacy promotes paradigmatic forms of privacy, it promotes privacy interests as well as liberty interests.

68. Walter Berns, "Privacy, Liberalism, and the Role of Government," in *Liberty and the Rule of Law*, ed. Robert C. Cunningham (Texas A&M Univ. Press, 1979) (a distinction may be drawn between private and public, and liberalism rests on such a distinction). *But see* Howard B. Radest, "The Public and the Private: An American Fairy Tale," *Ethics* 89 (1979): 280–91.

CHAPTER 2

1. See, for example, Barrington Moore, *Privacy: Studies in Social and Cultural History* (M. E. Sharpe, 1984); Carl D. Schneider, *Shame, Exposure and Privacy* (Beacon Press, 1977).

2. See, for example, Alan F. Westin, *Privacy and Freedom* (Atheneum, 1967); S. I. Benn, "Privacy, Freedom and Respect for Persons," in *Privacy: Nomos XIII*, ed. J. Roland Pennock and John W. Chapman (Atherton Press, 1971), p. 1; and Jeffrey Reiman, "Privacy, Intimacy, and Personhood," *Philosophy and Public Affairs* 6 (1976): 26; David A. J. Richards, *Toleration and the Constitution* (Oxford Univ. Press, 1986).

3. Cf. Louis Brandeis and Samuel Warren, "The Right to Privacy," *Harvard Law Review*, 4 (1890): 193; Ruth Gavison, "Privacy and the Limits of Law," *Yale Law Journal* 89 (1980): 421.

4. The seven pieces of privacy protecting legislation enacted between 1970 and 1980 were the Fair Credit Reporting Act (1970), 15 U.S.C. 1691 *et seq.*, provisions of the Omnibus Crime Control and Safe Streets Act of 1974, 18 U.S.C. § 2510 *et seq.* Cum. Supp. 1985, the Privacy Act of 1974, 5 U.S.C. § 552a, the Family Education Rights and Privacy Act of 1976 (Buckley Amendment), 20 U.S.C. § 1232(g), provisions of the Tax Reform Act of 1976, 26 U.S.C. 6103, the Right to Financial Privacy Act of 1978, 12 U.S.C. § 3401 *et seq.*, and the Privacy Protection Act of 1980, 42 U.S.C. § 2000aa-§ 2000.

5. Catherine MacKinnon, "*Roe v. Wade*: A Study in *Male Ideology*," in *Abortion: Moral and Legal Perspectives*, ed. Jay Garfield and Patricia Hennessy (Univ. of Massachusetts Press: 1984), pp. 45–54.

6. Simone de Beauvoir, *The Second Sex*, trans. and ed. H. M. Parshley (Alfred A. Knopf, 1952), p. 670.

7. See, in general, Rem B. Edwards, "Intrinsic and Extrinsic Value," *Journal of Value Inquiry* 13 (1975): 133.

8. An exception is Gavison, "Privacy and the Limits of the Law," p. 427.

9. Carl D. Schneider, *Shame, Exposure, and Privacy* (Beacon Press, 1977), p. 41.

10. Sissela Bok, *Secrets* (Oxford Univ. Press, 1984).

11. See David M. O'Brien, *Privacy, Law and Public Policy,* (Praeger, 1979); Gavison, "Privacy and the Limits," p. 427.

12. Cf. Douglas P. Lackey, "Divine Omniscience and Human Privacy," *Philosophy Research Archives* 10 (1984): 383–92.

13. See, for example, T. M. Scanlon, "Rights, Goals and Fairness," in *Public and Private Morality,* ed. Stuart Hampshire (Cambridge Univ., 1978), p. 94; G. J. Warnock, *The Object of Morality* (Methuen & Co., 1971). For an overview of the central issues of ethical theory see, in general, James Rachels, *The Elements of Moral Philosophy* (Random House, 1986); Bernard Williams, *Moral Luck* (Cambridge Univ. Press, 1981); Alan Gewirth, *Reason and Morality* (Univ. of Chicago Press, 1978); Gilbert Harmon, *The Nature of Morality* (Oxford Univ. Press, 1977); Kurt Baier, *The Moral Point of View: A Rational Basis of Ethics* (Random House, 1958).

14. Cf. I. Kant, *Groundwork of the Metaphysic of Morals* (1785), trans. H. J. Paton (Harper & Row, 1958).

15. Does it mean, for example, that capital punishment is morally wrong? Cf. Jeffrie Murphy, *Retribution, Justice and Therapy* (D. Reidel Publishing Co., 1979).

16. Kant, *Groundwork.*

17. See, e.g., S. I. Benn, "Privacy, Freedom, and Respect for Persons," in *Privacy: Nomos XIII,* ed. J. Roland Pennock and John W. Chapman (Atherton Press, 1971), p. 1.

18. Cf. Richard Brandt, *Theory of the Right and the Good* (Oxford, 1979). Brandt advanced his own version of utilitarianism. See also J. J. C. Smart and Bernard Williams, *Utilitarianism: For and Against* (Cambridge Univ. Press, 1973).

19. I am referring to Bentham, *Principles of Morals and Legislation,* 1789, and Mill, *Utilitarianism,* 1861.

20. There are important differences between Bentham's and Mill's utilitarianism. See, in general, S. Gorovitz, ed., *Mill: Utilitarianism* (Bobbs-Merrill, 1971).

21. Aristotle, *The Nicomachean Ethics,* trans. Sir David Ross (Oxford Univ. Press, 1975).

22. An intriguing interpretation of Aristotle's ethics is Alasdair MacIntyre, *After Virtue: A Study of Moral Theory* (Univ. of Notre Dame Press, 1981).

23. See, for example, Judith Jarvis Thomson, "The Right to Privacy," *Philosophy and Public Affairs* 4 (1975): 295.

24. Ibid.

25. See James Rachels, "Why Privacy Is Important," *Philosophy and Public Affairs* 4 (1975): 321; Reiman, "Privacy, Intimacy, and Personhood,"; and Timothy Scanlon, "Thomson on Privacy," *Philosophy and Public Affairs* 4 (1975): 314.

26. See Westin, *Privacy and Freedom,* pp. 32–51.

27. Ibid.

28. Gavison, "Privacy and the Limits of the Law."

29. But not without protest. See Jenny Teichman, "The Definition of *Person,*" *Philosophy* 60 (1985): 175–86.

30. Hence it is sometimes argued that the unborn are not persons. See Richards, *Toleration and the Constitution;* Daniel Wikler, "Abortion, Privacy and Personhood," in *Abortion: Moral and Legal Perspectives,* ed. Jay L. Garfield and Patricia Hennessey (Univ. of Massachusetts Press, 1984), p.

238–59; Michael Tooley, "Abortion and Infanticide," *Philosophy and Public Affairs* 2 (1972): 52.

31. Benn, "Privacy, Freedom, and Respect," pp. 1, 8–13.
32. Ibid., p. 13.
33. Robert E. Lane, "Individualism and the Market Society," in *Liberal Democracy: Nomos XXV*, ed. J. R. Pennock and J. W. Chapman (New York Univ. Press, 1983), pp. 374–75.
34. Jeffrey Reiman, "Privacy, Intimacy, and Personhood," p. 26.
35. See Sally Ann Ketchum, "The Moral Status of the Bodies of Persons," *Social Theory and Practice* 10 (Spring 1984): 25–38; and Mark Wicclair, "The Abortion Controversy and the Claim That This Body Is Mine," *Social Theory and Practice* 7 (Fall 1981): 337–46.
36. Edward J. Bloustein, *Individual and Group Privacy* (Transaction Books, 1979), p. 42.
37. Tom Gerety, "Redefining Privacy," *Harvard Civil Rights–Civil Liberties Law Review* 12 (1977): 233.
38. Charles Fried, "Privacy," *Yale Law Journal* 77 (1968): 475.
39. Robert S. Gerstein, "Intimacy and Privacy," *Ethics* 89 (1978): 76.
40. Rachels, "Why Privacy Is Important."
41. Cf. Robert Nozick, *Anarchy, State, and Utopia* (Basic Books, 1984).
42. Carol Gilligan, *In a Different Voice* (Harvard Univ. Press, 1982).
43. See Moore, *Privacy*, pp. 71–72.
44. See Westin, *Privacy and Freedom*, pp. 11–22.
45. Ibid.
46. Ibid.
47. Ibid.
48. Moore, *Privacy*, p. 51.
49. See, in general, Michael A. Weinstein, "The Use of Privacy in the Good Life," in *Privacy: Nomos XIII*, ed. J. Roland Pennock and John W. Chapman (Atherton Press, 1971) p. 88, 92.
50. See, in general, Weinstein, "The Uses of Privacy." Accord, Boone C. Keith, "Privacy and Community," *Social Theory and Practice* 9 (1983): 1–30.
51. See, in general, Weinstein, "The Use of Privacy."
52. See, in general, Pennock and Chapman, *Liberal Democracy*.
53. What are rights? This question has intrigued and confounded moral and legal scholars. For example, cf. David Lyons, ed., *Rights* (Wadsworth Publishing Co., 1979); Jeremy Waldron, *Theories of Rights* (Oxford Univ. Press, 1984); Richard Tuck, *Natural Rights Theory* (Cambridge Univ. Press, 1979); Joel Feinberg, *Social Ethics* (Prentice-Hall, 1973). See also Duncan Kennedy, "The Structure of Blackstone's Commentaries," *Buffalo Law Review* 28 (1979): 209 (critique of legal conceptions of rights and wrongs).
54. See, in general, Ronald Dworkin, *A Matter of Principle* (Harvard Univ. Press, 1985), pp. 181–221; and Dworkin, *Taking Rights Seriously* (Harvard Univ. Press, 1977).
55. Cf. David A. J. Richards, *Toleration and the Constitution* (Oxford Univ. Press, 1986).
56. J. Roland Pennock, *Democratic Political Theory* (Princeton Univ. Press, 1979), p. 241.
57. Richard Posner, "Privacy, Secrecy and Reputation," *Buffalo Law Review* 28 (1979): 1.

58. Irving Howe, ed., *Essential Works of Socialism* (Yale Univ. Press, 1986) is a comprehensive anthology of readings that critique capitalism and liberalism, while also elaborating the principles of socialism.

CHAPTER 3

1. The privacy of the home was one of the major themes explored by feminist Charlotte Perkins Gilman in her book *Women and Economics* (Small, Maynard & Company, 1898). Gilman rejected the notion that the formal status of the household as private translated into personal privacy for individual members of nuclear families. She identified numerous respects in which family life and women's traditional roles at home stand in the way of individual privacy. Gilman proposed radical but sensible changes in domestic life that would obviate the need for women to devote so much of their lives to cooking, cleaning, and minding bric-a-brac.
2. See Catherine MacKinnon, *"Roe v. Wade:* A Study in Male Ideology," in *Abortion: Moral and Legal Perspectives,* ed. Jay L. Garfield and Patricia Hennessey (Univ. of Massachusetts Press, 1984), pp. 45–54, esp. 52; and Susan Okin Miller, "Women and the Making of the Sentimental Family," *Philosophy and Public Affairs* 11 (1982): 65 (hereinafter "Miller I"). Cf. Catherine MacKinnon, *Feminism Unmodified* (Harvard Univ. Press, 1987).
3. See, in general, Elizabeth Ewen, *Immigrant Women in the Land of Dollars* (New York Monthly Review Press, 1985); Lois W. Banner, *Women in Modern America: A Brief History* (Harcourt Brace Jovanovich, 1984); Ethel Klein, *Gender Politics* (Harvard Univ. Press, 1984); Ruth Schwartz Cowan, *More Work for Mother* (Basic Books, 1983); Susan Estabrook Kennedy, *If All We Did Was to Weep at Home: A History of White Working-Class Women* (Indiana University Press, 1979); Ellen Malos, ed., *The Politics of Housework* (Schocken Books, 1980); and Edward Shorter, *The Making of the Modern Family* (Basic Books, 1977). For general discussions of women's unequal status in the United States, also see Marlene Stein Wortman, ed., *Women in American Law* (Holmes & Meier, 1985); D. Kelly Weisberg, ed., *Women and the Law: A Social Historical Perspective* (Schenkman Publishing, 1982); and Leo Kanowitz, *Women and the Law: The Unfinished Revolution* (Univ. of New Mexico Press, 1969).
4. Throughout this book I make reference to the private sphere and the public sphere. "Private sphere" is sometimes used to designate a realm of conduct in which nongovernmental actors engage in activities that are or ought to be immune from governmental (or other "public") interference. The "public sphere," conversely, is sometimes used to designate a realm of conduct and affairs essentially involving governmental (or other "public") actors, law, and policy. I use the terms "public" and "private" loosely and without intending to imply that a sharp public-private distinction with inherent normative implications respecting the distribution of governmental power, economic assets, and legal rights can be drawn. I typically use "private sphere" to refer to home, to family life within the home, and to the kinds of intimate personal relationships and activities commonly associated with them. By "public sphere" I mean all else: all other sites, conduct, experiences, relationships, organizations and institutions. In the sense in which I use "public sphere," the term applies equally to what goes on behind closed doors between a nongovernmental employer and employee in a privately owned office building

and to what goes on in the open air in the middle of a municipal roadway.

5. See, for example, Jean Bethke Elshtain, *Public Man, Private Woman: Women in Social and Political Thought* (Princeton Univ. Press, 1981); MacKinnon, *"Roe v. Wade";* Susan Okin Miller, "Philosopher Queens and Private Wives: Plato on Women and the Family," *Philosophy and Public Affairs* 6 (1977): 345 (hereinafter "Miller II"); and Miller I, "The Sentimental Family."

6. MacKinnon, *"Roe v. Wade,"* p. 53. See *Roe v. Wade*, 430 U.S. 113 (1973). In *Roe* the U.S. Supreme Court declared unconstitutional Texas statutes criminalizing abortion. *Roe* established women's constitutional right to abortion.

7. For a survey and analysis of a variety of objections to privacy, see Boone C. Keith, "Privacy and Community," *Social Theory and Practice* 9 (1983): 1; Michael A. Weinstein, "The Uses of Privacy in the Good Life," in *Privacy: Nomos XIII*, ed. J. Roland Pennock and John W. Chapman (Atherton Press: 1971), p. 88; see also F. Schoeman, "Privacy: Philosophical Dimensions," *American Philosophical Quarterly* 21 (1984): 199, 211–12.

8. See, for example, Carol Gilligan, *In a Different Voice: Psychological Theory and Women's Development* (Harvard Univ. Press, 1982); and Jean Baker Miller, *Toward a New Psychology of Women* (Beacon Press, 1976).

9. Heinrich Böll, *The Lost Honor of Katharina Blum* (McGraw-Hill, 1976), p. 91.

10. Toni Morrison, *Sula* (Alfred A. Knopf, 1973), p. 44.

11. Ibid., p. 37.

12. Article 12 of the Universal Declaration of Human Rights, adopted by the United Nations General Assembly in 1948, provides that: "No one shall be subjected to arbitrary interference with his privacy, *family home* or correspondence, nor to attacks upon his honour and reputation. Everyone has the right to protection of the law against such interference or attacks" (emphasis added). Influenced by the United Nations document, Article 8 of the European Convention on Human Rights, a treaty binding fifteen European states, provides that: "Everyone has the right to respect for his private and family life, his *home,* and his correspondence" (emphasis added). The interpretation of the privacy rights ascribed in these documents is discussed in Jacques Velu, "The European Convention on Human Rights and the Right to Respect for Private Life, the Home and Communications," in *Privacy and Human Rights*, ed. A. H. Robertson (Manchester Univ. Press, 1973), p. 12.

13. "No Soldier shall, in time of peace be quartered in any house, without the consent of the Owner, nor in time of war, but in a manner to be prescribed by law." See in general David M. O'Brien, *Privacy, Law and Public Policy* (Praeger, 1979) on analyzing the privacy protections embodied in the Constitution.

14. See *Paxton's Case*, Quincy's Reports 51 (Mass. 1761); and T. T. F. Rudox, *Life of James Otis* (1823), p. 66. See also O'Brien, *Privacy, Law,* pp. 38–39.

15. It reads, in full: "The right of the people to be secure in their persons, houses, papers, and effects, against unreasonable searches and seizures, shall not be violated, and no warrants shall issue, but upon probable cause, supported by oath and affirmation, and particularly describing the place to be searched, and the persons or things to be seized."

16. See *Katz v. United States*, 389 U.S. 347 (1967). As *Katz* attests, difficulties for Fourth Amendment analysis have arisen chiefly where a right of

privacy is claimed respecting conduct or possessions located *outside* one's own home.

17. The Fifth Amendment provides, in relevant part: "No person . . . shall be compelled in any criminal case to be a witness against himself." Compulsory self-incrimination results in information disclosure, and hence informational privacy losses. *See* O'Brien, *Privacy, Law.* O'Brien devoted a full chapter of his book to the self-incrimination provisions of the Fifth Amendment.

18. *Boyd v. United States,* 116 U.S. 616, 630 (1885).

19. *Meyer v. Nebraska,* 262 U.S. 390, 399 (1923).

20. *Stanley v. Georgia,* 394 U.S. 557 (1969).

21. See *Griswold v. Connecticut,* 381 U.S. 479 (1965) (state laws criminalizing the use of contraceptives by married women are unconstitutional); *Roe v. Wade,* 410 U.S. 113 (1973) (state laws criminalizing abortion in the first trimesters of pregnancy are unconstitutional); *Thornburgh v. American College of Obstetricians and Gynecologists,* 737 F.2d 283 (1984), 106 S. Ct. 2169 (1986) (state abortion control laws that impede the right to choose abortion are unconstitutional). These cases could be read to protect constitutionally, by implication, the privacy of all sexual and reproductive intimacy in the home. Yet the Supreme Court has upheld the constitutionality of state laws criminalizing sodomy between consenting adults at home in their own beds. See *Bowers v. Hardwick,* 106 S. Ct. 2841 (1986). State laws prohibiting commercial sex (prostitution) in the home would probably be similarly upheld. Cf. *State v. Mueller,* 671 P.2d 1351 (Hi. 1985).

22. The Omnibus Crime Control and Safe Streets Act, 5 U.S.C. 3701. (The Crime Control Act was amended in 1986 to make accessing certain electronic communications a crime.) For an overview of the text of federal statutes relating to privacy, see Robert Smith, *Compilation of State and Federal Privacy Laws* (Privacy Journal, Washington D.C., 1984). Earlier editions of Smith's compilation are also helpful. See also James Rule, et al., *The Politics of Privacy* (Elsevier, 1980) (spirited critical overview of federal privacy statutes enacted prior to 1980).

23. See, in general, Smith, *Compilation.*

24. The invasion of privacy tort is now widely recognized in American law. As defended in 1890 by Samuel Warren and Louis Brandeis, *Harvard Law Review* 4 (1890): 193, the privacy tort protects the interest in "inviolate personality" through recognition of a right "to be let alone." William Prosser's influential analysis of law cases brought under right to privacy theories led him to view the privacy tort as four distinct torts: (a) intrusion upon seclusion; (b) publication of embarrassing facts; (c) publicity placing another in a false light; and (d) misappropriation of name, likeness or identity for commercial purposes. See Prosser, "Privacy," *California Law Review* 98 (1960): 383. This analysis of privacy was adopted by the American Law Institute in the Restatement (Second) of Torts, see Section 652A(2), and has been followed by a number of states. See, for example, *Vogel v. W. T. Grant Co.,* 488 Pa. 124, 327 A.2d 133 (1974) (Pennsylvania court adopts the Prosser/*Restatement* analysis). Some courts have redesignated Prosser's misappropriation tort as an altogether separate tort to which they give the name of "publicity." See, for instance, *Carson v. Here's Johnny Portable Toilets, Inc.,* 698 F.2d 831 (6th Cir. 1983). The right of publicity is held to protect purely economic

interests in name, likeness, and identity. The right of privacy is held to protect a person's dignitarian interests.

25. Of course, even under the best of circumstances the home is no perfect protector of the many forms of privacy to which Americans have a legal right and value. Computer and surveillance technologies have made it easier and less expensive for government and private industry to gather, store, access, and share vast quantities of information (and misinformation) about individuals. The abuse of information about education, health, debts and finances, criminal conduct, and morals obtained with or without our knowledge and consent by government, insurance companies, employers, creditors, hospitals and schools is becoming a major threat to personal privacy. See, in general, United States Privacy Protection Commission Report, *Personal Privacy in and Information Society* (U.S. Government Printing Office, 1977).

26. See, in general, Barrington Moore, *Privacy: Studies in Social and Cultural History* (M. E. Sharpe, 1984); and Alan F. Westin, *Privacy and Freedom* (Atheneum, 1967).

27. Moore, *Privacy*, p. 62.

28. See Westin, *Privacy and Freedom*, p. 16; John M. Roberts and Thomas Gregor, "Privacy: A Cultural View," in *Privacy: Nomos XIII*, ed. J. Roland Pennock and John W. Chapman (Atherton Press, 1971): 199, 225.

29. Moore, *Privacy*, p. 51; cf. Richard A. Epstein, "A Taste for Privacy? Evolution and the Emergence of a Naturalistic Ethic," *Journal of Legal Studies* 9 (1980): 665.

30. Kennedy, *If All We Did*, p. 97. See also Elizabeth Ewen, *Immigrant Women*, p. 151.

31. For fuller discussions of the social and the legal implications of obstacles to privacy caused by poverty, see Andrea M. Pearldaughter and Vivian Schneider, "Women and Welfare: The Cycle of Poverty," *Golden Gate University Law Review* 10 (1980): 1043. See also J. F. Handler and M. K. Roseheim, "Privacy in Welfare," *Law and Contemporary Problems* 31 (1966): 377; J. F. Handler and C. J. Hollingsworth, "Stigma, Privacy and Other Attitudes of Welfare Recipients," *Stanford Law Review* 2 (1969): 1. Cf. Albert M. Benedict, "Privacy, Poverty and the Constitution," *California Law Review* 54 (1966): 407 (civil rights include privacy rights); Margaret Greenfield, *Confidentiality and Public Assistance Records* (Univ. of California, Berkeley Bureau of Public Administration, 1952).

32. Roberts and Gregor, "Privacy," p. 225. The authors point out that in other countries "the management and functions of privacy may be quite different."

33. Millett's remark is anthologized in Elaine Partnow, ed., *The Quotable Woman* (Anchor Press/Doubleday, 1978), p. 336.

34. See Catherine Hall, "The History of the Housewife," in *The Politics of Housework*, ed. Ellen Malos (Schocken Books, 1980), p. 44, 60–61.

35. See, in general, David Flaherty, *Privacy in Colonial New England* (Univ. Press of Virginia, 1972).

36. See *Rule, Politics of Privacy*, pp. 13–15; Flaherty, *Colonial New England*, p. 172.

37. Kennedy, *If All We Did*, p. 8.

38. Ibid. See also Wortman, *Women in American Law*, pp. 22–24. For an account of the legal status of black women during and just after the Revolutionary War era, see A. Leon Higginbotham, Jr., *In the Matter of*

Color: Race and the American Legal Process: The Colonial Period (Oxford Univ. Press, 1978).

39. Cf. Eli Zaretsky's account: "This 'split' between the socialized labour of the capitalist enterprise and the private labour of women in the home is closely related to a second 'split'—between our personal lives and our place within the social division of labor. . . . While housewives and mothers continued their traditional tasks of production—housework, child-rearing, etc., their labour was devalued through its isolation from the socialized production of surplus value. In addition, housewives and mothers were given new responsibilities for maintaining the emotional and psychological realm of personal relations." In *Capitalism, the Family and Personal Life* (Harper & Row, 1976), p. 31.

40. See Kennedy, *If All We Did,* p. 44.

41. Ibid., p. 102.

42. Ibid., p. 69.

43. Ibid., "[T]he euphemism 'hooker' originated from the large number of prostitutes who followed [General Joe Hooker's army]."

44. Cf. Hall, "History of the Housewife," pp. 60–65; Barbara Welter, "The Cult of True Womanhood: 1820–1860," *American Quarterly* 18 (1966): 152; and Barbara J. Harris, *Beyond Her Sphere* (Greenwood Press, 1978). The labor statistics are from Wortman, *Women in American Law,* p. 214.

45. Welter, "True Womanhood," p. 174.

46. Thomas Gisborne, *Enquiry Into the Duties of the Female Sex* (T. Cadell Jr. and W. Davies, Successors to Mr. Cadwell, in the Strand, London, 1797), pp. 288–689.

47. Welter, "True Womanhood," p. 174.

48. Ruskin's lecture is quoted in Judith Hole and Ellen Levine, *The Rebirth of Feminism* (Quadrangle Books, 1971), p. 18.

49. Gilman, *Women and Economics,* p. 259.

50. Betty Friedan's *Feminine Mystique* (1963) chronicled the apartness of suburban housewives living lives too fragmented for meaningful work. See also Nancy Rubin, *The Suburban Woman* (McCann & Geoghegan, 1982). Rubin depicted suburban women as cloistered in their homes, frequently alcoholic, and unhappy. She contended that domestic chores, family care, community involvement, and a convenient life did not redeem the circumstance of the suburban wife in her heyday.

51. See, for example, MacKinnon, *"Roe v. Wade,"* p. 53.

52. Kennedy, "If All We Did," p. 94.

53. Westin, *Privacy and Freedom,* p. 21.

54. Kennedy; "If All We Did," p. 96.

55. Barclay, *Boarding Out: A Tale of Domestic Life* (Harper & Brothers, 1855), p. 14. The plot concerns a woman who, sick of domestic work, asks that her husband agree that they move from their own home and become boarders in an easy-to-maintain apartment. Boarding out proves to be a comic disaster. The husband, who knew all along that the experiment would fail, restores his grateful wife to their own home and enjoys the last laugh.

56. Moore, *Privacy,* pp. 51–52.

57. Linda Georgianno, *The Solitary Self: Individuality in the Ancrene Wisse* (Harvard Univ. Press, 1981).

58. Cf. J. Lieblich, "The Cloistered Life," *The New York Times Magazine,* July

10, 1983, p. 12. See Eileen Power, *Medieval Women* (Cambridge Univ. Press, 1975).

59. N. Sproat, *Family Lectures* (Samuel T. Armstrong, 1819). Readers will be relieved to know that Mrs. Sproat ended her earnest recitation of the wifely duties by observing that "no one is sufficient for these things . . . which are utterly impracticable without divine assistance."

60. These Bureau of Labor and Bureau of the Census statistics were cited in Andrew Hocke, "Women at Work," *New York Review of Books*, August 14, 1986, p. 26.

61. According to Edward Shorter, popular marriage in traditional European society was usually affectionless. Shorter, *Modern Family*, pp. 55–65.

62. Robert R. Ehrman, "Personal Love," *The Personalist* 49 (Winter 1968): 116.

63. Montaigne, "Of Solitude," *The Complete Essays of Montaigne*, trans. Donald M. Frame (Stanford Univ. Press, 1965), p. 174.

64. Gilman, *Women and Economics*, p. 259.

65. Ibid.

66. Moore, *Privacy*, p. 12.

67. MacKinnon, *"Roe v. Wade,"* p. 51.

68. Miller, *New Psychology*, p. 95.

69. Ibid., p. 18.

70. Gilligan, *In a Different Voice*.

71. George Eliot, *Middlemarch* (New American Library, 1964), p. 519.

72. There are noteworthy limitations to Gilligan's studies, although she was doubtless correct that expanding theories of development to include the approaches to moral reasoning typical of women and girls will provide a more accurate, fuller understanding of human development than Freud, Piaget and many other leading psychologists were able to achieve. Whether social experience shakes out neatly in terms of an "ethic of justice" and an "ethic of care" is another matter. Cf. Anne Colby, "Listening to a Different Voice: A Review of Gilligan's *In a Different Voice*," *Merrill-Palmer Quarterly* 29 (1983): 473–81.

Gilligan's empirical generalizations in *In a Different Voice* were largely based on three studies. A college student study involving 25 young women; an abortion decision study involving 29 women, and a rights and responsibility study involving 144 men and women. These are very small groups—perhaps too small to lend a high degree of support to some of her broad empirical contentions. Another problem is that Gilligan is not clear about the mechanism of mother-child individuation and gender formation. Just how individuation and gender formation differ in the case of boys and girls was not made clear. Nor was it made clear how her developmental account should be modified to accommodate co-parented children, children reared by the male parent, children reared in institutions, and so on.

A more serious problem lies in Gilligan's use of the concepts of rights, fairness, justice, reciprocity, and equality. I believe most moral philosophers would be uncomfortable with her classification of all of the aforenamed concepts as belonging to an ethic of "justice," and in particular her description of the "ethic of justice" as an "ethic of rights." The concept of justice, which has roots in classical antiquity, predated the concept of individual rights by many centuries. Liberalism equates justice with respecting abstract universal human rights. Another Aristotelian philosophical tradition equates justice with a happy, whole society wherein individuals possess appropriate virtues and exercise role-based, contextual responsibilities. It is interesting that female and male moralists have been critical of the rights-based liberal conception of justice. Two books, Alaisdair MacIntyre's *After Virtue* (Univ. of Notre Dame Press, 1981) and Michael Sandel's *Liberalism and the Limits of Justice* (Cambridge Univ. Press, 1982), are vigorous rejections of rights and individual autonomy-based ethics as these are often understood, in favor of ethics that stress identity, affiliation, and context.

A final criticism. Care-taking concerns can be couched in rules and "right-respecting" language. We can say children *need* stable environments and continuous nurture, or we can say they have a *right* to it. We can say, women need free choice in the area of reproductive concerns, or that they have a right to it. But if this is so, we have to rethink the reliability of Gilligan's methodology. Perhaps some of the men whom she studied who used the "masculine voice" did so in spite of underlying "feminine" ethical concerns. The converse is also true. Women perhaps used the "feminine voice" in spite of underlying "masculine" conceptions and concerns.

73. Gilligan, *In a Different Voice,* p. 70.
74. Catherine Talbot, *The Works of the Late Miss Catherine Talbot* (F. C. and J. Rivington, 1812).
75. See David A. J. Richards, *Toleration and the Constitution* (Oxford Univ. Press, 1980).
76. Gisborne, *Duties of the Female Sex,* p. 214.
77. Deidre Donahue, "Romance Novels Find Fans on the Rebound," *USA Today,* November 11, 1986.
78. Cf. Peggy Franklin, *Private Lines: Intimate Diaries of Women from the 1880's to the Present* (Ballantine, 1986); Lillian Schlissel, *Women's Diaries of the Westward Expansion* (Schocken Books, 1982).
79. Adrienne Rich, "Vesuvius at Home: The Power of Emily Dickinson" in *Critical Essays on Emily Dickinson,* ed. Paul J. Ferlazzo (G. K. Hall, 1984), pp. 175–95.
80. Ibid., p. 176. In "'Everyone Else Is Prose': Emily Dickinson's Lack of Community Spirit," pp. 223–38, Barbara A. C. Mossberg portrayed Dickinson as a woman who became an isolotta trapped on the horns of a dilemma: she wanted to transcend the usual female ambitions of marriage, but could not because she felt bound by family and social pressures to resist penetrating the world of male literrati. She was always a daughter, literally and figuratively locked in her father's house.
81. May Sarton, *Journal of Solitude* (W. W. Norton, 1973), p.11.
82. See Lisa R. Peattie and Martin Rein, *Women's Claims: A Study in Political Economy* (Oxford Univ. Press, 1983), p. 40; see in general C. Hall, "The History of the Housewife," in E. Malos, *Politics of Housework.*
83. Ruth Schwartz Cowan, "Housework: Why I Love/Hate My Clothes Washer," *Washington Post,* February 15, 1987, p. C31. Cf. Gilman, *Women and Economics,* p. 214, 215.
84. See David Finkelhor and Richard J. Gelles, eds., *The Dark Side of Families: Current Family Violence Research* (Sage Publications, 1983). Cf. M. Boulard, *Violence in the Family* (Humanities Press, 1976) and Karen MacKinnie, "Battered Wives," *University of California Law Review* 52 (1981): 587.

85. *Commonwealth v. Shoemaker,* 518 A.2d 591 (Pa. Super. 1986). See, in general, David Finkelhor and Kersti Yllo, *License to Rape, Sexual Abuse of Wives* (Holt, Rinehart & Winston, 1985).

86. R. Seidenberg and K. DeCrow, *Women Who Marry Houses: Panic and Protest in Agoraphobia* (McGraw-Hill, 1983), p. 212.

87. See Elshtain, *Public Man;* MacKinnon, *"Roe v. Wade";* Miller I; and Miller II.

CHAPTER 4

1. For example, Ruth Gavison, "Privacy and the Limits of Law," *Yale Law Journal* 89 (1980): 421, 432, uses "anonymity" in the broader sense identified.

2. See, in general, Arnold H. Buss, *Self-Consciousness and Social Anxiety* (W. H. Freeman, 1980); C. Schneider, *Shame, Exposure and Privacy* (Beacon Press, 1977).

3. Charlotte Perkins Gilman, *Women and Economics,* ed. Carl N. Degler (Harper & Row, 1966; first published in 1898 by Small, Maynard and Company, Boston), p. 258.

4. See Paul Shorey, trans., *The Republic,* in *Plato: Collected Dialogues,* ed. Edith Hamilton and Huntington Cairns (Princeton Univ. Press, 1961), Book V.

5. John Rawls, *The Theory of Justice* (Belknap Press of Harvard Univ. Press, 1971), pp. 511–12. The problems of social justice created by the family and the "hands off" approach to the family associated with liberalism are admirably addressed in James S. Fishkin, *Justice, Equal Opportunity, and the Family* (Yale Univ. Press, 1983.)

6. Rawls asks (p. 511), "Is the family to be abolished then?" He answers: "Taken by itself and given certain primacy, the idea of equality inclines in this direction. But within the context of the theory of justice as a whole, there is much less urgency to take this course. The acknowledgment of the difference principle redefines the grounds for social inequalities as conceived in a system of liberal equality."

7. Frederick Engels, *The Origin of the Family, Private Property and the State,* ed. Eleanor Burke Leacock (International Publishers, 1972).

8. See Jean Bethke Elshtain, "Family Reconstruction," *Commonwealth* (August 1, 1980): 430–36. See also her *Public Man, Private Woman* (Princeton Univ. Press, 1981), p. 323.

9. See Seibert, "Hegel's Concept of Marriage and Family: The Origin of Subjective Freedom," in Hegel's *Social and Political Thought,* ed. D.P. Nerema (Humanities Press, 1980), pp. 177–210, 178. The quoted passage is a description of Hegel's conception of the consequences of familial love for individuality.

10. See Deborah Fallows, *A Mother's Work* (Houghton Mifflin, 1986). Fallows argues that the quality of day-care in the United States is so low that we should "create the circumstances that allow more parents to care for their children themselves."

11. *Griswold v. Connecticut,* 381 U.S. 479, 486–87 (1965). Were first-trimester abortions not lawful, availability of an abortion pill intended for home use, such as the "once a month" RU 486 tablet developed in France which blocks the action of progesterone and prevents implantation of fertilized ova, would necessitate an analogous question.

12. *See* F. Friendly and M. Elliot, *The Constitution, That Delicate Balance* (Random House, 1984), pp. 188–202.
13. *Eisenstadt v. Baird,* 405 U.S. 438, 453 (1972).
14. *Roe v. Wade,* 410 U.S. 113 (1973) (Texas statute restricting abortion access invalidated); *Doe v. Bolton,* 410 U.S. 179 (1973) (Georgia statute restricting abortion access invalidated). Later Supreme Court cases have defined the limits of *Roe* and *Doe.* See *Bigelow v. Virginia,* 421 U.S. 809 (1975) (statute prohibiting advertisements encouraging or prompting abortion violative of First Amendment); *Connecticut v. Merillo,* 423 U.S. 9 (1975) (statute prohibiting attempted abortion by nonphysician not violative of constitution); *Planned Parenthood v. Danforth,* 428 U.S. 52 (1976) (Missouri statute requiring spousal consent for abortion violates constitutional privacy); *Belliotti v. Baird,* 428 U.S. 132 (1976) (District Court should have abstained on question of constitutionality of Massachusetts statute governing the consent requirements for unmarried minors); *Franklin v. Fitzgerald,* 428 U.S. 901 (1976) (memorandum case) (affirming District Court in light of *Planned Parenthood v. Danforth,* 428 U.S. 52 (1976)); *Singleton v. Wulff,* 428 U.S. 107 (1976) (physicians have standing to bring suit challenging Missouri statute denying state funding for elective abortions); *Guste v. Jackson,* 429 U.S. 399 (1977) (District Court injunction against enforcement of provisions of Louisiana statute requiring parental or spousal consent for minor's abortions vacated and remanded); *Beal v. Doe,* 432 U.S. 438 (1977) (Social Security Act does not require funding of elective abortion as a condition of Pennsylvania's participation in Medicaid); *Maher v. Roe,* 432 U.S. 464 (1977) (Pennsylvania may limit state assistance to "medically necessary abortions"); *Poelker v. Doe,* 432 U.S. 519 (1977) (state hospital may refuse to perform abortions); *Reproductive Services v. Walker,* 439 U.S. 1307 (1978) (dissolution of stay of protective order aimed at preserving confidentiality of abortion patient records sought in malpractice litigation); *Colautti v. Franklin,* 439 U.S. 379 (1979); *Bellotti v. Baird,* 443 U.S. 622 (1979) (Massachusetts statute requiring parental consent to minor's abortion violates constitutional privacy); *Williams v. Zbaraz,* 448 U.S. 358 (1980) (Illinois statute prohibiting state medical assistance payments for elective abortions not violative of 14th Amendment); *Harris v. McRae,* 448 U.S. 297 (1980) (Hyde Amendment prohibiting federal Medicaid assistance for elective abortions not violative of the 1st or 14th Amendment, and New York may constitutionally refuse to fund elective abortions ineligible for federal coverage); *H. L. v. Matheson,* 450 U.S. 398 (1981) (Utah statute requiring parental notification prior to performing abortions on unemancipated minors not violative of constitutional privacy); *Simopolous v. Virginia,* 462 U.S. 506 (1983) (Virginia physician may be convicted for performing abortion outside a licensed hospital); *Akron v. Akron Center for Reproductive Health,* 462 U.S. 416 (1983) (city ordinances requiring, inter alia, that second trimester abortions be performed in a hospital; that minors obtain written consent from one parent or a court order prior to abortion; and that a woman be read a specific list of information and beliefs about abortion constitutionally invalid); *Planned Parenthood Assn. of Kansas City Mo., Inc. v. Ashcroft,* 462 U.S. 476 (1983) (Missouri statute requiring that all second-trimester abortions be performed in a hospital constitutionally invalid; but requirements that a second physician be present at abortion of viable fetus, that a pathology report be provided

for each abortion, and that minors obtain parental consent or a court order prior to abortion constitutionally valid); *Thornburgh v. American College of Gynecologists et al.,* 106 S. Ct. 2169 (1986) (Pennsylvania statute requiring that women seeking abortion be advised of medical assistance programs, of fathers' child support responsibilities, and of the detrimental physical, psychological and medical risks of abortion unconstitutional; statutes requiring reporting and requiring the presence of a second physician, even in emergencies, unconstitutional; and statute establishing care appropriate for post-viability abortions facially invalid).

15. *Roe,* 410 U.S. at 153.
16. For a discussion and analysis of abortion cases and the normative and policy issues raised by them, see Nanette J. Davis, *From Crime to Choice* (Greenwood Press, 1985); Jay L. Garfield and Patricia Hennessey, *Abortion: Moral and Legal Perspectives* (Univ. of Massachusetts Press, 1984); Rosalind Petchesky, *Abortion and Women's Choice* (Northeastern Univ. Press, 1985); Kristin Lukes, *Abortion and the Politics of Motherhood* (Univ. of California Press, 1984); Eva R. Rubin, *Abortion, Politics and the Courts* (Greenwood Press, 1982); Carl E. Schneider and Maris A. Vinovskis, *The Law and Politics of Abortion* (Lexington Books, 1980); Lynn D. Wardle, *The Abortion Privacy Doctrine: A Compendium and Critique of Federal Court Abortion Cases* (William S. Hein, 1980).
17. *Roe,* 410 U.S. at 159.
18. *Thornburgh v. American College of Obstetricians and Gynecologists,* 737 F.2d 283 (3rd Cir. 1984), 106 S. Ct. 2169 (1986).
19. Ibid. at 2185.
20. Jenny Teichman, "The Definition of Person," *Philosophy* 60 (1985): 175–86.
21. See, for example, Michael Tooley, "Abortion and Infanticide," *Philosophy and Public Affairs* 2 (1972): 37–65.
22. See, for example, Stanley Hauerwas, "The Moral Meaning of the Family," *Commonwealth* 1 (August 1980): 432–33.
23. Carol Gilligan, *In a Different Voice: Psychological Theory and Women's Development* (Harvard Univ. Press, 1982).
24. Michael Sandel, *Liberalism and the Limits of Law* (Cambridge Univ. Press, 1982), p. 135.
25. Judith Jarvis Thompson, "A Defense of Abortion," *Philosophy and Public Affairs* 1 (1971): 47–66. Thompson wrote: "You wake up in the morning and find yourself back to back in bed with [a] famous unconscious violinist. He has been found to have a fatal kidney ailment, and the Society of Music Lovers has canvassed all available medical records and found that you alone have the right blood type to help. They have therefore kidnapped you, and last night the violinist's circulatory system was plugged into yours. . . . The director of the hospital now tells you [that for you to unplug] would be to kill him. But never mind, it's only for nine months. . . . Is it morally incumbent on you to accede to this situation?" Thomson's hypothetical is designed to lead readers to conclude that it would be morally permissible for the woman to detach the violinist (and likewise a fetus) on the ground that she owns her own body and has a right to its exclusive possession and control. Cf. the references also in note 34 below.
26. Cf. *Matter of Quinlan,* 355 A.2d 647 (1976) (comatose woman without apparent hope for improvement may be removed from artificial life

support systems); *Weber v. Stony Brook Hospital,* 95 A.D. 587, 467 N.Y.S.2d 685, *aff'd* 60 N.Y.S.2d 208, 456 N.E.2d 1186, 469 N.Y.S.2d 63 (per curiam), *cert. denied,* 464 U.S. 1026 (1983) (parents entitled to order that severely impaired newborn be allowed to die). On the other hand, children born with birth defects have been unsuccessful in recovering damages for wrongful life and impaired childhoods against physicians whose negligence caused their mothers to forego an opportunity to abort. "One of the most deeply held beliefs of our society is that life—whether experienced with or without a major physical handicap—is more precious than non-life." *Berman v. Allan,* 404 A.2d 8 (N.J. 1979), overruled in part, by *Procanik v. Cillo,* 478 A.2d 755 (N.J. 1984).

27. Emphasis in the original. *Eisenstadt,* 405 U.S. at 253.
28. George Sher, "Subsidized Abortion: Moral Rights and Moral Compromise," *Philosophy and Public Affairs* 10 (1981): 361, 363.
29. See, for example, W. A. Parent, "Privacy, Morality and the Law," *Philosophy and Public Affairs* 12 (1983): 269; idem, "Recent Work on the Conception of Privacy," *American Philosophical Quarterly* 20 (1983): 341, 346; Gavison, "Privacy and the Limits of Law," p. 421; Sher, "Subsidized Abortion"; John Hart Ely, "The Wages of Crying Wolf: A Comment on *Roe v. Wade,"* Yale 82 (1973): 920, 932. But see David A. J. Richards, *Toleration and the Constitution* (Oxford, 1986).
30. See S. I. Benn and R. S. Peters, *The Principles of Political Thought: Social Foundations of the Democratic State* (Collier Macmillan, 1959), pp. 248–49. L. Tribe, *The Constitutional Protection of Individual Rights* (Foundation Press, 1978), § 15–2, p. 889. Cf. James Childress, "Negative and Positive Rights," *Hastings Center Report* 10 (1980): 19. The negative conception of liberty was defended as the sole liberty properly guaranteed by government by conservative F. A. Hayek in *The Constitution of Liberty* (Univ. of Chicago Press, 1960).
31. Related issues arose in *Harris v. McRae,* 488 U.S. 297 (1980) and *Maher v. Roe,* 432 U.S. 464 (1977) (state may withhold funds for non-therapeutic abortion even though childbirth would be funded). See also Sher, "Subsidized Abortion." The ultimate issues in *Harris* were the constitutionality of the Hyde Amendment and whether the right to privacy in the abortion context is a positive liberty or a negative liberty. The Hyde Amendment was an act of the U.S. Congress that denied federal reimbursement to states that authorize Medicaid funding for elective abortions: "none of the funds provided by this joint resolution shall be used to perform abortions except where the life of the mother would be endangered if the fetus were carried to term; or except for such medical procedures necessary for the victims of rape or incest when such rape or incest has been properly reported to a law enforcement agency or public health service" (Pub. L. 96–123, 109, 93 Stat. 926). The Court held that in enacting the Hyde Amendment "the Congress has neither invaded a substantive constitutional right or freedom, nor enacted legislation that purposefully operates to the detriment of a suspect class" (p. 326). In a concurring opinion, Justice White stressed that the right of *Roe v. Wade* is a right against coercive interference, and not a right to government benefits. Justice Brennan dissented, arguing that the "Hyde Amendment's denial of public funds for medically necessary abortions plainly intrudes upon [the pregnant woman's freedom to choose whether to have an abortion], for both by design and effect it serves to coerce

indigent pregnant women to bear children that they would otherwise elect not to have" (p. 330).

32. See, in general, Leslie Goldstein, "A Critique of the Abortion Funding Decision: On Private Rights in the Public Sector," *Hastings Constitutional Law Quarterly* 8 (1981): 313; David T. Hardy, *"Harris v. McRae:* Clash of a Nonenumerated Right with Legislative Control of the Purse," *Case Western Reserve Law Review* 31 (1981): 465; Note, "Abortion Funding Restriction: State Constitutional Protections Exceed Federal Safeguards," *Washington and Lee Law Review* 39 (1982): 1469, 1473–74, n.14; Note, "The Hyde Amendment: New Implications for Equal Protection Clause," *Baylor Law Review* 33 (1981): 295.

33. Richards, in *Toleration and the Constitution,* argued that the jurisprudential basis of the Court's constitutional "right to privacy" analysis is sound. He maintained that the right to privacy would support further judicial intervention to invalidate state laws, in particular, laws criminalizing consensual adult homosexuality. For sympathetic discussion of the Supreme Court's "substantive due process" approach in the reproductive rights cases, see Laurence Tribe, "Forward: Toward a Model of Roles in the Due Process of Life and Law," *Harvard Law Review* 87 (1973): 1, where he defended *Roe* on ground the Court was "choosing among alternative allocations of decision-making"; idem, "Structural Due Process," *Harvard Civil Rights-Civil Liberties Law Review* 10 (1975): 269 (Court may facilitate evolution of a new moral consensus). Cf. Laurence Tribe, *Constitutional Choices* (Harvard Univ. Press, 1985). For an unsympathetic discussion, see Ely, "Crying Wolf"; and cf. John Hart Ely, *Democracy and Distrust: A Theory of Judicial Review* (Harvard Univ. Press, 1980).

34. See Sara Ann Ketchum, "The Moral Status of the Bodies of Persons," *Social Theory and Social Practice* 10 (1984): 25, 26. Ketchum remarks that: "In 'A Defense of Abortion,' Judith Jarvis Thomson argues that, even if fetuses did have rights of life, the traditional anti-abortion argument would fail because the right to life does not entail that right to anything whatsoever that one needs in order to live; in particular, it does not entail a right to another person's body or other property. Thomson, I believe, is correct in asserting that 'if a human being has any just prior claim to anything at all, he has a just prior claim to his own body.' This claim of right to one's body, however, need not be a property right" (p. 36). She goes on to argue persuasively that, although they are not property rights, the rights we have over our bodies are so strong that "Vital need does not yield rights to other people's bodies; in other words, A's body cannot be the object of B's welfare right" (p. 36). See also Mark Wicclair, "The Abortion Controversy and the Claim That This Body Is Mine," *Social Theory and Practice* 7 (1981): 337. Wicclair also points to the difficulty of claims of self-ownership.

35. *Roe,* 410 U.S. at 154.

36. Ibid., at 159.

37. Ronald Dworkin, *A Matter of Principle* (Harvard Univ. Press, 1985), pp. 181–213. Cf. Immanuel Kant, *Groundwork of the Metaphysic of Morals,* trans. H. J. Paton (Harper & Row, 1964). According to Kant, "Man is not a thing—not merely something to be used merely as a means: he must always in all his actions be regarded as an end in himself" (p. 97).

38. Dworkin, *A Matter of Principle,* pp. 206–13.

39. Ibid., p. 205.

40. Ibid., pp. 209–10.
41. Ronald Dworkin, *Taking Rights Seriously* (Harvard Univ. Press, 1977), p. 198.
42. Dworkin, *A Matter of Principle,* pp. 205–6.
43. Ibid., p. 206.
44. Roger Wertheimer, "Understanding the Abortion Arguiment," *Philosophy and Public Affairs* 1 (1971): 67–95.
45. 651 F.2d 1198 (6th Cir. 1981), aff'd in part and rev'd in part, 462 U.S. 416 (1983).
46. *Thornburgh,* 106 S. Ct. 2169.
47. David A. Grimes, "Second-Trimester Abortion in the United States," *Family Planning Perspectives* 16 (1984): 260–66.
48. "Viability" is an inexact term. It refers, roughly, to the date after which a fetus could survive after removal from a woman's uterus. On some measures this date has shifted back four weeks since 1973, from 28 weeks to 24 weeks, due to advances in fetal life-support technology. Toward contrary ends, feminists and conservatives alike have argued that the "viability" limitation on women's right to abortion is untenable in light of the impact of technology. See "Late Abortion and Technological Advances in Fetal Viability," *Family Planning Perspectives* 17 (1985): 160–64. Cf. David A. Grimes, "Second-Trimester Abortion."
49. *Thornburgh,* 106 S. Ct. at 2183.
50. Stephen Ross, "The Death of the Fetus," *Philosophy and Public Affairs* 11 (1982): 234. It is not clear how far Ross would push his thesis. He defends it only with respect to embryos and fetuses in the earliest stages.
51. Missouri: Annotated Statutes, Section 188.040 (Vernon 1982).
52. Note, "Current Technology Affecting Supreme Court Abortion Jurisprudence," *New York Law School Law Review* 27 (1982): 1221, 1257. Cf. Comment, "Fetal Viability and Individual Autonomy: Resolving Medical and Legal Standards for Abortion," *UCLA Law Review* (1980): 1340, 1361.
53. Benschof is cited in Daniel Callahan, "How Technology Is Reframing the Abortion Debate," *Hasting Center Report* (February 1986), pp. 33, 40.
54. *Planned Parenthood v. Danforth,* 428 U.S. 52, 68 (1976) (a state cannot delegate power to veto abortion to a spouse). It has been argued that spousal notification statutes should be declared unconstitutional as well. See Note, "Spousal Notification: An Unconstitutional Limitation on a Woman's Right to Privacy in the Abortion Decision," *Hofstra Law Review* 12 (1984): 531. See also Note, "The Spousal Notice and Consultation Requirement: A New Approach to State Regulation of Abortion," *Nova Law Journal* 6 (1982): 457.
55. *Scheinberg v. Smith,* 482 F. Supp. 529, 538 (S.D. Fla. 1979).
56. *Roe,* 410 U.S. at 172 (Justice Rehnquist, dissenting).
57. *Carey v. Population Services Int'l,* 431 U.S. 678, 681 (1976); *Planned Parenthood v. Danforth,* 428 U.S. 52, 74 (1976). See Note, "Minors' Right of Privacy: Access to Contraceptives Without Parental Notification," *Journal of Juvenile Law* 7 (1983): 99; Digest Note, *Journal of Juvenile Law* 7 (1983): 238.
58. See *Belloti v. Baird,* 443 U.S. 622 (1968); *Planned Parenthood v. Danforth,* 428 U.S. 52, 68 (1976); cf. *Planned Parenthood Association of Kansas City v. Ashcroft,* 462 U.S. 476 (1983); and *Akron v. Akron Center for Reproductive Health, Inc.,* 462 U.S. 416 (1983). But see *H. L. v. Matheson,* 450 U.S. 398

(1980) (Court upheld Utah statute requiring physician to give notice to parents prior to performing abortions on unemancipated daughters living at home who make no claim or showing as to independence). See also Digest Note, "Minor's Right to Privacy," *Journal of Juvenile Law* 8 (1984): 170, 173. The case for parental involvement and against judicial involvement was made by the Hon. Walter H. Bennett, Jr., in "Rights and Interests of Parent, Child, Family and the State: A Critique of Development of the Law in Recent Supreme Court Cases and in the North Carolina Juvenile Code," *Campbell Law Review* 4 (1981): 86.

59. The regulations in question were 49 Fed. Reg. 3614 § 59.5[a][12][i][A] (1983), issued by the Department of Health and Human Services pursuant to, Title X of the Public Health Services Act, 42 U.S.C. §§ 300–300a–6a (1982), Pub. L. No. 91–572, 84 Stat. 1506 (1970). This regulation was challenged in *State of New York v. Schweiker,* 557 F. Supp. 354 (S.D.N.Y. 1983) (due to importance of minor's right to privacy and equal protection, injunction granted against enforcement of regulation requiring parental notification within ten days when unemancipated minors provided with prescription birth control drug or device in federally funded clinic).

60. See, for example, Note, "Parental Notice Statutes: Permissible State Regulation of a Minor's Abortion Decision," *Fordham Law Review* 49 (1980): 81, 100–101. See, in general, T. Ooms, ed., *Teenage Pregnancy in a Family Context: Implications for Policy* (Temple Univ. Press, 1981).

61. Note, "Parental Notification: A State-Created Obstacle to a Minor Woman's Right of Privacy," *Golden Gate Law Review* 12 (1982): 579, 584–85, 587. See also Note, "The Abortion Decision for Minnesota Minors: Who Decides?", *William Mitchell Law Review* 9 (1983): 194.

62. See B. Rothman, *In Labor: Women and Power in the Birthplace* (W. W. Norton, 1982). Cf. *Fitzgerald v. Porter Memorial Hospital,* 523 F.2d 716 (7th Cir. 1975) (husband not entitled to be present at childbirth if medical authorities do not permit it).

63. Charles Wolfson, "Midwives and Home Birth: Social, Medical, and Legal Perspectives," *Hastings Law Journal* 37 (1986): 909, 929 n.117; see also Note, "Respecting Liberty and Preventing Harm: Limits of State Intervention in Prenatal Choice," *Harvard Journal of Law and Public Policy,* 8 (Winter 1985): 19; Note, "Childbearing and Nurse Midwives: A Woman's Right to Choose," *New York University Law Review* 58 (June 1983): 661; Walker, "A Matter of the Quality of Birth: Mothers and Midwives Shackled by the Medical Establishment and Pennsylvania Law," *Duquesne Law Review* 23 (1984): 171.

64. *De May v. Roberts,* 46 Mich. 160, 9 N.W. 146 (1881).

65. Ibid. at 147.

66. *Gulf, C. & S. F. Ry. Co. v. Butcher et ux.,* 18 S.W. 583, 585, 83 Texas 309 (1892).

67. B. Rothman, In *Labor,* p. 15. The desire for private childbirth can be a desire to exclude not only non-family members but also unsupportive members of one's own family: "Nothing's private in a one-room house. . . . I had nine children in that room, back there, and I suppose I'll die there the same way—with all the men in the family sitting around the fire muttering, 'Why doesn't she hurry up about it.' My father, my brothers, my husband's brothers, they all sat there by the fire and drank wine and waited. If you make a sound, if a pain catches you by surprise, or the

baby won't come out and you can't stand it and you moan, you've disgraced yourself. You keep a towel shoved in your mouth, and everytime it hurts so bad, you bite down on it and pray to God no noise comes out. I always tied a knot in one end so I could bite real hard, and my sister had a way of crooning and stroking me that made it better. . . . So many times it was all for nothing too. Six of nine died. I could have wailed then—that's all right—but there are some hurts that stay inside. . . . Nothing's private here, not birth, not death, not anything. No matter what any one says, though, you never get used to it." See Lisa Leghorn and Katherine Parker, *Women's Worth: Sexual Economics and the World of Women* (Routledge & Kegan Paul, 1981).

68. J. Goldstein, A. Freud, J. Solnit, *Before the Best Interests of the Child* (Macmillan, 1979); cf. idem. *In the Best Interest of the Child* (Free Press, 1985).

69. Alan F. Westin, *Privacy and Freedom* (Atheneum, 1967), p. 27.

70. See, for example, *Meyer v. Nebraska*, 262 U.S. 390 (1923); *Pierce v. Society of Sisters*, 268 U.S. 510; *Prince v. Massachusetts*, 321 U.S. 510 (1925); and *Wisconsin v. Yoder*, 406 U.S. 205 (1972).

71. June A. Eichbaum, "Towards an Autonomy-Based Theory of Constitutional Privacy: Beyond the Ideology of Familial Privacy," *Harvard Civil Rights–Civil Liberties Law Review* 14 (1979): 361.

72. See David Finkelhor and Richard J. Gelles, eds., *The Dark Side of Families: Current Family Violence Research* (Sage Publications, 1983); M. Boulard, *Violence in the Family* (Humanities Press, 1976); Karen MacKinnie, "Battered Wives," *University of California Law Review* 52 (1981): 587.

73. Callahan, "How Technology Is Reframing," p. 34.

74. *In re Baby Doe*, No GU 8204–004A (Cir. Ct. Monroe County, Ind. Apr. 12, 1982); *State ex rel. Infant Doe v. Baker*, No. 482 5140 (Ind. Apr. 16, 1982), *cert. denied*, 464 U.S. 961 (1983). See, in general, "Symposium: Issues in Procreational Autonomy," *Hastings Law Journal* 37 (1986): 765–908 (examining legal issues raised by Baby Doe and Baby Jane Doe cases).

75. See *Weber v. Stony Brook Hospital*, 95 A.D.2d 587, 467 N.Y.S.2d 685, *aff'd*, 60 N.Y.2d 208, 456 N.E.2d 1186, 469 N.Y.S.2d 63 *(per curiam)*, *cert. denied*, 464 U.S. 1026 (1983).

76. Child Abuse Amendments of 1984, 42 U.S.C.A. Sections 5102–5106, 5111–5113, 5115 (West Supp. 1985). Regulations promulgated under the statute are contained in the Child Abuse and Neglect Prevention and Treatment Program, 45 C.F.R. Section 1340 (1985).

77. See Stephen Smith, "Disabled Newborns and the Federal Child Abuse Amendments: Tenuous Protection," *Hastings Law Journal* 37 (1986): 765, 824.

78. *United States v. University Hospital State University of New York at Stony Brook*, 575 F. Supp. 607 (E.D.N.Y. 1983), *aff'd*, 729 F.2d 144 (2d Cir. 1984). See also *Bowen v. American Hosp. Ass'n.*, 106 S. Ct. 2101 (1986).

79. In addition to Section 504 of the Rehabilitation Act—which provides, in relevant part, that no "otherwise qualified handicapped individual . . . shall, solely by reason of his handicap, . . . be subjected to discrimination under any program or activity receiving federal financial assistance,"—DHHS relied on 45 C.F.R. § 80.6(c), as incorporated by 45 C.F.R. § 84.61, which requires record access to investigate compliance with the Rehabili-

tation Act notwithstanding "considerations of privacy or confidentiality."
80. *Weber,* 469 N.Y.S.2d at 65.
81. Unwanted sterilization denies a woman who may want to bear children, the ability to choose to do so. In *Skinner v. Oklahoma,* 316 U.S. 535 (1942) the Supreme Court upheld decisional privacy over state-imposed sterilization. But see *Buck v. Bell,* 274 U.S. 200 (1927) (sterilization may be utilized as an antidote to the propagation of imbeciles).

In the celebrated Baby "M" surrogate mother case, Judge Sorkow opined that "if one has a [decisional privacy] right to procreate coitally, then one has the right to reproduce non-coitally. If it is the reproduction that is protected, then the means of reproduction are also to be protected. The values and interests underlying the creation of family are the same by whatever means obtained." See *In the Matter of Baby "M",* Superior Court of New Jersey, Chancery Division/Family Part, Bergen County, Docket No. FM–25314–86E (March 31, 1987), p. 91. The decision to uphold a surrogate mother contract is not clearly warranted by fundamental privacy rights of the biological father if, as is sometimes argued, such contracts amount to baby selling and female exploitation. Moreover, when a surrogate birth mother changes her mind there is an argument to be made that, by virtue of her fundamental decisional privacy right of procreation, she is entitled to parent her child notwithstanding a prior agreement to surrender the baby and renounce parental rights at birth.

In January 1986, Pamela Rae Stewart Monson, a 27-year-old San Diego woman, was criminally prosecuted under a state child welfare law originally intended to ensure that fathers paid child-support. Monson gave birth to a short-lived brain-damaged child on November 23, 1985. A judge of the San Diego Municipal Court dismissed charges that Mrs. Monson injured her child during pregnancy by engaging in sexual intercourse against her doctor's orders, taking amphetamines, and delaying medical care for six hours when she began to bleed heavily. See M. Chambers, "Case Against Woman in Baby Death Thrown Out," *New York Times,* February 27, 1987. Monson's attorney and the ACLU argued that the parental support law was improperly applied to her case and that the constitutional right of privacy outweighed the right of the state to act on behalf of the child.

CHAPTER 5

1. Cf. "An individual clearly has an interest in privacy within a toilet stall." See *Elmore v. Atlantic Zayre, Inc.,* 341 S.E.2d 905, 906 (Ga. App. 1986) (no unlawful invasion of privacy where retail manager observed store restroom through crack in ceiling to investigate customer complaints of criminal sodomy).
2. See *Harkey v. Abate,* 346 N.W.2d 74 (Mich. App. 1983).
3. *Joekel v. Samonig,* 75 N.W.2d 925 (Wis. 1956).
4. *Lewis v. Dayton Hudson,* 339 N.W.2d 857 (Mich. App. 1983) (no invasion of privacy found where retailer posted signs warning customers that fitting rooms were under surveillance).
5. *Henderson v. Ripperger,* 594 P.2d 251 (Ct. App. Kan. 1979).

6. See *Pemberton v. Bethlehem Steel,* 502 A.2d 1101, 1117 (Md. App. 1986).

7. See *Forster v. Manchester,* 189 A.2d 147, 149–50 (Pa. Sup. Ct. 1963).

8. See *Bennett v. Norban,* 151 A.2d 476, 477 (Pa. 1959).

9. *Bennett,* 151 A.2d at 479.

10. Ibid.

11. See *Neff v. Time,* 406 F. Supp. 858 (W.D. Pa. 1976).

12. See *Onassis v. Galella,* 487 F.2d 986 (2d Cir. 1973).

13. Cf. *Lewis,* 339 N.W.2d 857.

14. See, for example, *Mark v. King Broadcasting,* 618 P.2d 512 (Wash. App. 1980) (no intrusion upon seclusion where news station ran film of interview in a pharmacy in connection with news story about pharmacist charged with defrauding state).

15. Intentional harmful or offensive conduct aimed at a person in virtue of his or her sex is commonly described as "sexual harassment."

16. The examples are derived from the first-hand experiences of the author in New York City, Washington, D.C., and Chicago.

17. Cf. A. Ellis, "Offense and the Liberal Conception of the Law," *Philosophy and Public Affairs* 13 (1984): 3; J. Feinberg, "Harmless Immoralities and Offensive Nuisances," in *Legal Remedies,* ed. Norman C. Case and Thomas K. Trelogan (Case Western Reserve Univ. Press, 1973).

18. M. W. Barnes, "Vulgarity," *Ethics* 91 (1980): 74, 75.

19. See Arnold H. Buss, *Self-Consciousness and Social Anxiety* (W. H. Freeman, 1980), esp. p. 22.

20. Ibid., p. 5. Audience anxiety (stage-fright) and shyness are two additional forms of "social anxiety" identified by Buss.

21. T. Milburn and K. Watman, *On the Nature of Threat: A Social Psychological Analysis* (Praeger, 1981), p. 129.

22. Cf. S. Seagert, ed., *Crowding in Real Environments* (Sage Publications, 1976).

23. Janet Radcliffe Richards, *The Skeptical Feminist: A Philosophical Enquiry* (Routledge & Kegan Paul, 1980), attacked the feminist ideal of the unadorned woman. She argued that there is nothing wrong with being concerned with whether one is beautiful and stylish. It is not incumbent upon liberated women to be unconcerned with their packaging. "The question of how much effort is worth putting into beauty has nothing to do with feminism," she wrote (p. 196). She contended that men cannot be blamed if, *ceteris paribus,* they prefer conventional beauty and stylishness to their opposites. "Feminism is concerned with sexual justice, and not with the ultimate worth of one kind of preference over another" (p. 197). Richards overlooks ways in which men's preferences can sometimes have an impact on sexual justice. While it is normally attenuated, there is a discernible relationship between sexual justice and men's preferences about women's appearances. Suppose, for example, men's preferences for young, pretty faces, feminine styles, and hour-glass figures cause qualified job candidates to be turned down or aging employees to be fired.

24. See, in general, Clara Mayo and Nancy M. Henley, *Gender and Nonverbal Behavior* (Springer-Verlag: 1981).

25. Clara Mayo and Nancy M. Henley, "Nonverbal Behavior: Barrier or Agent for Sex Role Change?" in ibid., p. 7. See also J. Hall, "Gender, Gender Roles and Nonverbal Behavior," in *Skill in Nonverbal Communication,* ed. R. Rosenthal (Oelsgeschlage, Gunn, & Hain, 1979); R. Rosen-

thal, "Measuring Sensitivity to Non-Verbal Communication: The Pons Test," in *Non-Verbal Behavior,* ed. A. Wolfgang (Academic Press, 1979). Cf. *Women and Sex Roles: A Social Psychological Perspective* (W. W. Norton, 1978), pp. 321–24.

26. Rosenthal, *Nonverbal Communication.* See, in general, Rosenthal and J. Hall et al., *The Pons Test Manual: Profile of Non-Verbal Sensitivity* (Irvington Publishers, 1979).

27. Milburn and Watman, *The Nature of Threat,* p. 126.

28. Rosemarie Tong discusses the law of sexual harassment in detail in *Women, Sex, and the Law* (Rowman & Allanheld, 1984).

29. Kristin Lukes, *Abortion and the Politics of Motherhood* (Univ. of California Press, 1984), p. 100.

30. The Community Board Program, Inc., of San Francisco, executive director Raymond Shonholtz, was established to help neighborhoods govern their own conflicts. Shonholz believes that peaceful expression of local conflicts in a neighborhood justice forum where community volunteers hear, judge, conciliate, and mediate disputes can provide a basis for greater understanding, awareness, and mutual working-out of community-based problems.

31. Alan F. Westin, *Privacy and Freedom* (Atheneum, 1967), p. 14.

32. The gist of these points is argued by Barbara S. Bryant in "Sexual Display of Women's Bodies—A Violation of Privacy," *Golden Gate University Law Review* 10 (1980): 1211.

33. Andrea Dworkin attaches special significance to the etymology of the term. See her *Pornography: Men Possessing Women* (Pedigree Books, 1981).

34. See C. Schneider, *Shame, Exposure and Privacy* (Beacon Press, 1977), pp. 56–57.

35. Ibid.

36. Ibid.

37. Eva Feder Kittay, "Pornography and the Erotics of Domination," in *Beyond Domination,* ed. Carol C. Gould (Rowman & Allanheld, 1983), pp. 147–48.

38. "Really Socking It to Women," *Time,* February 7, 1977, pp. 58–59.

39. See, in general, B. Faust, *Women, Sex and Pornography* (Macmillan, 1980).

40. See, for example, A. Garry, "Pornography and Respect for Women," in *Philosophy and Women,* ed. S. Bishop and M. Weinzweig (Wadsworth Publishing, 1979).

41. S. Brownmiller, *Against Our Will* (Simon & Schuster, 1975), has objected to pornography on these grounds.

42. The Commission was formed by Attorney General Edwin Meese, III. Commission data was criticized as "worthless" and "one-sided." Evelina Kane, staff coordinator of Women Against Pornography, described the report as "a major breakthrough in raising the consciousness of the country." See Philip Shenon, "A Second Opinion on Pornography's Impact," *The New York Times,* May 18, 1986.

43. See *New York Daily News Sunday Magazine,* June 26, 1983, pp. 7–8. The article also cited the testimony of three girls who said they sexually assaulted a nine-year-old Californian after watching a similar attack in a television movie called "Born Innocent".

44. In *Miller v. California* (1983), the Supreme Court held that states may ban depictions or descriptions of sexual conduct as obscenity if they are part of "works which, taken as a whole, appeal to the prurient interest in sex,

which portray sexual conduct in a patently offensive way, and which, taken as a whole, do not have serious literary, artistic, political or scientific value." In *Pope v. Illinois*, No. 85-1973, decided May 5, 1987, the court held that First Amendment values require that the social worth of a work be assessed from the standpoint of a "reasonable person" standard rather than a community standard.

Public display of obscenity is prohibited in many localities. Whether obscenity display laws would reach all forms of pornography depicting women would depend upon how "obscenity" was defined under local law. For example, the city code of Pittsburgh, Pennsylvania, provides that "No person, knowing the obscene character of the materials involved, shall: (a) Display or cause or permit the display of any obscene materials in or on any window, showcase, newsstand, display rack, billboard, display board, viewing screen, motion picture screen marquee or similar place, in such manner that the display is visible from any public street, highway, sidewalk, transportation facility or other public thoroughfare." The Pittsburgh code goes on from the quoted passage to generally prohibit the sale and production of all obscene materials (see Pittsburgh Code, Article I, Title 6 Conduct, Chapter 613). The code does not appear to prohibit display of typical "soft-porn" magazine covers some feminists would say are pornographic because they degrade and humiliate women and are intended to arouse men. These are not "obscene." To qualify as "obscenity" under the Pittsburgh code, depictions of women's bodies would have to appeal to prurient interest, lack serious literary, artistic, political, educational, or scientific value, and, most important, constitute "patently offensive representations or descriptions of ultimate sexual acts, normal or perverted, actual or simulated, and patently offensive representations or descriptions of masturbation, excretory functions or lewd exhibitions of the genitals." Under this definition, typical "men's entertainment" magazine covers of semi-nude women are permitted. Public display of pornography is not categorically prohibited in Pittsburgh.

45. Cf. Bryant, "Sexual Display."
46. A firm believer in the inequality of the sexes, James Fitzjames Stephens was not altogether lacking in insight. He was a defender of privacy and understood that popular usage of "privacy" reflects a broad conception of the term: "Legislation and public opinion ought in all cases whatever scrupulously to respect privacy. To define the province of privacy distinctly is impossible, but it can be described in general terms. All the more intimate and delicate relations of life are of such a nature that to submit them to unsympathetic observation, or to observation which is sympathetic in the wrong way, inflicts great pain, and may inflict lasting moral injury. Privacy may be violated not only by the intrusion of a stranger, but by compelling or persuading a person to direct too much attention to his own feelings and to attach too much importance to their analysis. The common usage of language affords a practical test which is almost perfect upon this subject. Conduct which can be described as indecent is always in one or another an invasion of privacy." See R. J. White, *Liberty, Equality, Fraternity* (Cambridge Univ. Press, 1967), p. 160.
47. Cf. Catherine MacKinnon, *Sexual Harassment of Working Women* (Yale Univ. Press, 1979); and Lin Farley, *Sexual Shakedown: The Sexual Harassment of Women on the Job* (McGraw-Hill, 1978). See also Alice Montgom-

ery, "Sexual Harassment in the Workplace," *Golden Gate Law University Review* 10 (1980): 879; and Barbara N. White, "Job-Related Sexual Harassment and Union Women: What Are Their Rights?," *Golden Gate University Law Review* 1 (1980): 929. In general, see William F. Pepper and Florynce R. Kennedy, Sex Discrimination in Employment (The Michie Company, 1981); Ronnie Steinberg, ed., *Equal Employment Policy for Women* (Temple Univ. Press, 1980); Suzanne Reifers, *How to Hire and Supervise Women* (Executive Enterprises Publications Co., 1979); and Cynthia Stoddard, *Sex Discrimination in Educational Employment: Legal Alternatives and Strategies* (Learning Publication, 1981).

48. Cf. Myron Brenton, *The Privacy Invaders* (Coward-McCann, 1964), pp 97–98: "The ladies were applying for jobs in a pilferage-plagued department store which asked them to prove their own probity by taking polygraph examinations. Soon they discovered that the examiner had far more than pilferage on his mind, as they subsequently pointed out in angry letters to the Connecticut State Department of Labor." Adult women and teenage job-seekers were asked whether they were menstruating and whether they "go too far with boys."

49. See Lisa Leghorn and Katherine Parker, *Women's Worth: Sexual Economics and the World of Women* (Routledge & Kegan Paul, 1981), p. 161: "They [women] are treated worse than male inmates are because they are expected to conform to the role of the docile woman."

50. Cf. MacKinnon, *Sexual Harassment;* and Farley, *Sexual Shakedown.* Cf. also Montgomery, "Sexual Harassment" and White, "Job-Related Sexual Harassment."

51. MacKinnon, *Sexual Harassment,* pp. 29, 43.

52. *Philips v. Smalley Maintenance Services,* 435 So. 2d 705 (Ala. 1983). This notable case held that sexual prying is an invasion of privacy under the common law of Alabama even if no information is yielded or communicated to third parties. Philips was awarded damages for chronic anxiety caused by her employer's behavior.

53. The statistics are based on Bureau of Labor Statistics and National Center for Education Statistics studies. See Andrew Hacker, "Women at Work," *New York Review of Books,* August 14, 1986, pp. 26–31.

54. *Bodewig v. K-Mart,* 635 P.2d 657 (Or. App. 1981).

55. See Cynthia Fuchs Epstein, *Women In the Law* (Anchor/Doubleday, 1983); Eve Spangler, *Lawyers for Hire: Salaried Professionals at Work* (Yale Univ. Press, 1986).

56. *Pangallo v. Murphy,* 243 S.W.2d (Ct. App. Ky. 1951). Cf. *Froelich v. Werbin,* 548 P.2d 482 (Sup. Ct. Kan. 1976) (no intrusion upon seclusion found with respect to sample of hair taken from plaintiff's hospital room).

57. See *Ponton v. Scarfone,* 468 So. 2d 1009 (Fla. App. 2 Dis. 1985), at 1010, 1011.

58. Ibid.

59. See Paul Burstein, *Discrimination, Jobs and Politics: The Struggle for Employment Opportunity in the United States Since the New Deal* (Univ. of Chicago Press, 1985).

60. Cf. Note, "Equal Credit," *Journal of Legislation* 8 (1981): 121.

61. "Marian and the Elders," *Time Magazine,* March 26, 1984, p. 70. Nurse Marian Guinn sued the Church of Christ of Collinsville, Oklahoma, a small community near Tulsa, in state district court for $1.3 million. She alleged invasion of privacy and intentional infliction of emotional dis-

tress. She was awarded $390,000. Noting that "He was a man. She is a single lady. And this is America," her lawyer likened her branding to that of Hester Prynne in Hawthorne's *The Scarlet Letter.*

62. "Kings, and emperors, and presidents, and parliaments, and congresses, and assemblies, and courts, and legislators, and judges may labor in vain to influence or to reform mankind, so long as female influence is not what it should be." Wm. A. Alcott, *Young Woman's Guide to Excellence* (Charles H. Pierce, Birney and Otherman, W. J. Reynolds and Co., 1847).

63. Two privacy theorists, Westin, *Privacy and Freedom,* and Edward J. Bloustein, *Individual and Group Privacy* (Transaction Books, 1978), heartily embrace the notion of group and organizational privacy, defending it on grounds analogous to those on which the defense of individual privacy is based.

64. See, in general, Bobb, "The Private Clubs Issue: Irreconcilable Differences?" *Illinois Bar Journal* 74 (1986): 446; Note, "Roberts v. United States Jaycees," *Rutgers Law Review* 38 (1986): 341; Devins, "The Trouble With Jaycees," *Catholic University Law Review* 34 (1985): 901; Archer, "Blackballed! The Case Against Private Clubs," *Barrister* 10 (Spring 1983): 22; C. Goodwin, "Challenging the Private Club: Sex Discrimination Plaintiffs Barred at the Door," *Southwest University Law Review* 13 (1982): 237.

65. But see Feldblum, Krent and Watkin, "Legal Challenges to All-Female Organizations," *Harvard Civil Rights and Civil Liberties Law Review* 21 (1986): 171.

66. John M. Roberts and Thomas Gregor, "Privacy: A Cultural View," in *Privacy: Nomos XIII,* ed. J. Roland Pennock and John W. Chapman (Atherton Press, 1971), p. 182, 210.

67. Ibid., p. 210.

68. *Bell v. Maryland,* 378 U.S. 226 (1964) (concurring opinion).

69. *Moose Lodge No. 107 v. Irvis,* 407 U.S. 163, 179–80 (1972).

70. See *Civil Rights Cases,* 109 U.S. 3, 22 (1883) ("The Congress that enacted the 14th Amendment was particularly conscious that the 'civil rights' of man should be distinguished from his 'social rights.'")

71. Enacted as a title of the Civil Rights Act of 1964, the Federal Public Accommodations Act, 42 U.S.C. Section 2000a ("the Act"), prohibits discrimination or segregation in places of public accommodations by establishments whose operations effect commerce or are supported by state action. Section 2000a(e), however, exempts private clubs or establishments from the statute: "(e) The provisions of this subchapter shall not apply to a *private club* or other establishment *not in fact opened to the public* except to the extent that the facilities of such establishment are made available to customers or patrons of an establishment within the scope of subsection (b) of this section" (emphasis added). Self-description and de facto exclusiveness seem to be the implied criteria for determining what is a private club or organization. Self-described private clubs have generally been held to be "truly private" in the federal courts. One test for private club status in controversies arising under the Act is whether, without regard to the suspect classification, the club's membership policies and practices manifest a "plan or purpose of exclusiveness." See *Tillman v. Wheaton Haven Recreation Ass'n,* 410 U.S. 431, 93 (1973); *Sullivan v. Little Huntington Park, Inc.,* 396 U.S. 229 (1969); *Wright v.*

Salisbury, 479 F. Supp. 378, 80 (1979). A number of cases under the Act, however, suggest that a club whose membership and patronage are generally open or "for sale" to all but members of a protected class, is not truly private. See *Cornelius v. Benevolent Order of the Elks,* 382 F. Supp. 1182 (D.CT) (1974).

The constitutionality of the Act has been tested and upheld. *Hamm v. City of Rock Hill, Arkansas,* 379 U.S. 306 (1964) (Congress exercised constitutional power in enacting this subchapter). Some legislative history suggests that without a private club exemption like § 2000a(e), the Act would not have been constitutional. The Act has become a model for state and local governments.

72. *Statement by Counsel President Carol Bellamy,* Private Club Bill Press Conference, April 8, 1983.
73. *Administrative Code of New York,* Title B Commission on Human Rights, Section B1-2.0(9) (defining place of public accommodation).
74. Goodwin, "Challenging the Private Club," pp. 270–71.
75. Clarence Ruddy, "Personal Viewpoint: 'A Protest from Private Organizations'," *American Bar Association Journal* 68 (August 1982): 884.

CHAPTER 6

1. Bureau of Justice Statistics, U.S. Department of Justice, *Compendium of State Privacy and Security Legislation* (1984). See also Donald Marchand, *The Politics of Privacy, Computers, and the Criminal Justice Records* (Information Resources Press, 1980); United States Privacy Protection Study Commission, *Personal Privacy in an Information Society* (U.S.G.P.O., 1977), pp. 534–36.
2. Bureau of Justice Statistics, *Compendium,* p. iii.
3. Ibid., p. 3.
4. Ibid., p. 10.
5. See *Cox Broadcasting Corp. v. Cohn,* 420 U.S. 469 (1975); *In Re Oliver,* 333 U.S. 57 (1948); *United States v. Cianfrani,* 573 F.2d 835 (3rd Cir. 1978) (media appeals court order excluding public from pretrial suppression hearing in trial of a Philadelphia politician). Also see note 8, below. Cf. *Sheppard v. Maxwell,* 384 U.S. 333 (1966).
6. "I'm Sick, I'm Sick, and I Have No One," *The New York Times,* October 25, 1985, p. 2. See Charles M. Brodie, "Privacy and Mental Health," *The Right to Privacy Versus the Right to Know* (Institute of Government, Univ. of Georgia, 1979), p. 46. Brodie summarizes the information demands arising out of the desire of the public to assist in mental health services and the collateral demands for accountability.
7. Sixth Amendment policy is succinctly explained in *U.S. v. Cianfrani,* 573 U.S. at 835, 847–48. The complete text of the Sixth Amendment reads: "In all criminal prosecutions, the accused shall enjoy the right to a speedy and public trial, by an impartial jury of the State and district wherein the crime shall have been committed, which district shall have been committed, which district shall have been previously ascertained by law, and to be informed of the nature and cause of the accusation; to be confronted with the witnesses against him; to have compulsory process for obtaining witnesses in his favor, and to have the Assistance of Counsel for his defense."
8. *U.S. v. Cianfrani,* 573 U.S. at 852.
9. Franklyn S. Haiman, *Speech and Law in a Free Society* (University of

Chicago Press, 1980), pp. 71–72. Marc Franklin's view that rape victim anonymity policies have only weak "gallantry justification" and "law enforcement justification" is discussed. See, in general, E. Fishbein, "Identifying the Rape Victim: A Clash Between the First Amendment and the Right to Privacy," *John Marshall Law Review* 18 (1985): 987.

10. "Inviolate personality" was a term Samuel Warren and Louis Brandeis used to refer to the interests protected by the right to privacy. See Brandeis and Warren, "The Right to Privacy," *Harvard Law Review* 4 (1890): 193, 205. It is often said that the purpose of the right to privacy is to protect the feelings and sensibilities of natural persons. See Robert D. Sack, *Libel, Slander and Related Problems* (1980), p. 398; and Bruce W. Sandford, *Libel and Privacy: The Prevention and Defense of Litigation* (1983), p. 460.

11. Haiman, in *Speech and Law,* p. 71, takes a partly opposing view.

12. *Cox Broadcasting Corp. v. Cohn,* 420 U.S. 469 (1975).

13. Ibid., at 494–95.

14. *Cape Publications, Inc. v. Bridges,* 423 So. 2d 426, rev. denied, 431 So. 2d 988 (Fla. 1983), *cert. denied,* 464 U.S. 893 (1983).

15. *Doe v. United States,* 666 F.2d 43 (4th Cir. 1981).

16. 124 Congressional Record H.11.944 (Daily ed. October 10, 1978) (Congressman Mann). Congressman Holtzman was the chief architect of the bill that became Rule 412. Defending it before the Congress, she remarked that: "Too often in this country victims of rape are humiliated and harassed when they report and prosecute the rape. Bullied and cross-examined about their prior sexual experiences, many find the trial almost as degrading as the rape itself. Since rape trials become inquisitions into the victim's morality, not trials of the defendant's innocence or guilt, is not surprising that it is the least reported crime. It is estimated that as few as one in ten rapes is ever reported." See, in general, Susan Estrich, *Real Rape* (Harvard Univ. Press, 1987).

17. Federal Rules of Evidence, Title 28 U.S.C. Rule 412 (1984). Rule 412 reads in full:

(a) Notwithstanding any other provision of law, in a criminal case in which a person is accused of rape or of assault with intent to commit rape, reputation of opinion evidence of the past sexual behavior of an alleged victim of such rape or assault is not admissible.

(b) Notwithstanding any other provision of law, in a criminal case in which a person is accused of rape or of assault with intent to commit rape, evidence of a victim's past sexual behavior other than reputation or opinion evidence is also not admissible, unless such evidence other than reputation or opinion evidence is—

(1) admitted in accordance with subdivisions (c)(1) and (c)(2) and is constitutionally required to be admitted; or

(2) admitted in accordance with subdivision (c) and is evidence of—

(A) past sexual behavior with persons other than the accused, offered by the accused upon the issue of whether the accused was or was not, with respect to the alleged victim, the source of semen or injury; or

(B) past sexual behavior with the accused and is offered by the accused upon the issue of whether the alleged victim consented to the sexual behavior with respect to which rape or assault is alleged.

(c)(1) If the person accused of committing rape or assault with intent to commit rape intends to offer under subdivision (b) evidence of specific instances of the alleged victim's past sexual behavior, the accused shall make a written motion to offer such evidence not later than fifteen days before the date on which the trial in which such evidence is to be offered is scheduled to begin, except that the court may allow the motion to be made at a later date, including during trial, if the court determines either that the evidence is newly discovered and could not have been obtained earlier through the exercise of due diligence or that the issue to which such evidence relates has newly arisen in the case. Any motion made under this paragraph shall be served on all other parties and on the alleged victim.

(2) The motion described in paragraph (1) shall be accompanied by a written offer of proof. If the court determines that the offer of proof contains evidence described in subdivision (b), the court shall order a hearing in chambers to determine if such evidence is admissible. At such hearing the parties may call witnesses, including the alleged victim, and offer relevant evidence. Notwithstanding subdivision (b) of rule 104, if the relevancy of the evidence which the accused seeks to offer in the trial depends upon the fulfillment of a condition of fact, the court, at the hearing in chambers or at a subsequent hearing in chambers scheduled for such purpose, shall accept evidence on the issue of whether such condition of fact is fulfilled and shall determine such issue.

(3) If the court determines on the basis of the hearing described in paragraph (2) that the evidence which the accused seeks to offer is relevant and that the probative value of such evidence outweighs the danger of unfair prejudice, such evidence shall be admissible in the trial to the extent an order made by the court specifies evidence which may be offered and areas with respect to which the alleged victim may be examined or cross-examined.

(d) For purposes of this rule, the term "past sexual behavior" means sexual behavior other than the sexual behavior with respect to which rape or assault with intent to commit rape is alleged.

18. *Cox Broadcasting Corp. v. Cohn*, 420 U.S. 469 (1975).
19. See Harriett R. Galvin, "Shielding Rape Victims in the State and Federal Courts: A Proposal for the Second Decade," *Minnesota Law Review* 70 (1986): 763, 765 n.3, and 773. Utah has no rape shield statute and in Arizona the admissibility of evidence is restricted by case law.
20. See ibid.
21. Rule 412(b)(3).
22. *Doe v. United States*, 666 F.2d (4th Cir. 1981).
23. *United States v. Nez*, 661 F.2d 1203, 1205 (10th Cir. 1981).
24. *United States v. One Feather*, 702 F.2d 736 (8th Cir. 1983).
25. J. Tanford and A. Bocchino, "Rape Victim Shield Laws and the Sixth Amendment," *University of Pennsylvania Law Review* 128 (1981): 544.
26. Ibid., p. 545.
27. *U.S. v. One Feather*, 702 F.2d at 739.
28. See note 11, above.

29. See, in general, David O'Brien, *Privacy, Law and Public Policy* (Praeger, 1979).

30. See, for example, *United States v. Bear Ribs,* 722 F.2d 420 (8th Cir. 1983).

31. See *Doe v. U.S.,* 666 F.2d at 48, note 9.

32. Galvin, "Shielding Rape Victims," p. 887.

33. *U.S. v. Bear Ribs,* 722 F.2d at 423, n.1. For an overview of fabrication instructions in general, see 92 A.L.R.3d 886 (1979).

34. *U.S. v. Bear Ribs,* at 423, note 2.

35. See Estelle Freedman, *Their Sisters' Keepers: Women's Prison Reform in America, 1830–1930* (Univ. of Michigan Press, 1981); Sharon L. Fabian, "Women Prisoners: Challenge of the Future," in *Legal Rights of Prisoners,* ed., Goffrey Alpert (Sage Publications, 1980), pp. 184–85; John Ortez Smykley, *Coed Prison* (Human Sciences Press, 1980), p. 271; Ronald Goldfarb, *Jails: The Ultimate Ghetto of the Criminal Justice System* (Anchor Press/Doubleday, 1975), p. 379; Edna Walker Chandler, *Women in Prison* (The Bobbs-Merrill Company, 1973), p. 40; John Thornhill, *The Prison and the Group* (The Bruce Publishing Company, 1967).

   See also Rosemary Herbert, "Women's Prisons: An Equal Protection Evaluation," *Yale Law Journal* 94 (1985): 1182; Laurie A. Hanson, "Women's Prisoners: Freedom from Sexual Harassment—A Constitutional Analysis," *Golden Gate University Law Review* 13 (1983): 667; Anne T. Vitale, "Inmate Abortions—The Right to Government Funding Behind the Iron Gates," *Fordham Law Review* 48 (1980): 550; Sharon L. Fabian, "Toward the Best Interests of Women Prisoners: Is the System Working?," *New England Journal of Prison Law* 6 (1979): 1; Julie H. Jackson, "The Loss of Parental Rights as a Consequence of Conviction and Imprisonment: Unintended Punishment," *New England Journal of Prison Law* 6 (1979): 61; Note, "On Prisoners and Parenting: Preserving the Tie That Binds," *Yale Law Journal* 87 (1978): 1408; Richard D. Palmer, "The Prisoner-Mother and Her Child," *Capital University Law Review* 1 (1972): 127; Tom Goldstein, "Behind Prison Walls," *Cosmopolitan,* November 1984, pp. 259–61, 290; and Kenneth Sargoy, "Constitutional Law—Privacy—Prisons," *Whittier Law Review* 2 (1980): 619.

36. Jonathan R. Haden, "Constitutional Law: *Bell v. Wolfish* a Balk at Constitutional Protection for Pretrial Detainees," *UMKV Law Review* 48 (1980): 466; Catherine Mazankas, "Privacy for Pretrial Detainees: Will the California Courts Protect the Detainee from Surreptitious Surveillance by Jail Authorities?," *Criminal Justice Journal* 4 (1980): 199.

37. Selwyn Raab, "Strip Searches at Issue in Girl's Suit," *The New York Times,* June 22, 1986.

38. See *Hudson v. Palmer,* 468 U.S. 517 (1984); *Bell v. Wolfish,* 441 U.S. 520 (1978). In *Hudson* the Court held that there is no reasonable expectation of privacy in a prison cell that would preclude unannounced cell-searches aimed to detect contraband and disciplinary violations; but that there are Fourth Amendment limitations when bodily integrity is invaded, as in the case of strip searches. In *Bell,* visual body cavity searches conducted after every contact visit with a person from outside the institution were held not to be an unconstitutional invasion of privacy. Cf. *Ruffin v. Commonwealth,* 62 Va. (21 Gratt) 790 (1891).

39. Cf. Julie H. Jackson, "The Loss of Parental Rights As a Consequence of Conviction and Imprisonment: Unintended Punishment," *New England Journal of Prison Law* 6 (1979): 61.

40. See, for example, *Bell v. Wolfish*, 441 U.S. at 537.
41. See Barry K. Tagawa, "Prisoner Hunger Strikes: Constitutional Protection for a Fundamental Right," *American Criminal Law Review* 20 (1983): 569; G. M. M, "The Executioner's Song: Is There a Right to Listen?," *Virginia Law Review* 67 (1983); Stephanie Claven Powell, "Constitutional Law—Forced Feeding of a Prisoner on a Hunger Strike: A Violation of the Inmate's Right to Privacy," *North Carolina Law Review* 61 (1983): 714; Daniel Aronson, "Prisoners Rights," *Annual Survey of American Law* (1982): 79; Lynn Soodik, "Communications Behind Bars: Are We Finally Applying the Reasonable Expectation of Privacy Test to Custodial Conversations?," *Comment Law Journal* 4 (Winter 81/82): 327. "Prisoners . . . Hunger Strikes," *American Bar Association Journal* 68 (1982): 1161; Sharon C. Esposito, "Conjugal Visitation in American Prisons Today," *Journal of Family Law* 19 (1980–81): 313; Norman Elliot Kent, "The Legal and Sociological Dimensions of Conjugal Visitation in Prisons," *New England Journal of Prison Law* 2 (1975): 47; "Conjugal Visitation Rights and the Appropriate Standard of Judicial Review for Prison Regulations," *Michigan Law Review* 73 (1974): 398; Jonathan Brant, "Behavior Modification as a Potential Infringement on Prisoners' Right to Privacy," *New England Journal for Prison Law* 1 (1974): 180.
42. See, in general, *Hudson v. Palmer* and *Bell v. Wolfish.*
43. Ronald Dworkin, *Taking Rights Seriously* (Harvard Univ. Press, 1977).
44. "By paternalism I shall understand roughly the interference with a person's liberty of action justified by reasons referring exclusively to the welfare, good, happiness, needs, interests or values of the person being coerced." Gerald Dworkin, "Paternalism," *The Monist* 56 (June 1972): 64–84.
45. Note, "Women Prisoners: Freedom from Sexual Harassment."
46. See, in general, Note, "Conjugal Visitation and the Appropriate Standard of Judicial Review."
47. Ibid., p. 419.
48. See, in general, Vern Bullough and Bonnie Bullough, *Prostitution: An Illustrated Social History* (Crown Publishers, 1978); K. Barry, *Female Sexual Slavery* (Prentice-Hall, 1979); John Boswell, *Christianity, Homosexuality and Tolerance* (Univ. of Chicago Press, 1980).
49. "Recommendation and Report to the House of Delegates by the Section of Individual Rights and Responsibilities Concerning Prostitution and Solicitation," *Human Rights* 4 (1974): 77; Charles Rosenbleet and Barbara Parrente, "The Prostitution of the Criminal Law," *American Criminal Law Review* 11 (1973): 373. Daniel Wade, "Prostitution and the Law: Emerging Attacks on the 'Women's Crime,'" *UMKC* 43 (1975): 413. Therese M. Wandling, "Decriminalization of Prostitution: The Limits of the Criminal Law," *Oregon Law Review* 55 (1976): 553.
50. See NEV. REV. STAT. ANN. § 269.175 (Michie 1986): "The boards of county commissioners may in any unincorporated town in their respective counties license, tax, regulate, prohibit and suppress all . . . houses of ill fame."
51. See, for example, MINN. STAT. ANN. § 609.725 (West Supp. 1987): "Any of the following are vagrants and are guilty of misdemeanor: . . . (3) A prostitute who loiters on the street or in a public place or in a place open to the public with intent to solicit for immoral purposes."
52. See, for example, OHIO REV. CODE ANN. § 2907.25 (Anderson 1982):

"(A) No person shall engage in sexual activity for hire. (B) Whoever violates this section is guilty of prostitution, a misdemeanor of the third degree."

53. See, for example, N.Y. PENAL LAW § 230.00 (McKinney 1980): "A person is guilty of prostitution when such person engages or agrees or offers to engage in sexual conduct with another person in return for a fee. Prostitution is a class B misdemeanor."

54. See, for example, COLO. REV. STAT. § 18–7–206 (1986): "Any person who knowingly lives on or is supported or maintained in whole or in part by money or other thing of value earned, received, procured, or realized by any other person through prostitution commits pimping, which is a class 3 felony."

55. See, for example, IOWA CODE ANN. § 725.3 (West 1979): Pandering defined: "A person who persuades or arranges for another to become an inmate of a brothel, or to become a prostitute, such person not having previously engaged in prostitution, or to return to the practice of prostitution after having abandoned it, or who keeps or maintains a brothel, commits a class D felony."

56. See, for example, MO. ANN. STAT. § 567.060(1) (Vernon 1979): "A person commits the crime of promoting prostitution in the second degree if he knowingly promotes prostitution by managing, supervising, controlling or owning, either alone or in association with others, a house of prostitution or a prostitution business or enterprise involving prostitution activity by two or more prostitutes."

57. See, for example, ARK. STAT. ANN. § 41–2914 (1977): "(1) A person commits the offense of loitering if he: (e) lingers or remains in a public place for the purpose of engaging or soliciting another person to engage in prostitution or deviate sexual activity."

58. See, for example, N.Y. PENAL LAW § 240.37(2) (McKinney 1980): "Any person who remains or wanders about in a public place and repeatedly beckons to, or repeatedly stops, or repeatedly attempts to stop, or repeatedly attempts to engage passersby in conversation, or repeatedly stops or attempts to stop motor vehicles, or repeatedly interferes with the free passage of other persons, for the purpose of prostitution, or of patronizing a prostitute . . . is guilty of a class B misdemeanor."

59. See, for example, COLO. REV. STAT. § 18–7–202 (1986): "(1) A person commits soliciting for prostitution if he: (a) Solicits another for the purpose of prostitution; or (b) Arranges or offers to arrange a meeting of persons for the purpose of prostitution; or (c) Directs another to a place knowing such direction is for the purpose of prostitution. (2) Soliciting for prostitution is a class 3 misdemeanor."

60. See, for example, NEV. REV. STAT. ANN. § 202.140 (Michie 1986): "(2) Any physician or other person, knowing that any common prostitute is afflicted with any infectious or contagious venereal disease, who fails to notify immediately the police authorities . . . is guilty of a misdemeanor."

61. See *State v. Mueller,* 671 P.2d 1351 (Hi. 1983). See also D. B. M., "Constitutional Law—Woman's Right to Have Sexual Relations for Hire in Her Home with Consenting Adults Is Not a Fundamental Privacy Right Protected by State or Federal Constitution: *State v. Mueller,* 671 P.2d 1351 (Hi 1983)," *Journal of Family Law* 22 (1983): 755.

62. The home knitting and sewing industries are unlawful below minimum wage employment under The Fair Labor Standards Act, legislation

implemented to eliminate sweatshop conditions found earlier in the century in big cities. See K. Nable, "U.S. Weighs End to Ban on Factory Homework," *New York Times*, August 20, 1986.

63. Susan Kennedy, *If All We Did Was Weep at Home: A History of White Working Class Women in America* (Indiana Univ. Press, 1979), pp. 98–99.

64. R. Rothman's remarks were quoted in a Boston-area newspaper, *Equal Times*, October 23, 1983, p. 7.

65. Ibid.

66. R. Symanski, *The Immoral Landscape: Female Prostitution in Western Societies* (Butterworths, 1981). Also see, in general, Bullough and Bullough, *Prostitution*.

67. See Marilyn Haft, "Hustling for Rights," *Civil Liberties Review* 1 (1974): 8; and M. Anne Jennings, "The Victim as Criminal: A Consideration of California's Prostitution Law," *California Law Review* 64 (1976): 1235.

68. Sayde Markowitz, "Criminal Law—Due Process—Statute Proscribing Loitering for the Purpose of Prostitution Is Not Unconstitutionally Vague," *Fordham Urban Law Journal* 6 (1977): 159; Ellen F. Murray, "Anti-Prostitution Law: New Conflicts in the Fight Against the Oldest Profession," *Albany Law Review* 43 (1979): 360; and Raymond Parnas, "Legislative Reform of Prostitution Laws: Keeping Commercial Sex Out of Sight and Out of Mind," *Santa Clara Law Review* 21 (1981): 669.

69. Perry, "Right to Privacy Challenges to Prostitution Statutes," *Washington University Law Quarterly* 58 (1980): 439; and Note, "Privacy and Prostitution: Constitutional Implications of State v. Pilcher," *Iowa Law Review* 63 (1971): 248.

70. *Bowers v. Hardwick*, 106 S. Ct. 2841 (1986).

71. See above, note 60.

72. Patrick Devlin, *The Enforcement of Morals* (Oxford Univ. Press, 1965). Devlin's view is that there is a public morality, constituted by the community of ideas about how individuals should be governed, and that society has a prima facie right to enforce them. His book was a response to the famous Wolfenden Report, which had concluded that prostitution and homosexuality ought not be criminal offenses in England.

73. See, in general, Bullough and Bullough, *Prostitution;* and Cheverir, "Victimless Crime Laws," *North Carolina Central Law Journal* 6 (1975): 258.

74. See Paul J. Goldstein, *Prostitution and Drugs* (Lexington Books, 1979).

75. This phrase inspired the name and acronym COYOTE, which is borne by an organization headed by Margo St. James. COYOTE has actively promoted the rights of women in prostitution.

76. See, in general, R. Arrington, "On Respect," *Journal of Value Inquiry* 12 (1978): 1.

77. See Martin O'Brien, *All the Girls* (St. Martin's Press, 1982). This book is written as a sexually explicit account of the experience of a man who patronized prostitutes in diverse milieus around the globe.

78. See Sydney Biddle Barrows, *Mayflower Madam: The Secret Life of Sydney Biddle Barrows* (Arbor House Publishing Co., 1986).

79. John Stuart Mill, *On Liberty* (1859).

Table of Cases Cited

Index

Abortion: cost of, 107; decisional-privacy case for, 97–110; facilities, 91, 106, 111, 112; fetal death, 109; number performed, 86; patient privacy, 91; privacy case for, 85, 89–97; public opinion, 87, 89; record-keeping and reporting, 33, 111; statutes limiting, 96–108; studies of, 199 *n.* 16; Supreme Court cases, 198–99 *n.* 14

Access control, definitions of "privacy" based on, 11, 25–26

Adoption, 87

Affiliation, valued by women, 56, 72, 74

Aggression, caused by harassment, 132

Agoraphobia, 80

Aid to Dependent Children, 118

Ambiguity, in social behavior, 133

Amnesia, as inaccessibility, 17

Ancillaries, women as, 141–43, 151

Anonymity: abortion for sake of, 111; attention paid at home, 82, 83, 84, 86, 92, 124, 126, 128; of celebrities, 124; defined, 23–24; as domestic privacy, 60; information non-disclosure, 31, 32, 33, 106, 107, 109, 111; of Onassis, 127; of politician, 124; and vagrancy, 62; value of, 35, 37, 42

Aristotle, 40

Arrest, 162. *See also* Prisons

Athena, myth of, 122

Attractiveness, concern about, 133, 206

Authority, 33, 115, 116, 117

Autonomy: by choice, 56, 71, 74, 82; through privacy, 42, 46, 47, 50, 101

Avoidance, as privacy mechanism, 48, 61

Baby Doe, 119–22

Baby Jane Doe, 119–22

Baby M, 205 *n.* 81. *See also* Surrogate mothering

Beauty, 206 *n.* 23. *See also* Attractiveness

Being let alone, 7, 8, 9

Birth control: pill, 87; policies and practice of, 74, 94, 103, 105, 111, 181. *See also* Abortion; Contraception

Black women, 64, 94–95, 135

Bodily integrity, 33, 92, 101, 102. *See also* Self-ownership

Bok, S., 23, 24, 25, 27, 38

Boundary-drawing, 45

Breast-feeding, 136

Call-girl, 169. *See also* Prostitution

Capitalism, 49, 51, 194 *n.* 39

Caretaking roles: effect on women's privacy, 49, 72, 73, 81; fathers', 87; ideals respecting, 56; too much time spent on, 75

Cat-calling, 129

Causal access, 17

Character: and abortion choice, 92, 94; developed by privacy, 40, 48

Child abuse and neglect, 117, 119, 120

Childbirth, privacy in, 82, 113–15, 180

Childcare, options for, 87

Children, as bars to privacy, 67, 75, 86

Children's privacy, 62. *See also* Teenagers

Christianity: doctrines, 92; and fornication, 146; God of, 77; and private